MULTIMODAL COMPOSING
AND WRITING TRANSFER

MULTIMODAL COMPOSING AND WRITING TRANSFER

EDITED BY
KARA POE ALEXANDER,
MATTHEW DAVIS,
LILIAN W. MINA, AND
RYAN P. SHEPHERD

UTAH STATE UNIVERSITY PRESS
Logan

© 2023 by University Press of Colorado

Published by Utah State University Press
An imprint of University Press of Colorado
1580 North Logan Street, Suite 660
PMB 39883
Denver, Colorado 80203-1942

All rights reserved

 The University Press of Colorado is a proud member of the Association of University Presses.

The University Press of Colorado is a cooperative publishing enterprise supported, in part, by Adams State University, Colorado State University, Fort Lewis College, Metropolitan State University of Denver, University of Alaska Fairbanks, University of Colorado, University of Denver, University of Northern Colorado, University of Wyoming, Utah State University, and Western Colorado University..

ISBN: 978-1-64642-532-7 (hardcover)
ISBN: 978-1-64642-533-4 (paperback)
ISBN: 978-1-64642-534-1 (ebook)
https://doi.org/10.7330/9781646425341

Library of Congress Cataloging-in-Publication Data

Names: Alexander, Kara Poe, editor. | Davis, Matthew, PhD, editor. | Mina, Lilian W., editor. | Shepherd, Ryan P., editor.
Title: Multimodal composing and writing transfer / edited by Kara Poe Alexander, Matthew Davis, Lilian W. Mina, and Ryan P. Shepherd.
Description: Logan : Utah State University Press, [2023] | Includes bibliographical references and index.
Identifiers: LCCN 2023023490 (print) | LCCN 2023023491 (ebook) | ISBN 9781646425327 (hardcover) | ISBN 9781646425334 (paperback) | ISBN 9781646425341 (ebook)
Subjects: LCSH: English language—Rhetoric—Study and teaching (Higher)—Computer-assisted instruction. | Academic writing—Study and teaching (Higher)—Computer-assisted instruction. | Modality (Linguistics) | Computers and literacy.
Classification: LCC PE1404 .M8467 2023 (print) | LCC PE1404 (ebook) | DDC 808/.0420711—dc23/eng/20231016
LC record available at https://lccn.loc.gov/2023023490
LC ebook record available at https://lccn.loc.gov/2023023491

This book was supported in part by Baylor University, University of Massachusetts Boston, and Northern Illinois University.

Cover art: Shutterstock/Lightspring

CONTENTS

Acknowledgments vii

Foreword: Dimensions of Transfer and the Role of Multimodality
 Chris M. Anson ix

Introduction: Mapping the Histories, Definitions, Methods, and Conversations of Multimodal Transfer
 Kara Poe Alexander, Matthew Davis, Lilian W. Mina, and Ryan P. Shepherd 3

PART I: MULTIMODALITY AND TRANSFER IN THE FIRST-YEAR WRITING CURRICULUM

1. Seeing It, Hearing It, Feeling It: Digital Methods for the Study of Transfer across Media
 Crystal VanKooten 27

2. Making Transfer Matter across Digital Media Platforms: First-Year Writers' Design of Multimodal Campaigns for Social Advocacy
 Jialei Jiang 48

3. On the Labor of Writing Transfer: Bodies and Borderlands Discourses in Translation
 Joseph Anthony Wilson and Josie Rose Portz 66

PART II: MULTIMODALITY AND TRANSFER IN THE VERTICAL CURRICULUM

4. Equipping Tutors to Transfer Multimodal Writing Knowledge to Writing Center Contexts
 Kara Poe Alexander, Becca Cassady, and Michael-John DePalma 85

5. "It's Not Like I Can Put a Picture of a Paper on Instagram, You Know?": Genre and Multimodality in Writing Knowledge Transfer across Contexts
 Anna V. Knutson 104

6. The Other Curriculum: Social Media and Its Connection to University Writing
   Ryan P. Shepherd   125

PART III: MULTIMODALITY AND TRANSFER ACROSS THE WRITERLY LIFE

7. Drawing Worlds Together: Tracing Semiotic Practices along Histories of Literate Activity
   Kevin Roozen   145

8. Rhetoric in its Fullness: Metalanguage and Multimodal Transfer
   Logan Bearden   170

9. A Curriculum Delivered, a Curriculum Remembered: Multimodal Transfer in Writing and Rhetoric Major Alumni
   Travis Maynard   190

10. If You Build It, Will They Use It: Composing Infrastructures, Communities of Practice, and Instructor Dispositions
    Jeff Naftzinger   209

    Afterword: Transfer Happens; Transfer Doesn't Happen: Maps, Tensions, Questions, and Ways Forward
    Kathleen Blake Yancey   227

    Index   235
    About the Authors   245

ACKNOWLEDGMENTS

This edited collection has its origins in numerous conversations among the editors, contributing authors, and others at conferences and over virtual sessions. Most of our conversations occurred during the Covid-19 pandemic, which meant they took place virtually, over Zoom. We would like to thank each of our universities—Baylor University, University of Massachusetts–Boston, the University of Alabama at Birmingham, and Northern Illinois University—for supporting this work in various ways. Thank you to the authors who contributed to this collection. Each one of them contributed ideas, methods, and theories that broadened our own thinking and expanded the possibilities of what this book could be. We are deeply grateful for your belief in this book and for working with us throughout the revision and editing process. Thank you to the anonymous manuscript reviewers who offered thoughtful feedback, which helped strengthen the entire collection. Thanks to Rachael Levay at Utah State University Press for seeing potential in this project and for guiding us through the publication process. We thank each of our partners—Shane Alexander, Samantha Regan, Ehab Abouseif, and HyeSook Kim—for their ongoing love and their support of our professional work. Finally, we want to thank one another. Each of us experienced many different individual and professional challenges during the time we were working on this book, and collaborating on this collection has brought a great amount of joy and encouragement into each of our lives.

Foreword
DIMENSIONS OF TRANSFER AND THE ROLE OF MULTIMODALITY

Chris M. Anson

Early in my study of the concept of "transfer,"[1] I became puzzled about the difference between transfer and learning. Learning means being able to use new knowledge, or adapt it, or build on it elsewhere. Why is "transfer" not simply the result of learning? Don't people learn, then use that knowledge to do things like theorize, create, study, or convey?

Eventually, I came to some new understandings. Learning can involve informational content (re)constructed by the learner and integrated into prior knowledge. For example, an architecture student can learn about the work of Frank Lloyd Wright—studying his intellectual and personal history, looking at photos of the buildings and houses he designed (or visiting them), and placing Wright into broader architectural movements such as the Prairie School. Of course, this kind of knowledge is never just passive; it interacts with and informs prior and further learning. But it's a different order of knowledge—a kind of "knowing that"—than the knowledge required for the same student to create her own architectural designs perhaps faintly invoking or revising Wright's—a kind of "knowing how" influenced by the "that" (see Ryle 1946, 1949). In the context of transfer in writing, "knowing that," or *declarative knowledge*, might be concepts such as the often taught rhetorical appeals, but that knowledge could be used *procedurally* to write a text whose persuasive success has its origins in those appeals.

Declarative knowledge is usually conscious: you are aware that you know what it means to use *pathos* as an emotional appeal in a piece of writing; you can define it and point to examples of it. Procedural knowledge may also be conscious: you craft a piece of writing drawing explicitly on your knowledge of *pathos*, deliberately tapping into people's emotions to persuade them to do something or think a certain way. But much procedural knowledge is also *tacit*, driven into the background

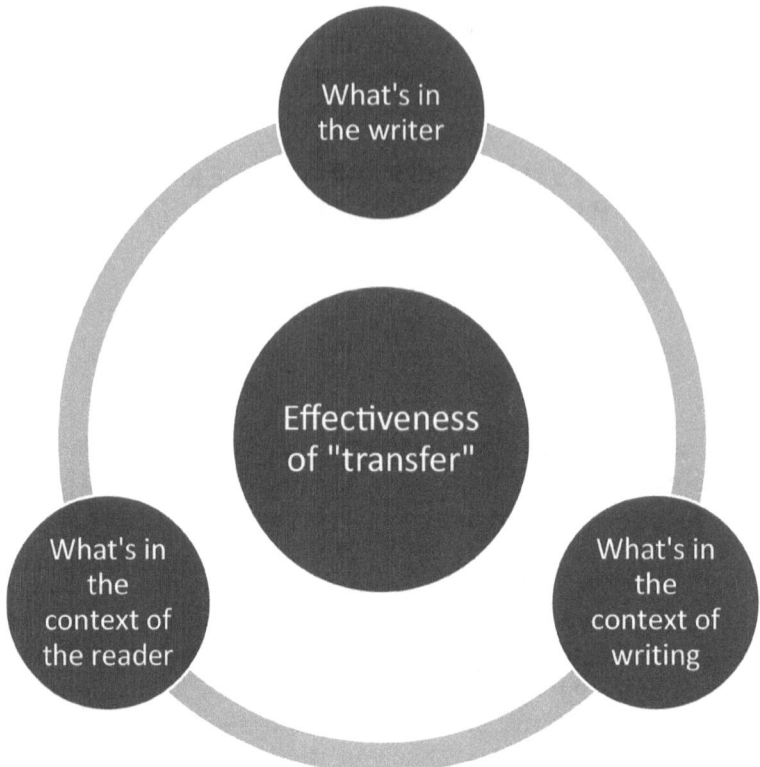

Figure 0.1. Dimensions of writing and transfer

or into automaticity because of repeated practice and experience, like braking before a stoplight while focusing all of your attention on a conversation you're having with another passenger. For most writers, gaining expertise means being able to push some processes into the background—into tacit automaticity—in an effort to focus consciously on higher-order matters such as assessing whether choices of language, structure, or the development of ideas conform to the expectations of a particular genre. The problem solving required for transfer usually attends to these higher-order questions.

This focus on the mind of the individual writer (as shown at the top of figure 0.1) characterizes much of the scholarship on transfer in writing studies. How do novice and experienced writers take what they have learned (both declarative and procedural) in one context and deploy it in another? The question is central to composition instruction because the pedagogy is thought to be worthless if students can't apply what they've learned in other settings. That learning includes, for example, threshold writing concepts (Adler-Kassner and Wardle 2015), strategies for producing and refining text, skills of giving and receiving generative feedback or discovering and integrating new knowledge into current thinking, and recognizing patterns of genre embedded in the language of texts and in their social and disciplinary functions. The strongest immediate source of accountability for foundational writing courses comes from instructors in other courses, who expect students to adapt effortlessly to whatever idiosyncratic writing projects they assign there—to *transfer* what they learned in first-year composition. Later, accountability comes from future employers who assume that because a student has a college degree, they are ready to effortlessly take on whatever specialized kinds of writing may be the discursive norm. Because of these expectations, transfer has become a subject of much interest and even urgency as composition programs assess how well they prepare individual students to write effectively in other contexts (Anson and Moore 2016).

Addition 1: But there's more—much more—about the individual. So far our description of what's in the writer is all about what they know and can do, a mostly cognitive orientation. Imagine a scenario: a writer is working on a project, but something happens along the way that changes how the writer *feels* about the project. Loss of interest and lassitude. Too much bewildering complexity in the subject matter. A turn in expectations about the focus, such as discovering that the person being studied for a (positive) biographical account was a eugenicist. Or a life event that pushes the project into the background. Also in the writer, then, is what Alice G. Brand (1987, 1989), Susan McLeod (1987, 1997), and other scholars claim the field does not always recognize: emotion and affect. In addition to what a writer knows and can do, emotions, attitude, beliefs about one's own abilities, incentive, energy or exhaustion, feelings about how and from whom prior knowledge was learned, feelings about how and from whom a task is assigned, and a host of other affective states can influence the ability to transfer prior knowledge. What might be effective transfer in one situation becomes troubled in another; or what starts out effectively takes a turn for the worse, the struggle then negatively influencing the relationship between the writer and the project. Studying transfer means not just finding out what a writer knows but tracing the development and effects of these emotional states.

Addition 2: So far, then, transfer depends on both knowledge or skill and emotion and affect. But focusing transfer on the individual writer assumes what Brian V. Street (1984), David Barton (1994), and other scholars call an "autonomous" view of literacy, which is preoccupied with individual knowledge and performance without regard to social context. The New Literacy scholars (Street 1997) remind us that writing is an ecological concept involving shifting social practices, genres, contexts, readers, and relationships of actors. It's misguided to think of the complex discourse processes of adapting existing skill and knowledge to new contexts as something wholly in the writer's control. When we acknowledge that the *context* of writing transfer is as important as what the writer brings *to* that context, things get more complicated. These complications have generated different theories of transfer in writing, some more optimistic than others (see Brent 2011). In one orientation, developing the individual writer's abilities takes precedence; the better prepared with metacognitive and analytic skills through a "Teaching for Transfer" approach (see Yancey, Robertson, and Taczak 2014), the more easily the learner will adapt to new contexts and genres. In a more pessimistic orientation, no matter how well prepared the learner is to adapt to new settings and genres, if the task is distant enough from what they have experienced before, little of what they know will help them perform effectively, at least at first (see Russell 1995). Some years ago, in a study of interns deemed excellent writers by English department standards, Laurie Lee Forsberg and I (Anson and Forsberg 1990) found that they were dismayingly unable to perform when asked to write unfamiliar genres in their internship programs at local businesses and nonprofits. Not much from their successful, extensive writing experiences as English majors was useful, with the exception of a decent control of grammar and mechanics (but which occasionally allowed them to write complex sentences that were then eschewed by members of their organizations). Taught over and over to elaborate and extend their ideas and provide supporting details in their literary analyses, some students were shocked to find that their supervisors wanted them to eliminate over half the material in their "overwritten" documents and get to the point. In a more recent account of a highly experienced writer, I further documented the paralyzing effect of a new genre and context on the writer's abilities to transfer existing knowledge and experience (Anson 2018). Others, such as Graham Smart (2000), have shown similar patterns in the challenges people in businesses face when writing in unfamiliar genres.

This suggests that what's in the context of writing—the bottom right of the diagram in figure 0.1—strongly influences the effectiveness of transfer. When a student moves from one course that requires an annotated bibliography to another that assigns the same genre, with perhaps a few differences of teacher preference for the length and detail of the annotations and the reference style used, the contexts of transfer are "near" (Perkins and Salomon 1989). But when a student moves from a first-year composition course where they have written a literacy autobiography, an argumentative essay, and a brief term paper to a sociology course requiring a country migration report or a history course requiring a new historical analysis of a cultural conflict from the perspective of both groups, the distance stretches, as does the student's ability (without support) to write effectively. They can ask good questions and study models, but they won't write effortlessly without trial and error and without learning the habits and discursive practices expected of them.

Addition 3: To make matters more complicated, contexts of transfer don't sit still. They are themselves constantly changing and adapting to local circumstances, new information, new norms and practices, or feedback they get both from within and without. (We might imagine the contextual circle in figure 0.1 spinning with activity and change.) From an ecological perspective, contexts behave like living environments with discursive microclimates and organisms interacting with each other. The writer new to an environment can't adapt instantly to it but must instead become acclimated, which takes time and is facilitated if there are guides and mentors there.

Addition 4: But understanding how transfer works or happens doesn't involve only the writer and the context of the writing. It's impossible for someone to judge how successfully they have met the norms and expectations of a particular community of practice without a *context of readers*, as shown on the bottom left of figure 0.1. The context of readership may have stable (known) audiences or diverse and unpredictable ones, as in a **PR** division when writers address their colleagues as well as those outside the organization. When writers such as the interns in the Anson and Forsberg study receive feedback from others in an organization, it usually focuses on how effectively the writer has met the standards of the community or context in which the writing will be read. Mentors, anticipating the response of those beyond the organization, can gauge how close a piece of writing is to being acceptable. Without intermediaries, writers risk final judgments by unknown audiences that can show them how off the mark they are—how ineffectively they have adapted to the genre and context. In classroom settings, these complications are usually "closed," to the extent that a teacher represents the judge of transfer and the arbiter of its effectiveness. But the response, when transfer is not effective, is no less unsettling to the writer.

THE BIG ADDITION: COMPLICATING THE MODEL WITH MULTIMODALITY

In view of what the present collection contributes to our understanding of transfer, let's admit that the model in figure 0.1 is all wrong. First, it's a conventional alphabetic model that theorizes the roles of the *writer*, the *context of writing*, and the *context of reader(s)*. Everything above considers transfer as the ability of a writer to use knowledge, meta-knowledge, and prior experience to write in other settings for readers. And most of the prior scholarship on transfer in writing studies has focused on these relationships.

When we transition from the assumptions of the New Literacy Studies to the New *Literacies* Studies, transfer takes on much greater and more interesting complexity. As Gee (2015, 44) puts it:

> The NLS [New Literacy Studies] was about studying literacy in a new way. "The New Literacies Studies" is about studying new types of literacy beyond print literacy, especially "digital literacies" and literacy practices embedded in popular culture . . . Like the NLS, the New Literacies Studies also argues that the meanings to which these technologies give rise are determined by the social, cultural, historical, and institutional practices of different groups of people. And, as with the NLS, these practices almost always involve more than just using a digital tool—they involve, as well, ways of acting, interacting, valuing, believing, and knowing, as well as often using other sorts of tools and technologies, including very often oral and written language.

From this perspective, transfer involves not just text but the use and manipulation of still and moving images, video, sound, and iconographic material. Decisions are no longer restricted to writing alphabetic text, which puts the writer into the role of a *designer*, as shown in figure 0.2. The context of writing becomes a context of *production* involving a potentially vast array of technological tools that can create, manipulate, arrange, animate, and provide options for exploring language and media. The context of the reader becomes a context of *reception*, which includes watching, reading, listening, navigating, sampling, and moving from the digital artifact to wherever it might link beyond itself.

When we look at transfer through the lens of multimodality, all the dimensions previously described become further layered with constructs

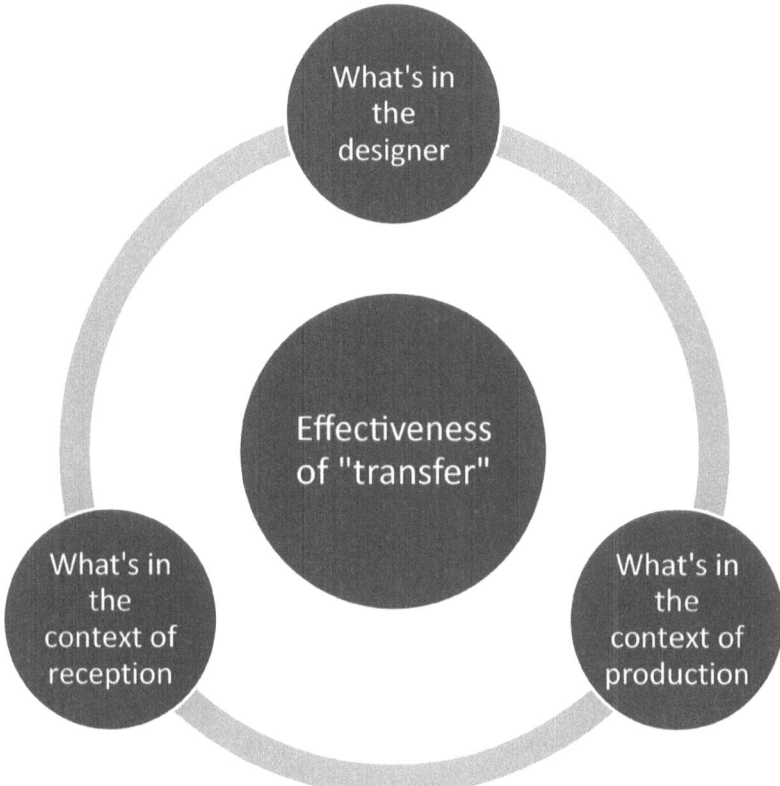

Figure 0.2. Dimensions of multimodality and transfer

that invite research. Prior knowledge and ability include both formally learned multimodal practices and those learned from engaging in self-sponsored digital work. Those practices are affected by access, the nature of formal schooling, and material conditions. How do multimodal literacies intersect with alphabetic literacies? What rhetorical understandings and skills are fostered—consciously or not—from using digital tools and participating in online experiences? How do students' experiences with digital technologies inform—transfer into—their subsequent projects? What new aspects of emotion and affect arise when we add multimodality to the process of design and production? How does multimodality affect L2 students, since the need for linguistic meaning is offset or augmented by visual and other forms of meaning? How does learners' varied prior access to the internet and to digital tools affect levels of their self-efficacy when they are asked to apply what they know—or lack knowledge of—to new projects in new settings?

Just as "what's in the designer" begs to be studied, so do contexts of production, where students may be asked to create multimodal projects requiring, variously, the adaptation of prior knowledge and experience—or, lacking it, the use of the projects as the vehicles for experimenting with and learning to apply new digital tools. If the need is great to support students who face transfer challenges when asked to write in unfamiliar genres, it may be even greater—or at least more complicated—when they are asked to transfer knowledge of conventional written discourse into multimodality. The reverse also needs far more research: what do students experience, rhetorically and otherwise, in their formal as well as self-sponsored digital work that informs their academic work, especially their conventional writing assignments?

Studying students' transfer of knowledge ("knowing that") and ability ("knowing how") through the lens of multimodality is not without significant challenges. First, although it might be possible to track or document students' progress as they work on different projects within a course, it's impossible to hold their experiences still to gauge how much their learning can be attributed to what happens in the course. Beyond, they are constantly experiencing the products of digital technology in other courses and, more significant, in their self-sponsored explorations and participation in multiple media. Focusing on specific contexts is a start, but more ethnographically oriented and longitudinal studies are needed.

It is these and other questions and challenges that the present volume confronts—across methodologies (qualitative and case studies, close analyses of digital tools and programmatic metalanguage, surveys and coded interviews, and mixed methods studies), across the curricular landscape of higher education and beyond (first-year composition, the vertical curriculum, the institutional infrastructure, the extracurriculum and social media, and contexts of work), and across genres and linguistic traditions. It is a bold and generative collection that answers some new questions but, more important, sets a path for continued and much-needed research on the nature of transfer in a digital world.

NOTE

1. Almost everyone in writing studies thinks the term *transfer* is too limited to capture the complex processes of deploying knowledge and skill across contexts and occasions, but they use it anyway because of its widespread recognition.

REFERENCES

Adler-Kassner, Linda, and Elizabeth Wardle, eds. 2015. *Naming What We Know: Threshold Concepts of Writing Studies*. Logan: Utah State University Press.

Anson, Chris M. 2018. "The Pop Warner Chronicles: A Case Study of Contextual Adaptation and the Transfer of Writing Ability." *College Composition and Communication* 67 (4): 518–549.

Anson, Chris M., and Laurie Lee Forsberg. 1990. "Moving beyond the Academic Community: Transitional Stages in Professional Writing." *Written Communication* 7 (2): 200–231.

Anson, Chris M., and Jessie L. Moore, eds. 2016. *Critical Transitions: Writing and the Question of Transfer*. Fort Collins, CO: WAC Clearinghouse.

Barton, David. 1994. *Literacy: An Introduction to the Ecology of Written Language*. Oxford: Blackwell.

Brand, Alice G. 1987. "The Why of Cognition: Emotion and the Writing Process." *College Composition and Communication* 38 (4): 436–443.

Brand, Alice G. 1989. *The Psychology of Writing: The Affective Experience*. New York: Greenwood.

Brent, Doug. 2011. "Transfer, Transformation, and Rhetorical Knowledge: Insights from Transfer Theory." *Journal of Business and Technical Communication* 25 (4): 396–420.

Gee, James Paul. 2015. "The New Literacy Studies." In *The Routledge Handbook of Literacy Studies*, edited by Jennifer Rowsell and Kate Pahl, 35–48. London: Routledge.

McLeod, Susan. 1987. "Some Thoughts about Feelings: The Affective Domain and the Writing Process." *College Composition and Communication* 38 (4): 426–435.

McLeod, Susan. 1997. *Notes on the Heart: Affective Issues in the Writing Classroom*. Carbondale: Southern Illinois University Press.

Perkins, David N., and Gavriel Salomon. 1989. "Are Cognitive Skills Context-Bound?" *Educational Researcher* 18 (1): 16–25.

Russell, David R. 1995. "Activity Theory and Its Implications for Writing Instruction." In *Reconceiving Writing, Rethinking Writing Instruction*, edited by Joseph Petraglia, 51–77. Hillsdale, NJ: Erlbaum.

Ryle, Gilbert. 1946. "Knowing How and Knowing That." *Proceedings of the Aristotelian Society* XLVI. Repr. in *Collected Papers*, vol. 2, 212–225 (1971). London: Hutchinson.

Ryle, Gilbert. 1949. *The Concept of Mind*. London: Hutchinson.

Smart, Graham. 2000. "Reinventing Expertise: Experienced Writers in the Workplace Encounter a New Genre." In *Transitions: Writing in Academic and Workplace Settings*, edited by Patrick Dias and Anthony Paré, 223–252. Cresskill, NJ: Hampton.

Street, Brian V. 1984. *Literacy in Theory and Practice*. Cambridge: Cambridge University Press.

Street, Brian V. 1997. "The Implications of the 'New Literacy Studies' for Literacy Education." *English in Education* 31 (3): 45–59.

Yancey, Kathleen, Liane Robertson, and Kara Taczak. 2014. *Writing across Contexts: Transfer, Composition, and Sites of Writing*. Logan: Utah State University Press.

MULTIMODAL COMPOSING AND WRITING TRANSFER

Introduction

MAPPING THE HISTORIES, DEFINITIONS, METHODS, AND CONVERSATIONS OF MULTIMODAL TRANSFER

Kara Poe Alexander, Matthew Davis,
Lilian W. Mina, and Ryan P. Shepherd

MAPPING THE CONVERSATION

Since the start of the twenty-first century, research on multimodality and writing transfer has transformed rhetoric and composition. Separately and simultaneously, these two strands of research have impacted theory, pedagogy, research methods, programmatic infrastructures, and teacher training. They have reshaped writing courses and curricula across the institutional locations of composing—including the first-year writing classroom, the vertical curriculum, writing centers, graduate programs, and writing curriculum development. From the pages of journals and position statements to assignment design and assessment practices, research on both multimodality and writing transfer expands the discipline's sense of what writing is, what it can be, what it can do, how it is learned and taught, and how it can be studied. There are many reasons for the disciplinary impact of scholarship on multimodality and transfer, among them: (1) an epistemological focus, (2) an orientation to improving teaching and learning, (3) a view of writing as a dynamic rhetorical activity, (4) an expansion of the context and methods of disciplinary study, and (5) a shared focus on the crucial role of language in teaching, learning, and researching writing.

Both multimodality and writing transfer focus on epistemology: that is, what we know about writing and how we know it. Multimodality provides scholars, teachers, and students with an expanded sense of writing—not bounded by the written word but not wholly separate from it either. It is also focused on a range of meaning-making modes, each with its own affordances and limitations, genres and materiality, composing practices, and necessary technical and technological knowledge and resources. This expanded sense of writing is grounded in the theory that composing—in whatever modes— is an "epistemological commitment" to certain modes and media as the appropriate means of meaning making in a given situation (Kress 2010, 16). Transfer research is similarly grounded in an epistemological approach to studying writing, often focusing on the knowledge domains from which writers draw as they encounter new meaning-making tasks. These knowledge domains include content, genre, process, discourse community, and rhetorical knowledges composers bring to their attempts to write in new situations (see Beaufort 2007 for more on knowledge domains). Reflection also works as a sixth knowledge domain (Taczak and Robertson 2016). The study of writing transfer provides scholars, teachers, and students with a sense of writing and learning to write that is not necessarily bounded by the classroom where prior knowledge, context, agency, and reflective capacity come together in moments of composing. Research on writing transfer, then, studies the epistemological dispositions composers have, how they draw on prior knowledge, and how those dynamics change and develop across time and context (Adler-Kassner and Wardle 2015; Robertson, Taczak, and Yancey 2012; Yancey, Robertson, and Taczak 2014).

Both multimodality and writing transfer emerge from scholarly contexts oriented to improved teaching and learning. Multimodality, with its roots in the New London Group's (NLG) (1996) work on "social futures," was a framework for reconceiving pedagogy to meet the needs and demands of a twenty-first-century communication landscape. Writing transfer, with its roots in psychology, education, and the study of workplace writing, has focused on how understanding writers' struggles (McCarthy 1987) and successes (Beaufort 1999, 2007) in new composing situations can lead to transformed teaching and learning of writing. In this sense, multimodality and writing transfer clearly have (and have had) much to offer the teaching of writing.

In addition, both emerge from scholarly starting points that treat writing as a complex, socially embedded, purpose-driven activity and prompt scholars and teachers to attempt to push past moments in which writing is treated or studied as if it were singular, static, monomodal, or immutable. That is, both multimodality and writing transfer point to multiplicity: of texts and contexts, languages and materials, and processes and possibilities. This emphasis on multiplicity not only results in a much broader view of literacy and learning but also underscores the importance of teaching such literacies, knowledge, and skills in classrooms.

To understand multimodality and writing transfer, scholars have adjusted the context(s) of their studies, the kinds of texts they study, and the methods by which texts are studied in those contexts. The result—as is evident below and in the chapters that follow— is a deeper understanding of composing processes and practices, a clearer picture of how those look across a range of mutually informative contexts, and a more varied set of tools for how to study them. In other words, multimodality and writing transfer have both broadened the reach of writing research methods and inspired researchers to develop new methods altogether.

Finally, both multimodality and writing transfer focus on the role of language in teaching, learning, researching, and practicing a range of composing practices. Both are vocabulary-building and reshaping projects aimed at creating a more expansive set of terms for describing how we study, teach, learn, and practice communication. Such a focus underscores the value of exposing writers to a range of composing practices, processes, genres, and situations.

Even given these shared starting points, readers unfamiliar with research on multimodality, writing transfer, or both may sometimes find both areas of inquiry difficult to grasp, not only because of the multiple, sometimes confusing definitions offered in the literature but also because the massive increase in publications on both topics has made it daunting to keep pace with the shared terms (and abundant synonyms) both areas of study hope to engender. For this reason, we start with a partial review of the literature that includes definitions of both terms. We hope this brief overview will make the possible work at the intersection between multimodality and writing transfer more visible to the readers.

WHERE WE ARE NOW

In this section, we provide brief literature reviews of both multimodality and transfer as they have operated independently of each other; then we bring these topics together and situate the need for *Multimodal Composition and Writing Transfer*. This brief literature review does not attempt to cover the history of either concept or its development over years; a full history of both is beyond the scope of this volume.[1] We encourage readers who are interested in learning more about the history of either term to refer to two comprehensive CompPile bibliographies on transfer (Snead 2011) and transfer and multimodality (Snead et al. 2022).

Multimodality

The term *multimodality* (in its modern meaning) is perhaps best known from its influential appearance in the NLG's (1996) "A Pedagogy of Multiliteracies: Designing Social Futures." In the context of the NLG's multiliteracies theory, multimodality signals a shift in defining literacy and conceptualizing writing and composing. The NLG scholars argue that "all meaning-making is multimodal" (81), theorizing that multimodality is a theory that "relates all the other modes in quite remarkably dynamic relationships" (82). Two of the NLG scholars, Bill Cope and Mary Kalantzis (2000, 5), later elaborated: "Meaning is made in ways that are increasingly multimodal" or in ways where the linguistic, visual, aural, and spatial modes work together to communicate unique meanings. The call of this group to expand the conceptualization of literacy beyond alphabetic text to include the various modes of communication (e.g., images, sound, movement, and text) was welcomed by numerous writing studies scholars who embraced multiliteracies and multimodality theoretically, scholarly, and pedagogically.[2]

For instance, Cynthia L. Selfe (2004, 43) defined multimodality in the context of new-media texts, describing them as "texts created primarily in digital environments, composed in multiple media (e.g., film, video, audio, among others), and designed for presentation and exchange in digital venues." This definition suits the context of Selfe's research on designing and producing digital texts to be circulated in digital environments. In a later account, Pamela Takayoshi and Cynthia L. Selfe (2007, 1) labeled texts as multimodal when they "exceed the alphabetic" by "includ[ing] still and moving images, animations, color, words, music and sound." This second definition emphasizes specific modes—the status of images and sound in multimodal composing—situating the visual and aural modes as equally essential to composition as the verbal mode.

Numerous scholars have related multimodality to the discipline of composition (e.g., Alexander 2013; Alexander and Rhodes 2014; Anderson 2008; Bowen and Whithaus 2013; Haas 1996; Palmeri 2012; Powell, Alexander, and Borton 2011; Selber 2004; Selfe 2007, 2009; Sheppard 2009; Shipka 2011; Snyder 1998; Yancey 2004). Kathleen Blake Yancey (2004) called on writing teachers to have students' needs at the center of our attention and to change our conceptualizations of literacy, composing, and pedagogy to respond to those changing needs. Her argument to meet students where they are and to cater to their needs challenges writing teachers and researchers to think not only of students' self-sponsored digital practices outside our classrooms but also of students' future multimodal composing contexts (see also Rosinski 2017).

Similarly, Jonathan Alexander and Jacqueline Rhodes (2014, 5) warned that overlooking "the specific rhetorical and production capabilities of new and multimedia may hamper our ability to understand the challenges that multimedia bring to understanding 'literacy' and communicative possibilities in the twenty-first century." In other words, ignoring multimodal composing and continuing to leave it at the doorstep of our writing classrooms means we may "fail to meet our students' most pressing needs as communicators" who use those technologies every day (5).

To summarize, multimodal composition pedagogies enable writers to (1) develop digital, rhetorical, linguistic, technological, and composing skills; (2) merge their composing practices outside the classroom with those in the classroom; (3) help students become more critical readers and writers; and (4) encourage students to see the multimodality of all texts, including print-based reading and writing that traditionally has not been thought of as multimodal (Alexander 2013; Alexander, Powell, and Green 2012; Bernhardt 1986; Hill 2004; Jewitt 2005; Shepherd 2018; Takayoshi and Selfe 2007; Trimbur 2002; Wysocki 2004). Multimodal composition is also inherently multicultural, inclusive, and democratic because it bridges digital divides, draws on multiple learning styles and semiotic modes, and focuses attention away from grammar and error (Klages and Clark 2009; Smith 2008).

Beyond these outcomes, multimodal composition has helped scholars and students better understand and explore the concept of affordances. Affordances are the unique representational capacities of a mode, including both its possibilities and its limitations. According to Gunther Kress (2000, 157), "Semiotic modes have different potentials, so that they afford different kinds of possibilities of human expression and engagement with the world, and through this differential engagement with the world they facilitate differential possibilities of development." For example, the affordances of school-based uses of alphabetic language as represented in print typically includes linear, sequential presentations of logic and evidence, an unfolding of time in sequence, and, therefore, a tendency to present an argument explicitly (i.e., through a thesis statement) (Ball 2004; Walsh 2006). Audio affordances include accent, tone of voice, mood, music, and an appeal to pathos, among others (Ball and Moeller 2008; Halbritter 2006). Still visual images represent space and simultaneity differently, which affords "showing" meaning to an audience rather than explicit argumentation (Kress 1998; Walsh 2006). Moving image—like video—incorporates the affordances of static visual images and includes others, such as movement, process, and passage of time (Burn and Parker 2003). Because these modes are always combining to create meaning within the structure of one composition, multimodal texts are less linear and more flexible in their presentation. Meaning is thus made through all of the modes deployed and their interrelations, which has the effect of encouraging different ways of making meaning (Alexander 2013; Ball and Moeller 2008; Blair 2004; Kress and van Leeuwen 2001; Sorapure 2006). That said, each mode's affordances are a function of its material affordances, the technologies through and with which we deploy them, *and* the way those materials are deemed appropriate for use in certain composing situations (Kress 1998). So any list of modes or of modal affordances is shaped by what modes are capable of *and* what we are capable of imagining doing with them (for examples that blur the boundaries of modes, see Wysocki 2005).

The impact of multimodal composition has been felt at all levels of curriculum development in writing studies. Many universities now require a multimodal assignment in first-year writing courses (Anderson et al. 2006; Reid et al. 2016). Others have added digital or new-media writing courses in their undergraduate majors as ways for students to expand their thinking and practice composing multimodal texts (Alexander et al. 2019; Lee 2020). Many courses and programs also assign PowerPoint presentations, videos, posters, visual texts, and other multimodal forms of communication across the curriculum, and definitions of writing have expanded. Of course, technical communication was one of the first to adopt visual and multimodal theories into its courses, but it too has benefited from multimodal composition theories (e.g., Bourelle, Bourelle, and Jones 2015; Cook 2009; Walters 2010). In spite of such integration into the curriculum, students and faculty in writing studies and beyond have sometimes been slow to expand their understanding of writing to include multimodal and digital texts (Melzer 2014).

In addition to its incorporation into writing classes, multimodality has also made its way into writing center contexts, as writing centers have broadened their missions to include multimodal compositions. These writing centers—sometimes known as multiliteracy centers—have updated their tutor education structures, training, and physical spaces to accommodate a more extensive range of texts and genres (e.g., Carpenter and Apostel 2016; Carpenter and Lee 2016; Fishman 2010; Inman 2010; Lee and Carpenter 2017, 2019; McKinney 2009, 2010; Sheridan and Inman 2010). Unfortunately, like faculty, writers have also been slow to utilize writing centers as places that can help with multimodal composing, even when writing centers are equipped with the hardware, software, marketing resources, and training required to accommodate such projects (Lee 2012; McKinney 2012). In addition, tutors themselves have struggled with anxieties related to giving feedback on multimodal composition (Sheridan 2012), especially when they are not regularly composing such texts themselves (Lee 2012). Faculty have also been slow to recognize writing centers as places that assist these kinds of texts, and they are often unaware themselves of how to assign and evaluate multimodal compositions (Balester 2012). Writing centers can play a unique role in the university context in teaching and supporting multimodal composition assignments—and in helping faculty better teach multimodal composition—but this shift requires time, money, and resources, to which many writing centers and writing center staff do not have access.

Building bridges between practices inside and outside the writing classroom is one foundation of integrating multimodal composing into courses and curricula; similarly, building bridges between writing knowledge and practices students learn in the writing classroom and those they learn in other writing contexts is the cornerstone of transfer in writing studies.

Transfer

Learning transfer has been classically defined as "the ability to extend what has been learned in one context to new contexts" (Donovan, Bransford, and Pellegrino 1999, 52). That traditional conceptualization of transfer has focused on moving and extending learning from one situation to another, a sense of transfer that risks seeing what one knows as a thing—or a container—that can be transported around. While this conception of transfer as reuse of prior knowledge is still common in some circles, it presents a disposition toward knowledge as static, which can stymie writing transfer (Driscoll and Jin 2018). Therefore, recent research on writing transfer draws attention to two significant aspects of transfer: (1) a more dynamic epistemological understanding of the nature of transfer and (2) attention to transfer as a pedagogical goal.

Several scholars have suggested that the nature of transfer is more complex than simply reusing prior knowledge, and they nuanced the term *transfer* and its definition in the process. Michael-John DePalma and Jeffrey Ringer (2011, 135), for instance, define writing transfer as "writers' conscious or intuitive processes of applying or reshaping learned writing knowledge and practices in order to negotiate new and potentially unfamiliar writing situations." This definition implies applying, reshaping, adapting, resituating, recontextualizing, and remixing prior writing knowledge and practices to new writing settings (Elon Statement 2015; Nowacek 2011; Robertson, Taczak, and Yancey 2012). DePalma and Ringer (2011, 141) elaborate this new relationship between knowledge and transfer through six characteristics, seeing "adaptive transfer" as dynamic, idiosyncratic, cross-contextual, rhetorical, multilingual, and transformative.

In addition to DePalma and Ringer, Doug Brent (2011) described transfer as the transformation of prior knowledge that can be facilitated and made possible through pedagogy and instruction. Elizabeth Wardle and Doug Downs (2012) argued that to facilitate such dynamic transfer—or what they called "creative repurposing"—for student writers, scholars need to examine and understand the influence of the educational system on individual writers' dispositions about learning. Similarly, in *Writing across Contexts*, Kathleen Blake Yancey, Liane Robertson, and Kara Taczak (2014, 33) define writing transfer as "a dynamic rather than static process, a process of using, adapting, and repurposing the old for success in the new," relating this definition to the emergence of a curriculum designed to facilitate transfer. The shift in defining and researching transfer has also acknowledged the active and agentive role of the writer— especially student writers—to "both draw from and reshape writing knowledge to suit and influence writing contexts" (DePalma 2015, 616).

Because transfer is a dynamic process that aims at enhancing future writing situations and contexts by repurposing the knowledge writers have, studying writing transfer involves acknowledging the dynamic and fluid writing contexts and situations in which writers compose. Writers move back and forth between modalities and languages or language varieties, and they cross the already blurring boundaries between modalities as they negotiate their communication, literacy, and work choices.

This awareness brings us to the second aspect of transfer research: the pedagogical *goal* of transfer. DePalma (2015, 616) argues that the goal of transfer is to "influence writing contexts," while Yancey, Robertson, and Taczak (2014, 33) emphasize "success in the new [context]." Similarly, DePalma and Ringer (2011) theorize that the goal of transfer is to provide students with the means by which they navigate new writing situations using their writing knowledge. As a pedagogical matter, then, the goal of transfer research is to provide students with the conceptual frameworks and compositional tools that enable them to understand and negotiate future writing situations and contexts through rhetorical repurposing of the knowledge learned.

In 2012, Jessie Moore mapped the terrain of writing transfer research, establishing a foundation for understanding the questions, methods, contexts of study, framing theories, and outcomes of the emerging area of interest. This terrain subsequently expanded through large, multi-institutional efforts (e.g., the Elon University Research Seminars in 2013 and 2019; the Teaching for Transfer multi-institutional research projects) and by numerous studies of specific, often individualized, contexts for writing. Several edited volumes explored transfer in and outside the classroom, considering the multiplicity of locations and prompts for writing transfer (Anson and Moore 2017; Moore and Bass 2017). Other research focused on the knowledge dynamics of writing transfer, finding that reflection (Taczak and Robertson 2016), metacognition (Gorzelsky et al. 2016), prior knowledge uptake (Walwema and Driscoll 2015), writerly agency (Nowacek 2011), and process knowledge (Cleary 2013) all play a role in how writers develop and repurpose what they know for new writing challenges.

As the topography of writing transfer research became clearer, scholars also began creating, implementing, and assessing transfer-oriented courses and curricula to facilitate writing transfer for students. Building on early work by Lucille Parkinson McCarthy (1987) and Anne Beaufort (2007), scholars engaged with the question of whether and how writing curricula might foster transfer. Doug Downs and Elizabeth Wardle's Writing about Writing approach proposed that composition courses should be an introduction to the disciplinary texts and approaches of rhetoric and composition; one operative assumption there is that building this knowledge would transfer into students' other classes and (like other disciplines) into their potential work in the major (Downs and Wardle 2007; Wardle and Downs 2022). The Teaching for Transfer (TFT) curriculum developed and tested a writing curriculum specifically oriented to fostering transfer, finding that key terms, reflection, and theorizing writing helped students develop and transform what they know about writing for success in different writing contexts (Yancey, Taczak, and Robertson 2014). Subsequently, research into TFT showed its success in fostering transfer across a range of contexts and composing situations: across assignment types, including portfolios (Yancey 2017); across institutional types, including community colleges (Andrus, Mitchler, and Tinberg 2019); and for concurrent writing contexts across disciplines and outside of school (Yancey et al. 2019). Key to this success was students' ability to develop a "transfer mind-set"—a framework for thinking about writing as a broad, capacious phenomenon that incorporated their experiences of writing both inside and outside school (Yancey et al. 2018).

Contemporaneous to these large curricular projects, a robust body of research emerged focusing on transfer through and across a multiplicity of interconnected sites of writing, both in and outside classrooms. In collegiate writing classrooms, writing researchers were exploring evidence-based pedagogy and curricular designs attentive to student agency at various sites of writing, including in writing in the disciplines (Hayes et al. 2018), in the vertical writing curriculum (Melzer 2014), in technical communication (Brent 2011; Ford 2004), in disciplinarity more generally (Bergmann and Zepernick 2007; Driscoll and Jin 2018), with respect to writerly dispositions in the humanities (Driscoll and Wells 2012), and in the natural sciences (Baird and Dilger 2018). Still other researchers mapped the connections between writing education and non-classroom or non-academic writing contexts, including writing centers (Alexander, DePalma, and Ringer 2016; Bromley, Northway, and Schonberg 2016; Devet and Driscoll 2020), student athletics (Rifenburg 2018), internships (Baird and Dilger 2017), and co-op learning contexts (Brent 2012).

As the map of writing transfer has become clearer, researchers and teachers have gained insight into what happens before, during, and after college writing courses. This, in turn, opens newer avenues for research, including attention to the longitudinal view of writing development beyond the first year of college (Fraizer 2010), focus on prior knowledge (Robertson, Taczak, and Yancey 2012), and consideration of writing across one's life span (e.g., Bazerman et al. 2018). The connection between transfer and disciplinarity also continues to interest researchers, specifically as it relates to the "threshold concepts" that students need to know and develop for entry into the discipline (Adler-Kassner and Wardle 2015).

TRANSFER ACROSS MODALITIES OF COMPOSING

As alluded to above, multimodality and learning transfer share a great deal in terms of epistemology and connection to writing pedagogy. In 1996, the NLG used the term *transfer* relative to the "transformed practice" component of a pedagogy of multiliteracies "in which students transfer and re-create Designs of meaning from one context to another" (New London Group 1996, 83). One goal of this kind of transfer was to help students "engage critically with the conditions of their working lives," and the NLG suggested that a teacher's role was to create an environment "in which the students can demonstrate how they can design and carry out, in a reflective manner, new practices embedded in their own goals and values" (67, 87). Since the conditions of meaning production constantly change through the ongoing emergence of text technologies, a major goal of transfer within a pedagogy of multiliteracies is to prepare students to adapt their learning for those fluid and changing conditions. According to Cope and Kalantzis (2000), this preparation starts in the writing classroom, where students learn to create meaning from the various modes of communication and to reflect on their learning so they can transfer these communicative practices and multimodal composing processes to their "social futures." In addition, as students reflect on their own learning experiences with multimodal design and production and on ways that allow them to "carry out" that learning to "work in other contexts or cultural sites," students become more aware of their writing and learning goals and values around multimodality, which is likely to foster and enhance their ability to transfer that learning to those new contexts (New London Group 1996, 87–88).

Although the NLG linked transfer and multimodal composition conceptually more than two decades ago, our field has only recently bridged transfer and multimodality in research. For example, in his study of remediation of alphabetic personal essays into digital stories, DePalma (2015) shifts research on transfer to multimodal composing and to students' perceptions of the transfer of their writing practices across modalities of composing. DePalma concluded that there is a need to adjust pedagogical choices to suit students' fluid, evolving, and multifaceted needs. Subsequently, Jonathan Alexander, Michael-John DePalma, and Jeffrey Ringer (2016, 34) developed their adaptive remediation theory and argued that when students are prompted to think about their rhetorical choices while composing, they are able to "reshape and remediate their composing knowledge from one medium into another" or from alphabetic to multimodal texts.

The importance of perceptions and reflection for facilitating multimodal transfer has been echoed by a growing number of researchers. Irene L. Clark (2014), Paula Rosinski (2017), Ryan P. Shepherd (2018), and others have found that students often need pedagogical intervention to connect writing in digital spaces to writing in academic ones. Connecting students' current digital practices and future writing contexts is a form of transfer that writing teachers can scaffold and facilitate through multimodal pedagogies and encouraging reflection. If students feel that their self-sponsored digital media practices have no place in the writing classroom, teachers miss the opportunity to engage them in rhetorical and critical media practice and in meaningful metacognition that would facilitate transferring those practices to future writing.

In addition, researchers have begun to connect transfer and multimodality through new methods and methodologies, not only developing methods for capturing transfer of students' digital writing processes (Pigg 2020) and social media practices (Shepherd 2018) but using multimodal methods—like video—in the study of transfer across media (VanKooten 2020).

Drawing from work in multimodality and transfer, *Multimodal Composition and Writing Transfer* employs these theoretical and pedagogical frameworks to further develop the concept of "multimodal transfer." This concept builds off of the concept of writing transfer, or adapting writing knowledge learned in one writing context to develop and enhance writing in other writing contexts. Multimodal transfer involves adapting knowledge of communicative modes to understand, develop, and enhance communication across other modes and contexts. Because multimodal transfer is not limited to writing as it has been traditionally defined (that is, alphabetic writing in print), multimodal transfer may involve adaptation from one mode to another—such as using visual design principles to help organize an analytical essay—or adapting from one context to another, such as using rhetorical knowledge learned in first-year writing to help write effective comments in a computer coding class.

This sense of multimodal transfer continues efforts to expand the definitions of writing and composing that undergird and guide our teaching. When students draw on communicative practices beyond traditional, alphabetic writing to inform their composing and rhetorical practices, they learn to hone practices not historically valued in school contexts: writing for digital spaces, creating multimedia texts, visual and spatial learning, multimodal thinking, and other "home" literacies. As important, students learn about writing in ways that help them connect those literacies—and transfer knowledge and practice from those contexts—to situations often not thought of as "writing." We believe multimodal transfer can extend writing theory, pedagogy, research, and application beyond what either multimodal composition or writing transfer could do alone. We hope that by bringing these conversations together, we extend them both.

SITUATING THE COLLECTION

Multimodal Composition and Writing Transfer stands at the intersection of two important conversations happening in writing studies: multimodality and writing transfer. As noted above, both of these conversations have been covered extensively and well by others in the field. We now have more than twenty years of research and scholarship on multimodal composition. Similarly, we now have more than twenty years of writing transfer research. In fact, there has even been a trend in recent years that looks at this overlap between the two conversations, including the work of the editors and authors of this collection (Alexander, DePalma, and Ringer 2016; DePalma and Alexander 2015; Mina 2017, 2021; Shepherd 2018; Yancey et al. 2019) as well as others contributing to it (DePalma 2015; Jiang 2020; Roozen 2012; VanKooten 2020; Yancey 2017). We hope to continue and expand that conversation in these pages.

Part of how *Multimodal Composition and Writing Transfer* continues the conversation is through looking at multimodality, writing transfer, *and* specific topics—such as the role of language in multimodal composition, the different exigencies and contexts in which people compose multimodally, and the ways these composing practices inform and are informed by classroom writing practices. The editors and authors of this collection have put forth every effort to provide data-informed research. The volume includes chapters that use multiple methods of inquiry, such as case studies, interviews, surveys, classroom practice, and combinations of these and other methods. These chapters also draw on a variety of analytical lenses for making sense of their data. Some chapters even provide new methods for researching multimodal composition. We hope these methods, frames, and data help change the way the field sees multimodality and writing transfer.

This collection leaves many roads unexplored and many questions open. We hope that the chapters presented here will lead to other areas of inquiry, and we invite the scholars reading *Multimodal Composition and Writing Transfer* to explore ways to address the questions that remain. These chapters represent what we saw when we stood at the intersection of multimodality and writing transfer research. We hope you might see different things at and beyond that same intersection. We hope to one day read about views we could not see from here, like work on multimodal transfer in different disciplines, in technical and professional writing contexts, and in additional transnational contexts.

CHAPTER SUMMARIES

Multimodal Composition and Writing Transfer begins with the foreword, "Dimensions of Transfer and the Role of Multimodality," by Chris M. Anson. Anson explores the nature of writing transfer and its relationship to multimodal composing. He offers five "additions" to our understanding of writing, transfer, and multimodality. This foreword complicates the notion of what transfer is and how we perceive it, but it also introduces why *multimodality* is important to the discussion of writing transfer.

From here, the collection proceeds in three sections: "Multimodality and Transfer in the First-Year Writing Curriculum," "Multimodality and Transfer in the Vertical Curriculum," and "Multimodality and Transfer across the Writerly Life." The first section, "Multimodality and Transfer in the First-Year Writing Curriculum," starts with first-year writing, the most studied area of writing transfer. However, these chapters shed new light on this familiar ground. Crystal VanKooten's chapter, "Seeing It, Hearing It, Feeling It," introduces a new method of data collection for writing transfer scholars. VanKooten uses analysis of student video compositions and videos of interviews with students about their compositions to look for evidence of writing transfer. She demonstrates the use of expanded research methods, such as her video approach, as scholars continue to explore multimodal transfer. In "Making Transfer Matter across Digital Media Platforms," Jialei Jiang explores the affordances of three online composing tools for facilitating writing transfer. Drawing on mixed methods data from seventy-three students' reflections on using these platforms, Jiang concludes that some platforms may facilitate learning transfer more easily and presents four pedagogical recommendations for how to maximize potential benefits and minimize potential drawbacks. Joseph Anthony Wilson and Josie Rose Portz offer an alternative view of exploring multimodal writing transfer in their chapter, "On the Labor of Writing Transfer." Instead of looking primarily at digital texts, they explore the idea of "multimodality" as it occurs through the textual practices of translation and linguistic boundary crossing by following the case study of Zhannat as she composes in different semiotic modes and different languages. Together, these chapters offer new approaches to first-year writing, multimodality, and writing transfer not yet investigated in other research. VanKooten offers a method of video-based interviews that can be used beyond first-year writing to illuminate instances of writing transfer, Jiang explores specifically how the uses of different platforms may facilitate learning transfer, and Wilson and Portz offer a view of first-year writing approaches from outside the US and with a focus on non-native speakers of English.

In the second section, "Multimodality and Transfer in the Vertical Curriculum," the focus of multimodal transfer shifts to the vertical writing curriculum. Building on and expanding out from first-year writing, these chapters show, collectively, how multimodal transfer looks in the broader university context and why it is important in developing writers. In "Equipping Tutors to Transfer Multimodal Writing Knowledge to Writing Center Contexts," Kara Poe Alexander, Becca Cassady, and Michael-John DePalma offer insights into how writing center consultants transfer prior multimodal composing knowledge to their consultations. Drawing on interviews with graduate and undergraduate consultants in two writing centers, they suggest that consultants may not always be able to adapt their prior knowledge, despite wide-ranging experience with multimodal composing, and they offer solutions to overcome this challenge. In the next chapter, "It's Not Like I Can Put a Picture of a Paper on Instagram," Anna V. Knutson illuminates the role of genre in writing transfer across modes by interviewing and collecting writing from eight undergraduate students taking part in feminist organizations on campus. She demonstrates that students can and do engage in multimodal transfer if they perceive the textual genres as related—a relationship often linked to the length of each genre—and she uses this knowledge to call for a greater emphasis on genre in composition classes. Ryan P. Shepherd's chapter, "The Other Curriculum," draws on a four-year longitudinal study in which he interviewed six university students about their social media usage over the course of their college careers. He uses these data to present "the other curriculum," or writing knowledge that students learn tacitly outside of school settings. He finds that students value the relationship between their university and "other" curricula less and less as their education progresses. To promote multimodal transfer, Shepherd argues for a greater emphasis on connecting students' composing experiences inside and outside of school. These chapters offer insights into how writing transfer continues for students beyond first-year writing contexts—as they work in the writing center, as they engage in student organizations, and as they write on social media. All three chapters present ways students' writing lives expand beyond the writing they are doing in school classrooms alone.

The final section, "Transfer across the Writerly Life," further branches out to connect multimodal transfer experiences across writers' lives. These chapters offer bigger-picture explorations of subjects such as writing majors, curricular development, extracurricular literate activity, and instructor disposition. Kevin Roozen frames multimodal transfer as literate activity, tracing multiple semiotic experiences in which learners make meaning across various times and contexts in his chapter, "Drawing Worlds Together." Roozen focuses on the case study of Laura and how her experiences with drawing informed her understanding of meaning making for medical illustration. In his chapter, "Rhetoric in Its

Fullness," Logan Bearden analyzes the use of metalanguage in composition curricula documentation to explore how these texts help students develop a meta-awareness of semiotic potentials that foster multimodal transfer. Looking at the curricular documents of ten university writing programs that integrate multimodal composition, Bearden finds that a rhetorical approach to constructing such documents could itself influence multimodal transfer. Travis Maynard's chapter, "A Curriculum Delivered, a Curriculum Remembered," explores how alumni of writing and rhetoric majors succeed (or fail) at multimodal transfer in composing beyond their major. Maynard draws on both survey data for a "macro-level" portrait of the program and six interviews with individual alumni to understand students' individual experiences. With special attention to extracurricular and career writing, Maynard offers three programmatic design strategies for writing majors seeking to promote multimodal transfer. The chapter by Jeff Naftzinger, "If You Build It, Will They Use It," provides a look at multimodal composition infrastructure on university campuses and details roadblocks to instructor use of this infrastructure. He focuses on four graduate instructor case studies to demonstrate how disposition and communities of practice may interfere with integrating multimodal composition assignments into courses. The chapters in this section highlight the extracurricular, non-academic, and professional influences on students' writing transfer and serve to broaden our understanding of how transfer may play out in non-writing contexts, in careers, and in learning to teach.

The collection ends with an afterword by Kathleen Blake Yancey, "Transfer Happens; Transfer Doesn't Happen." This chapter connects themes in the collection, offers a broad view of the state of writing transfer and multimodality, and provides paths forward for future research.

We hope this collection presents a broad view of writers' multimodal composing lives and how these multimodal composing practices in various contexts connect to other forms of writing and making meaning. As you read, please consider the ways your own writing and your writing pedagogy may be informed by the various types of composing you do both in and outside of academia. We also hope you will consider ways you can further these conversations in your classes, your institutions, and your research.

NOTES

1. For a history of multimodality in writing studies, see Palmeri (2012). An overview of writing transfer history is included in Yancey, Robertson, and Taczak (2014), but for a larger overview of the history of learning transfer more broadly, see Haskell (2001).

2. Notably, scholars in technical communication have been studying multimodality and visual rhetoric for years (e.g., Bernhardt 1986, 1993; Haas 1996; Handa 2004; Selber 1997), but they did not necessarily use the term. Moreover, the study of multimodality did not really cross over to rhetoric and composition at large until the New London Group's (1996) work, in spite of its emphasis in technical communication.

REFERENCES

Adler-Kassner, Linda, and Elizabeth Wardle, eds. 2015. *Naming What We Know: Threshold Concepts of Writing Studies.* Logan: Utah State University Press.

Alexander, Jonathan, and Jacqueline Rhodes. 2014. *On Multimodality: New Media in Composition Studies.* Urbana, IL: Conference on College Composition and Communication and National Council of Teachers of English.

Alexander, Kara Poe. 2013. "Material Affordances: The Potential of Scrapbooks in the Composition Classroom." *Composition Forum* 27 (Spring). compositionforum.com/issue/27/material-affordances.php.

Alexander, Kara Poe, Michael-John DePalma, and Jeffrey M. Ringer. 2016. "Adaptive Remediation and the Facilitation of Transfer in Multiliteracy Center Contexts." *Computers and Composition* 41: 32–45.

Alexander, Kara Poe, Michael-John DePalma, Lisa Shaver, and Danielle Williams. 2019. "Approaching the (Re)Design of Writing Majors: Contexts of Research, Forms of Inquiry, and Recommendations for Faculty." *Composition Studies* 47 (9): 16–37.

Alexander, Kara Poe, Beth Powell, and Sonya C. Green. 2012. "Understanding Modal Affordances: Student Perceptions of Potentials and Limitations in Multimodal Composition." *Basic Writing eJournal* 10 (11). bwe.ccny.cuny.edu/alexandermodalaffordances.html.

Anderson, Daniel. 2008. "The Low Bridge to High Benefits: Entry-Level Multimedia, Literacies, and Motivation." *Computers and Composition* 25: 40–60.

Anderson, Daniel, Anthony Atkins, Cheryl Ball, Krista Homicz Millar, Cynthia Selfe, and Richard Selfe. 2006. "Integrating Multimodality into Composition Curricula: Survey Methodology and Results from a CCCC Research Grant." *Composition Studies* 34 (2): 59–84.

Andrus, Sonja, Sharon Mitchler, and Howard Tinberg. 2019. "Teaching for Writing Transfer: A Practical Guide for Teachers." *Teaching English in the Two-Year College* 47 (1): 76–89.

Anson, Chris M., and Jessie L. Moore, eds. 2017. *Critical Transitions: Writing and the Question of Transfer.* Fort Collins, CO: WAC Clearinghouse.

Baird, Neil, and Bradley Dilger. 2017. "How Students Perceive Transitions: Dispositions and Transfer in Internships." *College Composition and Communication* 68 (4): 684–712.

Baird, Neil, and Bradley Dilger. 2018. "Dispositions in the Natural Science Laboratories: The Roles of Individuals and Contexts in Writing Transfer." *Across the Disciplines: A Journal of Language, Learning, and Academic Writing* 15 (4): 1–20.

Balester, Valerie. 2012. "The Multiliteracy Writing Center: Fostering Curricular Change." *Praxis: A Writing Center Journal* 9 (2): 1–10.

Ball, Cheryl E. 2004. "Show, Not Tell: The Value of New Media Scholarship." *Computers and Composition* 21: 403–425.

Ball, Cheryl E., and Ryan M. Moeller. 2008. "Converging the ASS[umptions] between U and ME; or How New Media Can Bridge a Scholarly/Creative Split in English Studies." *Computers and Composition Online.* http://cconlinejournal.org/convergence/index.html.

Bazerman, Charles, Arthur N. Applebee, Virginia W. Berninger, Deborah Brandt, Steve Graham, Jill V. Jeffery, Paul Kei Matsuda, Sandra Murphy, Deborah Wells Rowe, Mary Schleppegrell, and Kristen Campbell Wilcox. 2018. *The Lifespan Development of Writing*. Urbana, IL: National Council of Teachers of English. https://wac.colostate.edu/books/ncte/lifespan-writing/.

Beaufort, Anne. 1999. *Writing in the Real World: Making the Transition from School to Work*. New York: Teachers College Press.

Beaufort, Anne. 2007. *College Writing and Beyond: A New Framework for University Writing Instruction*. Logan: Utah State University Press.

Bergmann, Linda, and Janet Zepernick. 2007. "Disciplinarity and Transference: Students' Perceptions of Learning to Write." *WPA: A Journal of Writing Program Administration* 31 (1): 124–149.

Bernhardt, Stephen A. 1986. "Seeing the Text." *College Composition and Communication* 37 (1): 66–78.

Bernhardt, Stephen A. 1993. "The Shape of Text to Come: The Texture of Print on Screens." *College Composition and Communication* 44 (2): 151–175.

Blair, J. Anthony. 2004. "The Rhetoric of Visual Arguments." In *Defining Visual Rhetorics*, edited by Charles A. Hill and Marguerite H. Helmers, 41–62. Mahwah, NJ: Lawrence Erlbaum.

Bourelle, Andrew, Tiffany Bourelle, and Natasha Jones. 2015. "Multimodality in the Technical Communication Classroom: Viewing Classical Rhetoric through a Twenty-First Century Lens." *Technical Communication Quarterly* 24 (4): 306–327.

Bowen, Tracey, and Carl Whithaus, eds. 2013. *Multimodal Literacies and Emerging Genres*. Pittsburgh, PA: University of Pittsburgh Press.

Brent, Doug. 2011. "Transfer, Transformation, and Rhetorical Knowledge: Insights from Transfer Theory." *Journal of Business and Technical Communication* 25 (4): 396–420.

Brent, Doug. 2012. "Crossing Boundaries: Co-op Students Relearning to Write." *College Composition and Communication* 63 (4): 558–592.

Bromley, Pam, Kara Northway, and Eliana Schonberg. 2016. "Transfer and Dispositions in Writing Centers: A Cross-Institutional, Mixed-Methods Study." *Across the Disciplines: A Journal of Language, Learning, and Academic Writing* 13 (1): 1–15.

Burn, Andrew, and David Parker. 2003. "Tiger's Big Plan: Multimodality and the Moving Image." In *Multimodal Literacy*, edited by Carey Jewitt and Gunther Kress, 56–72. New York: Peter Lang, 2003.

Carpenter, Russell G., and Shawn Apostel. 2016. "A Space to Play, a Space to Compose: A Model for Creative Collaborations and Composition Practices." In *Making Space: Writing Instruction, Infrastructure, and Multiliteracies*, edited by James P. Purdy and Dànielle Nicole DeVoss. Ann Arbor: University of Michigan Press and Sweetland Digital Rhetoric Collaborative. https://www.digitalrhetoriccollaborative.org/makingspace/ch6.html.

Carpenter, Russell, and Sohui Lee, eds. 2016. "Pedagogies of Multimodality and the Future of Multiliteracy Centers." Special issue of *Computers and Composition* 41.

Clark, Irene L. 2014. "Print/New Media Transfer: Genre Issues." *Journal of Teaching Writing* 29 (1): 21–44.

Cleary, Michelle Navarre. 2013. "Flowing and Freestyling: Learning from Adult Students about Process Knowledge Transfer." *College Composition and Communication* 64 (4): 661–687.

Cook, Kelli Cargile. 2009. "Layered Literacies: A Theoretical Frame for Technical Communication Pedagogy." *Technical Communication Quarterly* 11 (1): 5–29.

Cope, Bill, and Mary Kalantzis, eds. 2000. *Multiliteracies: Literacy Learning and the Design of Social Futures*. London: Routledge.

DePalma, Michael-John. 2015. "Tracing Transfer across Media: Investigating Writers' Perceptions of Cross-Contextual and Rhetorical Reshaping in Processes of Remediation." *College Composition and Communication* 66 (4): 615–642.

DePalma, Michael-John, and Kara Poe Alexander. 2015. "A Bag Full of Snakes: Negotiating the Challenges of Multimodal Composition." *Computers and Composition* 37: 182–200.

DePalma, Michael-John, and Jeffrey Ringer. 2011. "Toward a Theory of Adaptive Transfer: Expanding Disciplinary Discussions of 'Transfer' in Second-Language Writing and Composition Studies." *Journal of Second Language Writing* 22 (2): 134–147.

Devet, Bonnie, and Dana Lynn Driscoll. 2020. *Transfer of Learning in the Writing Center: A WLN Digital Edited Collection*. wlnjournal.org/digitaleditedcollection2/index.html.

Donovan, M. Suzanne, John D. Bransford, and James W. Pellegrino. 1999. *How People Learn: Bridging Research and Practice*. Washington, DC: Committee on Learning Research and Educational Practice, National Research Council.

Downs, Douglas, and Elizabeth Wardle. 2007. "Teaching about Writing, Righting Misconceptions: (Re)Envisioning 'First-Year Composition' as 'Introduction to Writing Studies.'" *College Composition and Communication* 58 (4): 552–585.

Driscoll, Dana Lynn, and Daewoo Jin. 2018. "The Box under the Bed: How Learner Epistemologies Shape Writing Transfer." *Across the Disciplines* 15 (4): 1–21.

Driscoll, Dana Lynn, and Jennifer Wells. 2012. "Beyond Knowledge and Skills: Writing Transfer and the Role of Student Dispositions in and beyond the Writing Classroom." *Composition Forum* 26 (Fall). https://www.compositionforum.com/issue/26/beyond-knowledge-skills.php.

Elon Statement on Writing Transfer. 2015. https://www.centerforengagedlearning.org/elon-statement-on-writing-transfer/.

Fishman, Teddi. 2010. "When It Isn't Even on the Page: Peer Consulting in Multimedia Environments." In *Multiliteracy Centers: Writing Center Work, New Media, and Multimodal Rhetoric*, edited by David M. Sheridan and James Inman, 59–73. Cresskill, NJ: Hampton.

Ford, Julie Dyke. 2004. "Knowledge Transfer across Disciplines: Tracking Rhetorical Strategies from a Technical Communication Classroom to an Engineering Classroom." *IEEE Transactions on Professional Communication* 47 (4): 301–315.

Fraizer, Dan. 2010. "First Steps beyond First Year: Coaching Transfer after FYC." *WPA: Writing Program Administration* 33 (3): 34–57.

Gorzelsky, Gwen, Dana Lynn Driscoll, Joe Paszek, Ed Jones, and Carol Hayes. 2016. "Cultivating Constructive Metacognition: A New Taxonomy for Writing Studies." In *Critical Transitions: Writing and the Question of Transfer*, edited by Chris M. Anson and Jessie L. Moore, 215–246. Fort Collins, CO: WAC Clearinghouse.

Haas, Christina. 1996. *Writing Technology: Studies on the Materiality of Literacy*. Mahwah, NJ: Lawrence Erlbaum.

Halbritter, Bump. 2006. "Musical Rhetoric in Integrated-Media Composition." *Computers and Composition* 23 (3): 317–334.

Handa, Carolyn, ed. 2004. *Visual Rhetoric in a Digital World: A Critical Sourcebook*. Boston: Bedford/St. Martin's, 2004.

Haskell, Robert E. 2001. *Transfer of Learning: Cognition, Instruction, and Reasoning*. San Diego: Academic Press.

Hayes, Carol, Ed Jones, Gwen Gorzelsky, and Dana L. Driscoll. 2018. "Adapting Writing about Writing: Curricular Implications of Cross-Institutional Data from the Writing Transfer Project." *WPA: Writing Program Administration* 41 (2): 65–88.

Hill, Charles A. 2004. "Reading the Visual in College Writing Classes." In *Visual Rhetoric in a Digital World: A Critical Sourcebook*, edited by Carolyn Handa, 107–130. Boston: Bedford/St. Martin's.

Inman, James A. 2010. "Designing Multiliteracy Centers: A Zoning Approach." In *Multiliteracy Centers: Writing Center Work, New Media, and Multimodal Rhetoric*, edited by David M. Sheridan and James Inman, 19–32. Cresskill, NJ: Hampton.

Jewitt, Carey. 2005. "Multimodality, 'Reading' and 'Writing' for the Twenty-First Century." *Discourse: Studies in the Cultural Politics of Education* 26 (3): 315–331.

Jiang, Jialei. 2020. "'I Never Know What to Expect': Aleatory Identity Play in Fortnite and Its Implications for Multimodal Composition." *Computers and Composition* 55: 1–14.

Klages, Marisa A., and J. Elizabeth Clark. 2009. "New Worlds of Errors and Expectations: Basic Writers and Digital Assumptions." *Journal of Basic Writing* 28 (1): 32–49.

Kress, Gunther. 1998. "Visual and Verbal Modes of Representation in Electronically Mediated Communication: The Potentials of New Forms of Text." In *Page to Screen, Taking Literacy into the Electronic Era*, edited by Ilana Snyder, 53–79. London: Routledge.

Kress, Gunther. 2000. "Design and Transformation: New Theories of Meaning." In *Multiliteracies: Literacy Learning and the Design of Social Futures*, edited by Bill Cope and Mary Kalantzis, 153–161. New York: Routledge.

Kress, Gunther. 2010. *Multimodality: A Social Semiotic Approach to Contemporary Communication*. New York: Routledge.

Kress, Gunther, and Theo van Leeuwen. 2001. *Multimodal Discourse: The Modes and Media of Contemporary Communication*. London: Arnold.

Lee, Rory. 2020. "Making the Case: The Implementation of Multimodality within Undergraduate Major Programs in Writing and Rhetoric." In *Writing Changes: Alphabetic Text and Multimodal Composition*, edited by Pegeen Reichert Powell, 253–273. New York: Modern Language Association.

Lee, Sohui. 2012. "'Multimodal Thinking' and New Media Tutor Training Practices." In "The Idea of a Writing Center: Six Responses," by Valerie Balester, Nancy Grimm, Sohui Lee, Jackie Grutsch McKinney, David Sheridan, and Naomi Silver. *Praxis: A Writing Center Journal* 9 (2): 5–6.

Lee, Sohui, and Russ E. Carpenter. 2017. "Design and Pitch: Introducing Multiliteracies through Scientific Research Posters." *Writing Center Journal* 36 (2): 205–232.

Lee, Sohui, and Russell Carpenter. 2019. "Startup Multiliteracy Centers and Faculty Collaboration on Multimodal Pedagogy." *WLN: A Journal of Writing Center Scholarship* 44 (1–2): 11–18.

McCarthy, Lucille Parkinson. 1987. "A Stranger in Strange Lands: A College Student Writing across the Curriculum." *Research in the Teaching of English* 21 (3): 233–265.

McKinney, Jackie Grutsch. 2009. "New Media Matters: Tutoring in the Late Age of Print." *Writing Center Journal* 29 (2): 28–51.

McKinney, Jackie Grutsch. 2010. "The New Media (R)evolution: Multiple Models for Multiliteracies." In *Multiliteracy Centers: Writing Center Work, New Media, and Multimodal Rhetoric*, edited by David M. Sheridan and James Inman, 207–223. Cresskill, NJ: Hampton.

McKinney, Jackie Grutsch. 2012. "Tastes Change." *Praxis: A Writing Center Journal* 9 (2): 3–4.

Melzer, Dan. 2014. *Assignments across the Curriculum: A National Study of College Writing*. Logan: Utah State University Press.

Mina, Lilian W. 2017. "Social Media in the FYC Class: The New Digital Divide." In *Social Writing/Social Media: Publics, Presentations, and Pedagogies*, edited by Douglas M. Walls and Stephanie Vie, 263–282. Fort Collins, CO: WAC Clearinghouse.

Mina, Lilian W. 2021. "A Transmodal Framework for Teaching Multimodal Composing Practices to Multilingual Students." In *Plurilingual Pedagogies for Multilingual Writing Classrooms: Engaging the Rich Communicative Repertoires of U.S. Students*, edited by Kay M. Losey and Gail Shuck, 45–57. New York: Routledge.

Moore, Jessie L., and Randall Bass, eds. 2017. *Understanding Writing Transfer: Implications for Transformative Student Learning in Higher Education*. Sterling, VA: Stylus.

New London Group. 1996. "A Pedagogy of Multiliteracies: Designing Social Futures." *Harvard Educational Review* 66 (1): 60–92.

Nowacek, Rebecca S. 2011. *Agents of Integration: Understanding Transfer as a Rhetorical Act*. Carbondale: Southern Illinois University Press.

Palmeri, Jason. 2012. *Remixing Composition: A History of Multimodal Writing Pedagogy*. Carbondale: Southern Illinois University Press.

Pigg, Stacey. 2020. *Transient Literacies in Action: Composing with the Mobile Surround*. Fort Collins, CO: WAC Clearinghouse.
Powell, Beth, Kara Poe Alexander, and Sonya Borton. 2011. "Interaction of Author, Audience, and Purpose in Multimodal Texts: Students' Discovery of Their Role as Composer." *Kairos* 15 (2). kairos.technorhetoric.net/praxis/tiki-index.php?page=Student_Composers.
Reid, Gwendolynne, Robin Snead, Keon Pettiway, and Brent Simoneaux. 2016. "Multimodal Communication in the University: Surveying Faculty across Disciplines." *Across the Disciplines* 13 (1): 1–28.
Rifenburg, J. Michael. 2018. *The Embodied Playbook: Writing Practices of Student-Athletes*. Logan: Utah State University Press.
Robertson, Liane, Kara Taczak, and Kathleen Yancey. 2012. "Notes toward a Theory of Prior Knowledge and Its Role in College Composers' Transfer of Knowledge and Practice." *Composition Forum* 26. https://files.eric.ed.gov/fulltext/EJ985812.pdf.
Roozen, Kevin. 2012. "Comedy Stages, Poets Projects, Sports Columns, and Kinesiology 341: Illuminating the Importance of Basic Writers' Self-Sponsored Literacies." *Journal of Basic Writing* 31: 99–132.
Rosinski, Paula. 2017. "Students' Perceptions of the Transfer of Rhetorical Knowledge between Digital Self-Sponsored Writing and Academic Writing: The Importance of Authentic Contexts and Reflection." In *Critical Transitions: Writing and the Question of Transfer*, edited by Chris M. Anson and Jessie L. Moore, 247–271. Fort Collins, CO: WAC Clearinghouse.
Selber, Stuart A. 1997. *Computers and Technical Communication: Pedagogical and Programmatic Perspectives*. Greenwich, CT: Ablex, 1997.
Selber, Stuart A. 2004. *Multiliteracies for a Digital Age*. Carbondale: Southern Illinois University Press.
Selfe, Cynthia L. 2004. "Students Who Teach Us: A Case Study of a New Media Text Designer." In *Writing New Media: Theory and Applications for Expanding the Teaching of Composition*, edited by Anne Frances Wysocki, Johndan Johnson-Eilola, Cynthia L. Selfe, and Geoffrey Sirc, 43–66. Logan: Utah State University Press.
Selfe, Cynthia L. 2009. "The Movement of Air, the Breath of Meaning: Aurality and Multimodal Composing." *College Composition and Communication* 60 (4): 616–663.
Selfe, Cynthia L., ed. 2007. *Multimodal Composition: Resources for Teachers*. Cresskill, NJ: Hampton.
Shepherd, Ryan P. 2018. "Digital Writing, Multimodality, and Learning Transfer: Crafting Connections between Composition and Online Composing." *Computers and Composition* 48: 103–114.
Sheppard, Jennifer. 2009. "The Rhetorical Work of Multimedia Production Practices: It's More than Just Technical Skill." *Computers and Composition* 26 (2): 122–131.
Sheridan, David M. 2012. "'You Have Made Me Very Angry!' Mapping Writing Center Anxieties about Multiliteracies." In "The Idea of a Writing Center: Six Responses," by Valerie Balester, Nancy Grimm, Sohui Lee, Jackie Grutsch McKinney, David Sheridan, and Naomi Silver. *Praxis: A Writing Center Journal* 9 (2): 2–3.
Sheridan, David M., and James A. Inman, eds. 2010. *Multiliteracy Centers: Writing Center Work, New Media, and Multimodal Rhetoric*. Cresskill, NJ: Hampton.
Shipka, Jody. 2011. *Toward a Composition Made Whole*. Pittsburgh, PA: University of Pittsburgh Press.
Smith, Cheryl C. 2008. "Technologies for Transcending a Focus on Error: Blogs and Democratic Aspirations in First-Year Composition." *Journal of Basic Writing* 27 (1): 35–60.
Snead, Robin. 2011. "'Transfer-Ability': Issues of Transfer and FYC." WPA-CompPile Research Bibliographies 18. *WPA-CompPile Research Bibliographies*. http://comppile.org/wpa/bibliographies/Bib18/Snead.pdf.

Snead, Robin, Kara Poe Alexander, Matthew Davis, Lilian W. Mina, and Ryan P. Shepherd. 2022. "Rethinking Transfer: The Rise of *Writing Transfer* across Contexts." *WPA-CompPile Research Bibliographies*. https://wac.colostate.edu/docs/comppile/wpa/rethinking_transfer.pdf.

Snyder, Ilana. 1998. *Page to Screen: Taking Literacy into the Electronic Era*. London: Routledge.

Sorapure, Madeleine. 2006. "Between Modes: Assessing Student New Media Compositions." *Kairos* 10 (2). https://kairos.technorhetoric.net/10.2/coverweb/sorapure/.

Taczak, Kara, and Liane Robertson. 2016. "Reiterative Reflection in the Twenty-First Century Writing Classroom: An Integrated Approach to Teaching for Transfer." In *A Rhetoric of Reflection*, edited by Kathleen Blake Yancey, 42–64. Logan: Utah State University Press.

Takayoshi, Pamela, and Cynthia L. Selfe. 2007. "Thinking about Multimodality." In *Multimodal Composition: Resources for Teachers*, edited by Cynthia L. Selfe, 1–12. Cresskill, NJ: Hampton.

Trimbur, John. 2002. "Delivering the Message: Typography and the Materiality of Writing." In *Rhetoric and Composition as Intellectual Work*, edited by Gary A. Olson, 188–202. Carbondale: Southern Illinois University Press.

VanKooten, Crystal. 2020. *Transfer across Media: Using Digital Video in the Teaching of Writing*. Logan: Computers and Composition Digital Press and Utah State University Press. https://ccdigitalpress.org/book/transfer-across-media/index.html.

Walsh, Maureen. 2006. "The 'Textual Shift': Examining the Reading Process with Print, Visual, and Multimodal Texts." *Australian Journal of Language and Literacy* 29 (1): 24–37.

Walters, Shannon. 2010. "Toward an Accessible Pedagogy: Dis/ability, Multimodality, and Universal Design in the Technical Communication Classroom." *Technical Communication Quarterly* 19 (4): 427–454.

Walwema, Josephine, and Dana Lynn Driscoll. 2015. "Activating the Uptake of Prior Knowledge through Metacognitive Awareness: An Exploratory Study of Writing Transfer in Documentation and Source Use in Professional Writing Courses." *Programmatic Perspectives* 7 (1): 21–42.

Wardle, Elizabeth, and Doug Downs. 2022. *Writing about Writing*. 5th edition. Boston: Bedford/St. Martin's.

Wysocki, Anne Frances. 2004. "Opening New Media to Writing: Openings and Justifications." In *Writing New Media: Theory and Applications for Expanding the Teaching of Composition*, edited by Anne Frances Wysocki, Johndan Johnson-Eilola, Cynthia L. Selfe, and Geoffrey Sirc, 1–41. Logan: Utah State University Press.

Wysocki, Anne Frances. 2005. "awaywithwords: On the Possibilities in Unavailable Designs." *Computers and Composition* 22 (1): 55–62.

Yancey, Kathleen Blake. 2004. "Made Not Only in Words: Composition in a New Key." *College Composition and Communication* 56 (2): 297–328.

Yancey, Kathleen Blake. 2017. "Writing, Transfer, and ePortfolios: A Possible Trifecta in Supporting Student Learning." In *Understanding Writing Transfer: Implications for Transformative Student Learning in Higher Education*, edited by Jessie L. Moore and Randall Bass, 39–48. Sterling, VA: Stylus.

Yancey, Kathleen Blake, Matthew Davis, Liane Robertson, Kara Taczak, and Erin Workman. 2018. "Writing across College: Key Terms and Multiple Contexts as Factors Promoting Students' Transfer of Writing Knowledge and Practice." *WAC Journal* 29: 42–63.

Yancey, Kathleen Blake, Matthew Davis, Liane Robertson, Kara Taczak, and Erin Workman. 2019. "The Teaching for Transfer Curriculum: The Role of Concurrent and Inside- and Outside-School Contexts in Supporting Students' Writing Development." *College Composition and Communication* 71 (2): 268–295.

Yancey, Kathleen Blake, Liane Robertson, and Kara Taczak. 2014. *Writing across Contexts: Transfer, Composition, and Sites of Writing*. Logan: Utah State University Press.

PART I

Multimodality and Transfer in the First-Year Writing Curriculum

1
SEEING IT, HEARING IT, FEELING IT
Digital Methods for the Study of Transfer across Media

Crystal VanKooten

First-year writing student Tiara learned a lot about writing and herself as a writer through the work she completed in Composition I. This work included several written papers and a multimodal project in which she composed a short video and a Prezi and did an in-class presentation about a future career in sociology. When I talked with Tiara about what she learned through these assignments, she revealed evidence that she had transferred knowledge across media: from written paper, to video, to Prezi, to presenting in class, and back again to other written papers. She told me that the video and the Prezi, situated between papers, helped her develop an "understanding that I am very creative, and I am very visual, and I am very detailed when I'm writing." This understanding was something she could take with her during and after the course and apply as she wrote and designed in other contexts.

As a researcher, I gained insight into Tiara's experiences through listening to and rereading her own spoken accounts of her learning and written transcripts of interviews. But I also built knowledge through watching Tiara's mannerisms and actions, seeing her gestures, and hearing her tone of voice and speech through video recordings of interviews and in-class work. I watched, on video, as Tiara composed her Prezi, finding images online and making visual design choices. I listened to her confident voice as she presented to peers in class. I felt her joy as she laughed, describing how making a "little video" could help her stand out against others in the job market who only knew how to write papers. Then, using a video editor, I layered clips of many of these moments with excerpts from her interview or her products. Video was a key aspect of a research methodology that helped me see, hear, and feel moments of multimodal transfer or the beginnings of transfer in Tiara's compositional experiences.

https://doi.org/10.7330/9781646425341.c001

Rhetoric and composition has been interested for several decades in if and how transfer—the act of connecting different writing tasks or contexts—works for student writers like Tiara (Moore 2012; Nowacek 2011; Wardle 2012). Tiara's acts of transfer are further complicated because they involve the recontextualization of multimodal compositional knowledge, one area into which the field has recently started to inquire (Alexander, DePalma, and Ringer 2016; DePalma 2015; Rosinski 2017; Shepherd 2018; VanKooten 2020). My analysis of Tiara's experiences and those of several other students in writing courses indicates that digital and multimodal methods of data collection, data analysis, and data presentation—particularly involving video—can help us better study and understand transfer across media.

In this chapter, I ask researchers to consider alternate, more expansive digital methods for the study of writing transfer. To illustrate what a research methodology that includes multimodal video methods can bring to inquiry about transfer, I discuss the composition experiences of five students—Mikayla, John, Tiara, Samuel, and Evan—all of whom composed videos and written essays in college writing classrooms. Within these students' experiences, evidence of transfer across media was revealed not only through talking with students about their work but also through analyzing student-authored digital products, observing process and bodies (in person and on video), listening to recorded student voices, and creating videos in which combinations of this evidence could be seen, heard, and felt. These findings suggest that our research methodologies and methods for studying transfer should include digital ways to observe, analyze, and present data and that video recording and editing offer exciting possibilities.

DIGITAL METHODOLOGIES AND METHODS FOR THE STUDY OF MULTIMODAL TRANSFER

Past research on writing transfer and research on digital media writing point to the importance of further examining multimodal and digital transfer, but few studies have employed digital methods to do so. Transfer researchers Kathleen Blake Yancey, Liane Robertson, and Kara Taczak (2014) and digital media scholar Jason Palmeri (2012) discuss the *potential* for multimodal and digital transfer, but empirical evidence of such transfer is hard to find in published studies. Michael-John DePalma (2015) focuses on two interview-based case studies where students transformed a written essay into a digital story; his study with Kara Poe Alexander and Jeffrey Ringer explores one student's process of remediation from print essay to digital story through the lens of multiliteracy centers (Alexander, DePalma, and Ringer 2016). Paul Baepler and Thomas Reynolds (2014) look for evidence of Henry Jenkins's "transmedia navigation" through surveys in two intermediate writing courses, and Paula Rosinski (2017) and Ryan P. Shepherd (2018) use surveys and interviews to inquire into how students perceive intersections (or lack thereof) between academic and self-sponsored digital writing. Jialei Jiang (chapter 2, this volume) explores the affordances of various digital platforms in promoting writing transfer for first-year writers, concluding that the composition of websites provides notable opportunities for connection making. These few studies begin the work of looking and listening for multimodal and digital transfer; as in other writing transfer scholarship, the researchers rely on interviews and surveys to find evidence of transfer, and they present their work through written academic prose. This is important research, and I suggest that rhetoric and composition should build on these studies by using digital methods—in particular video methods—to expand where and how we look and listen for multimodal transfer, opening our inquiry to multimodal understandings and expression of knowledge.

Others in the field are using digital methodologies and methods for inquiry into areas not directly related to transfer. Some study digital and online communities, writing about the risks and rewards of analyzing online texts and diverse communities (Haywood 2022; Sapienza 2007; Sidler 2007; Sparby 2022) and inquiring into ethics of representation (Fancher and Faris 2022), informed consent (Banks and Eble 2007; McKee 2008), and copyright/fair use (Edwards 2018). Others have studied processes of writing and rhetoric through the use of various technologies, including mobile phones (Addison 2007), screen capture (Geisler and Slattery 2007), video cameras and video editing (Butler 2022; Rowell 2022), and coding (Miller 2022). Hip-hop scholars argue for digital research methodologies grounded in practices of hip-hop and Black and Brown DJs, where collaboration, remixing, sampling, and reaching across communities are key for engaging real-world concerns and ameliorating inequality (Craig 2022; Del Hierro 2018; Duthely 2018; House 2022).

Many of these and other scholars also demonstrate their findings through images, graphs, sound bites, remixes, and video along with alphabetic description (Craig 2022; Fancher and Faris 2022; Özyeşilpınar and Beltran 2022; Rowell 2022). Temptaous Mckoy (2022), for example, illustrates the use of amplification rhetorics within TRAP Karaoke through an academic video that features TRAP music and lyrics, recorded interviews, and TRAP Karaoke audience interactions. Reflecting on her use of digital/video methods, Mckoy explains that "by simply writing these ideas and discoveries, I feel I would have dismissed the authenticity of the TRAP Karaoke space andddd, I wanted to be sure that the voices of those I interviewed were heard loud and clear" (51). For Mckoy, the collection, analysis, and presentation of digital video data enabled her to highlight rhetorics, voices, and experiences that are commonly excluded or overlooked.

Mckoy's (2022) work is one example of how digital video has emerged as a useful and necessary medium for research in rhetoric and composition. Video recording and editing enable participatory and feminist compositional practices (Arroyo 2013; Hidalgo 2017), illuminate the complexities of literacy sponsorship and allow for multiple, multisensory representations of data (Halbritter and Lindquist 2012), and place attention on embodied literacies and rhetorics (Cardinal 2019). In another recent study, Ann Shivers-McNair (2019) describes the use of the body, time, communities, and various video cameras and other equipment to enact a methodology of "3D interviewing" in a maker space where the researcher attends to words, gestures, bodies, objects, relationships, actions, and positionalities. Alison Cardinal (2019) also uses video but places cameras into the hands of participants and asks them to compose their own videos as part of her research into literacy, a method similar to Bump Halbritter and Julie Lindquist's (2012) four-phase video-based interview methodology for the collection and distribution of literacy narratives in which participants also make videos. For Cardinal (2019, 35), participatory video was a method that opened opportunities to account for oppressions of bodies that have often been marginalized, and it served as a measure "to ensure power is shared with participants throughout the research process." Shivers-McNair (2019), Halbritter and Lindquist (2012), and Cardinal (2019) illustrate that an ethical and careful use of video can open access, redistribute power, address inequality, and allow deep inquiry into the multiple and complex factors that comprise writing and literacy experiences.

One study by Stuart Blythe and Laura Gonzales (2016) uses video to study transfer. Pointing to the "limited set of methods" we use in writing transfer scholarship (including a heavy reliance on interviews and focus groups), Blythe and Gonzales open up new methodological possibilities through the use of screencast video recordings combined with artifact-based interviews to document twelve students' work in response to a writing assignment in an interdisciplinary biology course (608–609). Through coding video data, the researchers identified patterns and categories they could then verify and ask participants to elaborate on in the interviews (614). Ultimately, Blythe and Gonzales found that "students are indeed adapting lessons learned in high school and first-year writing" but that the strategies they adapted were often related to structural and surface features such as the five-paragraph essay form (626–627). In particular, the visual and audio data that Blythe and Gonzales gleaned from the screencast videos allowed them to build graphs and "to first visualize the specific writing strategies students used to compose in the course being studied, and then to inquire about how these writing strategies were developed and transferred throughout students' education" (628–629). The collection of video data not only provided the researchers with information that guided the follow-up interviews, but it provided visual and oral access to information about students' composing processes that would not have been available otherwise.

While Blythe and Gonzales (2016) do not analyze or present any of the video data in their print article, Gonzales (2015) has used the presentation of images drawn from video data in other work. In a study of multilingual writers, video recordings of focus group discussions allowed Gonzales to observe and discuss gestures that paired with verbal descriptions of multimodality. Gonzales (2015) explained that "since most research about composition students is focused on what instructors say about students' writing practices or what the students say about their own writing practices, using video to capture the embodied and visual discussion taking place during the focus groups provides an additional layer of understanding." Most publication venues in rhet/comp already allow any researcher to begin to explore this "additional layer of understanding" through the inclusion of visuals. Digital journals such as *Kairos, Composition Forum, Enculturation, Literacy in Composition Studies,* and others, as well as digital presses such as Computers and Composition Digital Press and the University of Michigan's Sweetland Digital Rhetoric Collaborative book series, now allow for the peer-reviewed presentation of sound and video.

Digital methods and methodologies are thus expanding in the field, and video in particular has emerged as a useful medium for opening access to and greater participation in research; for seeing, hearing, and feeling data; and for combining modes as we analyze and present data. Research on transfer, and multimodal transfer in particular, would benefit from video and other digital method/ologies as we look and listen for transfer in more sites in the experiences of more and different kinds of students. Visuals, audio, and video can help us become aware of more aspects that characterize participants and their work; they provide opportunities for multimodal analysis of data, and through these forms we can more persuasively present evidence of transfer. Below, I discuss several examples where collecting, analyzing, and presenting video data provided key insights into how college writers transferred knowledge across media. I highlight the composition experiences of Mikayla, John, Samuel, Tiara, and Evan and describe how working with video data helped me interpret and better understand aspects of these students' learning.

METHODOLOGY AND METHODS

Mikayla, John, Samuel, Tiara, and Evan took composition courses in 2016 and 2017 at a regional state university in the Midwest. They were participants in a larger qualitative study focusing on the development of meta-awareness about composition and transfer across media. Mikayla, John, Samuel, and Tiara were classmates in one first-year writing course in 2016, and their course was selected for the study because the curriculum included written essays and a video project and their instructor volunteered to be part of the study. I was an external researcher in their classroom; I recruited participants, attended class, observed and video recorded interactions and lessons, and interviewed student participants as well as the course instructor on video several times. Evan was a student in an advanced writing course I taught in 2017. I added him as a participant in the study to provide insight into how transfer across media works for an advanced student, and his experiences serve as a comparative example to those of other participants who were enrolled in first-year writing. For Evan, I observed his learning in the course as his instructor, and then I interviewed him on video about his experiences after our course was completed. For all five students, I also collected their video compositions along with any reflective essays or documents.

To look and listen for evidence of transfer across media within the data, I approached data analysis with a methodology of interdependence, where I considered elements in the research scene as interwoven with one another and thus mutually influential: the participants' learning, their actions and interactions in class and in the interview room, the physical environments of the classrooms and the interview spaces, me as researcher, and the technologies I used to collect data and that participants used to compose products, to list a few of the elements involved. Conceptualizing the research scene as interdependent builds on Kristie S. Fleckenstein, Clay Spinuzzi, Rebecca J. Rickly, and Carole C. Papper's

(2008, 390) "ecological research enacted rhetorically," where technologies like video influence other aspects of the research scene—even exerting their own agency "apart from the conscious decision-making process of the researcher or participant," as Cardinal (2019, 36) points out. This methodology of interdependence, which I have written about extensively elsewhere (VanKooten 2019), prompted me to analyze data multimodally, looking and listening for insight from participant narratives and bodies but also from myself as the researcher (often captured on camera or speaking in an audio recording) or from the video cameras in the interview rooms and classrooms that recorded much data that I, as the researcher, did not see or hear until analysis began.

The multimodal analysis process involved the following. I used a grounded theory approach (Corbin and Strauss 2008; Merriam 2009) to perform several rounds of coding with interview transcripts. Then, using the codes and categories generated, I placed clips from interviews next to one another in a video editing program, along with other clips of student video products, recordings from class observations, clips from interviews with instructors, or my own recorded speech. I used grounded theory in combination with analysis with a video editor to see, hear, and *feel* the data with more of my senses. I use *feel* with two senses of the word: to experience emotion and to become aware through touch. Watching and listening to different combinations of the video data allowed me to experience emotions made more accessible through participants' tone of voice, body language, and selected music; at the same time, notes and voices in the video clips literally touched my eardrums and resonated in my body through sound waves. The multimodal analysis process was the beginning of the composition of my own research videos, in which I layered participants' voices with moments from their video work, created visual and aural juxtapositions, designed multimodal quotations, and used captions and narration to create persuasive research stories.

These research videos, some of which you can access at links provided in the sections to come, helped me better understand moments of transfer across media. Some moments were discussed by students in their interviews, and I was able to triangulate video data to corroborate those accounts. Other times, video data didn't exactly align with what students remembered, and I grappled with what this might mean for their learning. In many instances, I was able to see students move their bodies in ways that were revealing; I could hear their tones, accents, and speech pace as they spoke confidently or hesitantly; I could feel the beats of selected music in compositions and view colors and visual designs; I connected more directly with emotions as they recounted struggles and successes. Next, I describe some of these analytical moments where video as method and methodology was instrumental in identifying and understanding the complexities involved in transfer across media. Ultimately, these cases suggest that more transfer researchers should consider the possibilities of video and other digital tools when designing new research.

MIKAYLA AND JOHN: TRIANGULATING EVIDENCE WITH WORDS, VISUALS, AND SOUNDS

Classmates Mikayla and John gained compositional knowledge in Composition I that transferred across assignments in the course. Mikayla, an eighteen-year-old white student, learned about organizing the material she was writing about and herself as a writer, applying this learning to written essays and the final multimodal project that included a short video, a Prezi, and an in-class presentation. For John, an African American student, learning about the rhetorical appeals of logos, pathos, and ethos was meaningful; he, too, used this knowledge in his papers and in the final multimodal project. John commented that the appeals were important to his Animoto video on mechanical engineering, and he mentioned that instead of being written, in the video the appeals were *shown*. He described two examples of this showing: his use of images in the video that appealed to the audience's pathos, and his use of statistics that appealed to logos.

Both Mikayla and John spoke to me during interviews about the transfer of this writing knowledge, and I coded comments from each student with the label *transfer across assignments* during initial open coding. I turned to the video data as I sought to better understand their claims—that they had learned about and applied knowledge of organization and the rhetorical appeals across assignments and media in the course. To look and listen for evidence of learning beyond what I could observe from coding written transcripts, I began to review and juxtapose interview clips with a video editor and search for portions of video products and other work that might corroborate the spoken narratives. Because I coded both students' work with the *transfer across assignments* code, and they both described learning that was applicable across assignments in Comp I, I also decided to work with video data about Mikayla's and John's experiences together in the same video. The result of this analysis process is a research video that can be accessed at https://www.youtube.com/watch?v=yFkzGJqbllo.

In this video, I combined clips from Mikayla's and John's interviews with clips from their video products and Prezi presentations. Putting clips of Mikayla speaking back to back with clips of John speaking allowed me to compare and contrast the ways both students spoke about their learning, as well as their mannerisms and body language. Both are articulate, expressive, and positive about how they applied knowledge to new assignments, and each spoke about a different kind of knowledge becoming important and applicable. I then layered interview clips of both students with excerpts from their digital products: the beginning of both students' videos and some visuals from Mikayla's Prezi.

Overlaying products with student spoken narratives allowed me to see and hear moments in student work where their learning is demonstrated but also times when the product might not line up perfectly with how the student was talking about their learning. The start of Mikayla's video, for example, uses a template to combine short sentences and images and comes across as organized and visually pleasing, corroborating her claim to have learned about and applied organizational strategies. Mikayla puts this material together with the upbeat popular song "Hall of Fame" by the Script, which provides a quick, enjoyable pace. A zoomed-out view of her Prezi is visually stunning (figure 1.1), organized creatively around a visual of four keys aiming for a lock. When zoomed in on other visuals from the Prezi, though, Mikayla's work appears less organized and not as visually pleasing, with written text overlapping the circular border and slides overcrowded with words (figure 1.2). Placing these excerpts from Mikayla's product over the top of her spoken narrative allowed—even forced—me to make more comparisons and to triangulate the data across more modes: I examined Mikayla's words along with her body language and tone of voice, what I could see in the product, and what I could hear in the product.

Layering the beginning of John's video with him speaking about how the appeals function gave me an opportunity to triangulate and validate his claims as well: did he indeed use images for pathos or statistics for logos in the video? Could I spot evidence of his use of the rhetorical appeals in his video work? As I watched, listened, and edited, I found several meaningful examples, and I lined one of these up visually with John's dialogue to demonstrate it (access the image at 2:09 in my video). More exciting, though, was that the video analysis process allowed me to see and hear other elements in John's video that he hadn't mentioned in our interview: an appropriate and fitting technology-themed template and an upbeat song that drove the video forward and sent out positive vibes. For me, the music was so rhetorically effective and appropriate for John's chosen audience of prospective engineering majors that I chose to use it in my research video as well. After a clip from John's video, for

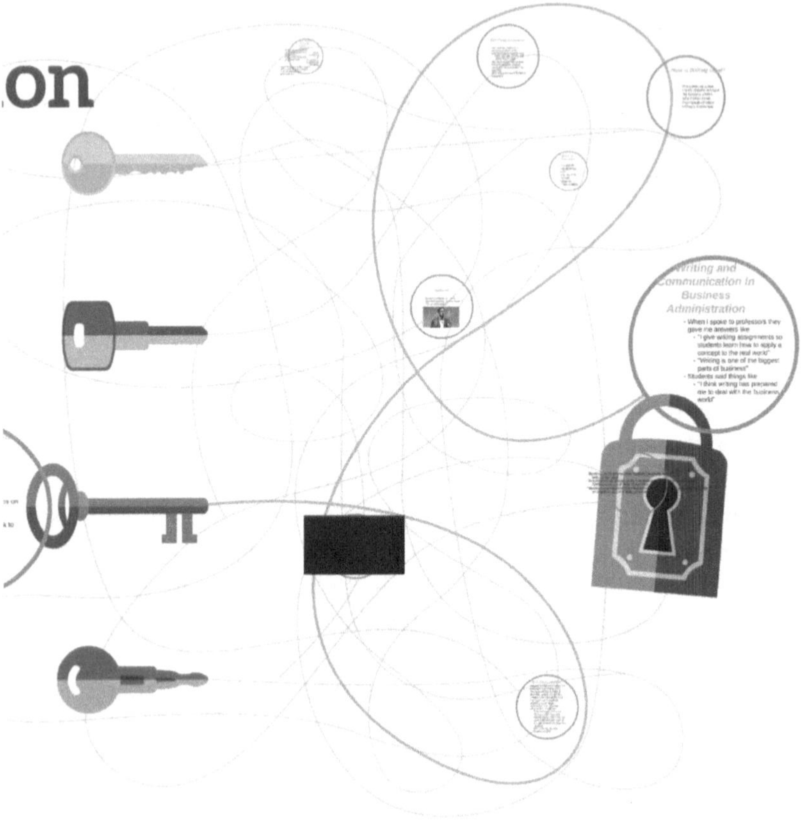

Figure 1.1. Zoomed-out view of Mikayla's Prezi. Author photo, used with participant permission.

Figure 1.2. Zoomed-in view of Mikayla's Prezi. Author photo, used with participant permission.

example, I stopped the visuals but continued to play his music, combining the song with a clip from a later interview of John and me speaking about what was most beneficial from the class for his learning (access this sequence from 2:20 to 2:50). The music served as a bridge between sections, and it did persuasive work for my analysis as it concluded with a bouncy, upbeat series of descending notes played by violins (listen at 2:35). In both John's video and my own, we used the music as an appeal to logos as we emphasized the positives of mechanical engineering (for John) and the positives of using multimodal elements like a song as rhetorical expression (for me).

SAMUEL AND TIARA: SEARCHING BEYOND DIGITAL VIDEO PRODUCTS

For student participants Samuel and Tiara, I analyzed data from their interviews and digital video products in a similar manner, beginning with the coding of interview transcripts and moving into an analysis with a video editor. With Mikayla's and John's work, I quickly saw examples in their videos that corresponded to claims they made about their learning during the interviews. But for Samuel and Tiara, connections between information discussed in interviews and the content of videos were not as obvious. Analyzing the data about Samuel's and Tiara's experiences multimodally, though, helped me again to look and listen across multiple data streams and search for evidence of learning and of transfer in more places, not just in student narratives.

Both participants were articulate and clear about their learning during interviews. Samuel, a Latino student from Pontiac, Michigan, for example, discussed the utility of rhetorical principles such as tailoring writing style to an audience and using *ethos, pathos, logos,* and *kairos*; he also thought forward to the future and discussed where he might use those concepts, such as in writing a business email (perhaps an early step in a transfer process). In Samuel's video on business management, though, he used written words to introduce the career, images related to the topic in an overly general way (a business newspaper, a group of workers in business attire seated around a table, several graphics using arrows), and a template and song that did not provide much rhetorical effect. In other words, I did not initially find much evidence in Samuel's video of the newly developed rhetorical knowledge he spoke so clearly about in interviews. In my own analysis video of Samuel's experiences (please access this video at https://www.youtube.com/watch?v=olin6AWMKAs), I combined Samuel's interview clips with one short clip from the beginning of his video (access the sequence from 0:18 to 0:57), but for Samuel, his learning was most evident to me through what he said during interviews and not in what I could observe in his product. This got me thinking more about the role of articulated awareness in transfer, even when that awareness may not be fully utilized or revealed in composition products.

African American first-year student Tiara spoke confidently about how her knowledge of research and video composition could help her stand out in her future career and how discomfort with learning to compose digital products ultimately resulted in learning benefits. Through these comments, she demonstrated a meta-awareness about the composition process and herself as a growing writer, but as I have explained elsewhere, in her video product about the field of sociology, the words "are hard to read, the organization of ideas is a bit awkward, and the chosen transportation theme (from Animoto, with subways, cabs, and road signs) seems to have little to do with her subject" (VanKooten 2020, section 4.3). In my analysis video about Tiara's experiences (access this research video at https://www.youtube.com/watch?v=KHRQW7uj7Z4), combining moments during class where Tiara worked on a computer with her interview comments provided insight into Tiara's learning that was not at first evident or obvious to me through her products. In classroom video data, Tiara worked on her video and Prezi in class; she alternated among the Prezi composing interface, a Google image search, and a "Change song" screen, where she listened to at least two musical samples that might have been included in her work (figure 1.3). It became clear to me as I watched Tiara compose that she was grappling with many multimodal compositional choices such as what color(s) to use, where to place images, and what song and sounds to use, if any. The results of these choices, visible and audible in her video and Prezi, may not have been at an advanced level, but what was impressive was the amount and kinds of multimodal compositional moves she was considering and making. Through video, we see Tiara cultivating a growing multimodal literacy as she composes a product through consideration of various resources, a literacy that may indeed carry on into other assignments or work. While Tiara's products themselves do leave room for improvement in her use of color, placement, and other design elements, putting together combinations of interview and classroom data reveals some of the complexity involved when students work with what Tiara called a "new experience of writing." Multimodal methods again point to seeds or first steps in a transfer across media process that is not yet fully realized in products.

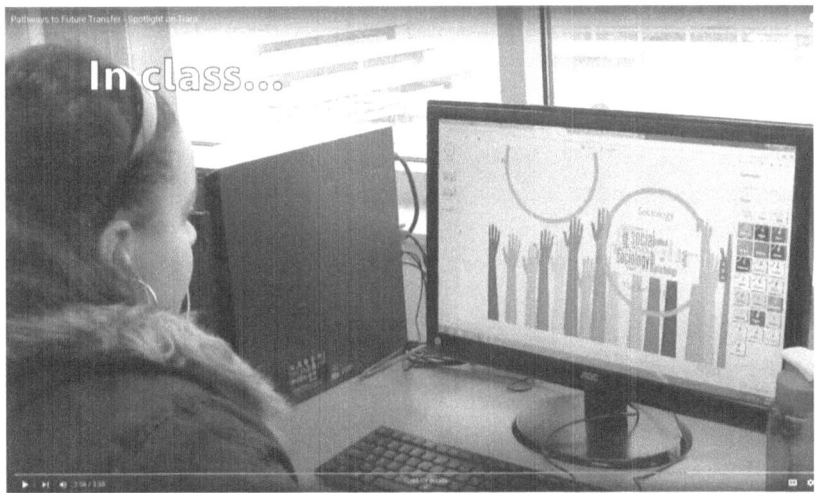

Figure 1.3. Image of Tiara working on her Prezi in class. Author photo, used with participant permission.

EVAN: SEEING IT, HEARING IT, FEELING IT

Evan was an advanced student in a Writing for Digital Media course I taught in 2017. He was a white student and a senior, and even though he was farther along in his studies and digital composition abilities than other first-year students, I added him as a participant and a comparative case after observing him move through a stunning composition and learning process for his *A College Collage: Not Going Back* video project. Not only was his video brilliantly composed and revised, but he displayed many different elements of a transfer across media process as he revised various drafts of the project: he considered, reused, discarded, applied, and adapted his skills and knowledge as he worked. Evan's experiences, while different from those of the freshmen in the study, provide one glimpse into what transfer across media can involve when it occurs after first-year writing for an advanced student.

For me as a researcher analyzing data about Evan's compositional experiences, being able to layer Evan's spoken narrative with his final video composition was an illuminating and stimulating process. It wasn't until I spent hours piecing together Evan's interview clips with his five-minute video composition that I began to more fully understand many of the compositional moves Evan made in his video and the amount of knowledge he transferred during the process of composing and revising the video four times (at least) during one semester. The data I collected about Evan's composition experiences included the final draft of his video, *A College Collage: Not Going Back* (access Evan's final draft at https://www.youtube.com/watch?v=RgX4U7Z25c0), three drafts of the video that preceded the final version, written and video reflections about *A College Collage* and our course, my written instructor comments to Evan on drafts, and a ninety-minute interview with Evan recorded on video. (For full access to all the drafts of Evan's video, see VanKooten 2020, section 5.1).

To begin to analyze these data, I coded the transcript of his interview along with the other interviews in the study. For this interview, however, instead of using the codes and categories to shape a video analysis process, I allowed Evan's final video product to guide me because I loved watching and listening to his video, and I wanted to start there. I placed *A College Collage* into my video editing software; as I watched and re-watched it, I went in search of interview clips in which Evan spoke to what I was seeing and hearing. I cut clips from Evan's interview and pasted them overtop and next to his product. I cut some more and rearranged, juxtaposing and illustrating what Evan said about his product during the interview and how a particular technique or skill could be seen and heard in the video. I tried a side-by-side view and a picture-in-picture view, where Evan could be seen speaking while the audience viewed and listened to his video (see figures 1.4 and 1.5).

One sequence in my analysis video (access this research video at https://www.youtube.com/watch?v=ApDtTeKxC6U) where weaving together Evan's interview footage with his video product revealed new insights about ways he considered, reused, or adapted his multimodal writing skills can be found at 2:57–3:23. In this section, we hear Evan speaking about how he edited images to pair strategically with the beats of the song in his video. The alignment of images with the song in Evan's composition is something that, as his instructor and the researcher, I first *felt* rather than noted explicitly. My ears and body literally felt the driving beats of the song timed perfectly with changing images; as I listened to the beats, melodies, harmonies, and lyrics and looked at images of Evan and his experiences, I also felt emotion: the pain of struggle, the difficulty of change, the triumph of perseverance and self-improvement. Early drafts of *A College Collage* didn't use this audio-visual juxtaposition technique, but as Evan revised, he worked more and more on the alignment of sounds and images as he adapted and reshaped knowledge from draft to draft.

At 3:07 in my analysis video, Evan confidently and physically describes his process of learning to edit sounds and visuals together across drafts, using his hands and gesturing to show how he used his software's editing interface to visually line up still images with strong beats in the

Seeing It, Hearing It, Feeling It   41

Figure 1.4. On the left, Evan gestures to describe how he lined up visuals with musical beats. On the right, an image of swirling leaves from his video is shown. Author photo, used with participant permission.

Figure 1.5. On the left, Evan continues to gesture as he speaks. On the right, an image of stacked pill bottles is shown. Author photo, used with participant permission.

audio track (see figures 1.4 and 1.5 to view his manner and some of his gestures). Then, from 3:16 to 3:23, I transition out of Evan's descriptive comment by showing one sequence where he did this so well. He alternates between images of his own face and images of stacked, empty pill bottles, the images switching exactly on the staccato, higher-pitched pinging beat in the song "Old Ways." In this sequence, we see, hear, and *feel* (with our bodies and with our emotions) how Evan actualized his authorial intent in his video: we hear his narrative spoken in his own voice and see his face and body (he's confident, he's proud, he shows with his hands); we bob our heads to the strong beat of the music; and we see images related to mental health, nature, and Evan himself quickly appear and disappear, the images colorized to match one another with the oranges and browns of medicine bottles and blowing leaves.

Truly, as I analyzed Evan's interview and video using editing software, I experienced his product and process in new—and multimodal—ways. I came to really like the song "Old Ways" by Demi Lovato as I listened to it again and again. I began to inadvertently memorize and sing the song's lyrics; I moved my body and arms around, dancing to the beat; and I appreciated its hard-hitting moments and the softer bridge. I even cried when I felt deeply the sadness or triumph expressed through Evan's use of Lovato's lyrics and voice, the song's rhythms and beats, and the audio-visual juxtapositions he crafted. While I sang, danced, cried, and edited, I noted more explicitly how Evan had used many musical moments in his own composition: he layered images of spinning and spilling pills overtop of Lovato's lyrics "I'm spiraling, I'm spiraling"; he showed footage of a toppling tower of pill bottles during the song's electronic, notes-descending interlude; he used color strategically for logical and emotional appeal, moving from black/white to red, to brown, to green, and finally to purple as Lovato sang "and I just keep changing these colors." Through this multimodal analysis process, I became aware of more aspects of Evan's learning and was able to more fully consider if and when he was (or was not) adapting or transferring knowledge across media. For me, using a multimodal analysis process was key to hearing, examining, and *feeling* many moments of transfer and multimodal expression, and digital video now allows me to present these moments to others visually and aurally.

CONCLUSION: A CALL FOR DIGITAL METHODS

Throughout this chapter, I've argued that transfer researchers, particularly those investigating multimodal and digital transfer, might expand the methodologies and methods we use to find evidence of student learning. In particular, the data, analysis, and findings from the student experiences here show that the collection of video data, digital processes for analyzing data, and multimodal presentation of findings on video are all methods we can explore and use more often and that these methods might help us better see, hear, and feel moments of transfer across media.

For me, collecting multimodal video data is important for several reasons. On video, I can see participants' facial expressions and body movements, and I can see their clothing, body, and mannerisms. I hear their voices, including their tone when they speak, emotion in their voices, and any starts and stops that occur. I hear how the participant interacts with others such as me as an interviewer and their peers or instructor in class. For classroom observational footage, I see and hear the environment around the student; my researcher presence is documented as I carry a camera, pass in front of a camera, or interact with participants on camera.

Analyzing data multimodally in a video editor allows me to see and hear these elements, of course, but also to begin to experience and feel their meanings as I combine them in different ways, both bodily and affectively. With Mikayla, John, Samuel, Tiara, and Evan, I experimented with simultaneous juxtaposition of data elements (placing a clip from Mikayla's or John's video over top of a clip from their interview, for example) and with side-by-side time-based juxtaposition (hearing Tiara speak and then watching a portion of her video product, or hearing Samuel speak at the beginning of the study and then again after some time has passed). As I described, I have used alphabetic coding processes as a first step toward multimodal analysis (in the cases of Mikayla, John, Tiara, and Samuel); conversely, I have let multimodal analysis come first (in the case of Evan). In all cases, though, I began to see, hear, and feel the data in different ways and to find more instances of what I considered transfer across media through analyzing words, visuals, and sounds together.

Presenting research findings on video has also been very important to me, and I hope more researchers will begin to explore the possibilities and affordances of digital scholarship. The multimodal presentation of data is needed within transfer studies because it allows our findings to not only be read by others but also to be seen, heard, and sometimes felt. Audiences can better make their own interpretations of data when they have access to the bodies, sounds, faces, musical selections, edited images, and words of participants in different combinations. Researchers can better present renditions of the findings and data that are both representational and persuasive, existing on what Halbritter and Lindquist (2012, 185) have labeled a "continuum of indexicality" that includes a range of "moments that convey a high degree of indexicality to moments that convey a high degree of authorial perspective and/or voice." Thus, we might begin to explore what different kinds of multimodal products along this range can offer us: glimpses, sound bites, unedited comments and conversations, and persuasive polished stories.

Working with video data about the experiences of Mikayla, John, Samuel, Tiara, and Evan has also highlighted for me the importance of paying more attention to intersections of identity and transfer. On video, important elements of these students' identities—including race, gender, and language use—were highlighted through the use of visuals and sounds. Race in particular has emerged as a critical component of teacher and student identity that deeply influences learning and that needs more explicit attention in the future. In the past, rhetoric and composition's methodologies and methods for studying all forms of transfer have been predominantly white. Not only are many published writing transfer researchers white (as am I), but so are many of the participants we have highlighted in published studies. While this whiteness does not invalidate the important work on transfer, we are in need of methodologies and methods that look beyond white student and white researcher experiences and positionalities and that engage the complexities of identities as they interact with transfer.

Joseph Anthony Wilson and Josie Rose Portz's (chapter 3, this volume) case study of Zhannat, a non-white multilingual first-year writer, provides one example of careful engagement with the role of identities within an enmeshed transfer process. Zhannat's experiences push us to rethink transfer as a political-rhetorical act of embodied resistance, where multimodality can play a part in disrupting transfer's "integration-aligned impulse" into violent (often white) academic discourse. Wilson and Portz helpfully use observations, textual analysis, and interviews in their study; yet evolving methods and technologies like video offer exciting and needed possibilities for even further engaging how identities, power, multimodality, and transfer interact for student writers. What might we learn within studies of digital and multimodal transfer if we sought to integrate digital methodological approaches grounded in Black, Brown, and Indigenous experience? What can we learn from hip-hop, where transfer happens often through the remix and sampling of sound? How might using digital tools and forms such as images, audio, and video help us recognize and observe more moments of writing transfer that *all* students experience in various ways and for different ends—white students, multilingual students, *and* students of color?

When we search for transfer, where is evidence of that transfer located, and how can we better observe and understand it? I urge writing researchers to look, listen, and feel their way through new and evolving digital methodologies and methods as we seek to more fully answer these questions.

REFERENCES

Addison, Joanne. 2007. "Mobile Technologies and a Phenomenology of Literacy." In *Digital Writing Research: Technologies, Methodologies, and Ethical Issues*, edited by Heidi A. McKee and Dànielle Nicole DeVoss, 171–183. Cresskill, NJ: Hampton.

Alexander, Kara Poe, Michael-John DePalma, and Jeffrey M. Ringer. 2016. "Adaptive Remediation and the Facilitation of Transfer in Multiliteracy Center Contexts." *Computers and Composition* 41 (September): 32–45.

Arroyo, Sarah J. 2013. *Participatory Composition: Video Culture, Writing, and Electracy*. Carbondale: Southern Illinois University Press.

Baepler, Paul, and Thomas Reynolds. 2014. "The Digital Manifesto: Engaging Student Writers with Digital Video Assignments." *Computers and Composition* 34 (December): 122–136.

Banks, Will, and Michelle Eble. 2007. "Digital Spaces, Online Environments, and Human Participant Research: Interfacing with Institutional Review Boards." In *Digital Writing Research: Technologies, Methodologies, and Ethical Issues*, edited by Heidi A. McKee and Dànielle Nicole DeVoss, 27–47. Cresskill, NJ: Hampton.

Blythe, Stuart, and Laura Gonzales. 2016. "Coordination and Transfer across the Metagenre of Secondary Research." *College Composition and Communication* 67 (4): 607–633.

Butler, Janine. 2022. "Strategies for Accessing and Articulating Voices through Digital Writing Research Projects." In *Methods and Methodologies for Research in Digital Writing and Rhetoric: Centering Positionality in Computers and Writing Scholarship*, vol. 1, edited by Crystal VanKooten and Victor Del Hierro, 65–85. Fort Collins, CO: WAC Clearinghouse.

Cardinal, Alison. 2019. "Participatory Video: An Apparatus for Ethically Researching Literacy, Power, and Embodiment." *Computers and Composition* 53 (September): 34–46.

Corbin, Juliet, and Anselm Strauss. 2008. *Basics of Qualitative Research: Techniques and Procedures for Developing Grounded Theory*, 3rd edition. Los Angeles: Sage.

Craig, Todd. 2022. "'Tell Virgil Write BRICK on My Brick: Doctoral Bashments, (Re)Visiting Hiphopography, and the Digital Discursivity of the DJ': A Mixed Down Methods Movement." In *Methods and Methodologies for Research in Digital Writing and Rhetoric: Centering Positionality in Computers and Writing Scholarship*, vol. 1, edited by Crystal VanKooten and Victor Del Hierro, 87–107. Fort Collins, CO: WAC Clearinghouse.

Del Hierro, Victor. 2018. "DJs, Playlists, and Community: Imagining Communication Design through Hip Hop." *Communication Design Quarterly* 7 (2): 28–39.

DePalma, Michael-John. 2015. "Tracing Transfer across Media: Investigating Writers' Perceptions of Cross-Contextual and Rhetorical Reshaping in Processes of Remediation." *College Composition and Communication* 66 (4): 615–642.

Duthely, Regina. 2018. "Hip-Hop Rhetoric and Multimodal Digital Writing." In *The Routledge Handbook of Digital Writing and Rhetoric*, edited by Jonathan Alexander and Jacqueline Rhodes, 352–360. New York: Routledge.

Edwards, Dustin W. 2018. "Circulation Gatekeepers: Unbundling the Platform Politics of YouTube's Content ID." *Computers and Composition* 47 (March): 61–74.

Fancher, Patricia, and Michael Faris. 2022. "Social Network Analysis and Feminist Methodology." In *Methods and Methodologies for Research in Digital Writing and Rhetoric: Centering Positionality in Computers and Writing Scholarship*, vol. 1, edited by Crystal VanKooten and Victor Del Hierro, 135–162. Fort Collins, CO: WAC Clearinghouse.

Fleckenstein, Kristie S., Clay Spinuzzi, Rebecca J. Rickly, and Carole Clark Papper. 2008. "The Importance of Harmony: An Ecological Metaphor for Writing Research." *College Composition and Communication* 60 (2): 388–419.

Geisler, Cheryl, and Shaun Slattery. 2007. "Capturing the Activity of Digital Writing: Using, Analyzing, and Supplementing Video Screen Capture." In *Digital Writing Research: Technologies, Methodologies, and Ethical Issues*, edited by Heidi A. McKee and Dànielle Nicole DeVoss, 185–200. Cresskill, NJ: Hampton.

Gonzales, Laura. 2015. "Multimodality, Translingualism, and Rhetorical Genre Studies." *Composition Forum* 31. http://compositionforum.com/issue/31/multimodality.php.

Halbritter, Bump, and Julie Lindquist. 2012. "Time, Lives, and Videotape: Operationalizing Discovery in Scenes of Literacy Sponsorship." *College English* 75 (2): 171–198.

Haywood, Constance M. 2022. "Developing a Black Feminist Research Ethic: A Methodological Approach to Research in Digital Spaces." In *Methods and Methodologies for Research in Digital Writing and Rhetoric: Centering Positionality in Computers and Writing Scholarship*, vol. 2, edited by Crystal VanKooten and Victor Del Hierro, 29–44. Fort Collins, CO: WAC Clearinghouse.

Hidalgo, Alexandra. 2017. *Cámara Retórica: A Feminist Filmmaking Methodology for Rhetoric and Composition.* Logan: Computers and Composition Digital Press and Utah State University Press. http://ccdigitalpress.org/camara/.

House, Eric A. 2022. "Reflections on a Hip-Hop DJ Methodology." In *Methods and Methodologies for Research in Digital Writing and Rhetoric: Centering Positionality in Computers and Writing Scholarship*, vol. 1, edited by Crystal VanKooten and Victor Del Hierro, 65–79. Fort Collins, CO: WAC Clearinghouse.

McKee, Heidi A. 2008. "Ethical and Legal Issues for Writing Researchers in an Age of Media Convergence." *Computers and Composition* 25 (1): 104–122.

Mckoy, Temptaous. 2022. "Flipping the Table and Redefining the Dissertation Genre with a Digital Chapter." In *Methods and Methodologies for Research in Digital Writing and Rhetoric: Centering Positionality in Computers and Writing Scholarship*, vol. 1, edited by Crystal VanKooten and Victor Del Hierro, 49–63. Fort Collins, CO: WAC Clearinghouse.

Merriam, Sharan B. 2009. *Qualitative Research: A Guide to Design and Implementation.* San Francisco: Jossey-Bass.

Miller, Benjamin. 2022. "The Pleasurable Difficulty of Programming." In *Methods and Methodologies for Research in Digital Writing and Rhetoric: Centering Positionality in Computers and Writing Scholarship*, vol. 2, edited by Crystal VanKooten and Victor Del Hierro, 159–183. Fort Collins, CO: WAC Clearinghouse.

Moore, Jessie. 2012. "Mapping the Questions: The State of Writing-Related Transfer Research." *Composition Forum* 26. http://compositionforum.com/issue/26/map-questions-transfer-research.php.

Nowacek, Rebecca. 2011. *Agents of Integration: Understanding Transfer as a Rhetorical Act.* Carbondale: Southern Illinois University Press.

Özyeşilpınar, Eda, and Diane Quaglia Beltran. 2022. "Digital Story-Mapping." In *Methods and Methodologies for Research in Digital Writing and Rhetoric: Centering Positionality in Computers and Writing Scholarship*, vol. 1, edited by Crystal VanKooten and Victor Del Hierro, 111–133. Fort Collins, CO: WAC Clearinghouse.

Palmeri, Jason. 2012. *Remixing Composition: A History of Multimodal Writing Pedagogy.* Carbondale: Southern Illinois University Press.

Rosinski, Paula. 2017. "Students' Perceptions of the Transfer of Rhetorical Knowledge between Digital Self-Sponsored Writing and Academic Writing: The Importance of Authentic Contexts and Reflection." In *Critical Transitions: Writing and the Question of Transfer*, edited by Chris M. Anson and Jessie L. Moore, 247–272. Fort Collins, CO: WAC Clearinghouse.

Rowell, Christina. 2022. "Multimodal Methods for Mapping Multimodal Composing Processes." In *Methods and Methodologies for Research in Digital Writing and Rhetoric: Centering Positionality in Computers and Writing Scholarship*, edited by Crystal VanKooten and Victor Del Hierro. Fort Collins, CO: WAC Clearinghouse.

Sapienza, Fil. 2007. "Ethos and Research Positionality in Studies of Virtual Communities." In *Digital Writing Research: Technologies, Methodologies, and Ethical Issues*, edited by Heidi A. McKee and Dànielle Nicole DeVoss, 89–106. Cresskill, NJ: Hampton.

Shepherd, Ryan P. 2018. "Digital Writing, Multimodality, and Learning Transfer: Crafting Connections between Composition and Online Composing." *Computers and Composition* 48 (June): 103–114.

Shivers-McNair, Ann. 2019. "Making Knowledge: A Kit for Researching 3D Rhetorics." *Enculturation: A Journal of Rhetoric, Writing, and Culture* 29. http://enculturation.net/3D_rhetorics.

Sidler, Michelle. 2007. "Playing Scavenger and Gazer with Scientific Discourse: Opportunities and Ethics for Online Research." In *Digital Writing Research: Technologies, Methodologies, and Ethical Issues*, edited by Heidi A. McKee and Dànielle Nicole DeVoss, 71–86. Cresskill, NJ: Hampton.

Sparby, Derek M. 2022. "Toward a Feminist Ethic of Self-Care and Protection When Researching Digital Aggression." In *Methods and Methodologies for Research in Digital Writing and Rhetoric: Centering Positionality in Computers and Writing Scholarship*, vol. 2, edited by Crystal VanKooten and Victor Del Hierro, 45–64. Fort Collins, CO: WAC Clearinghouse.

VanKooten, Crystal. 2019. "A Research Methodology of Interdependence through Video as Method." *Computers and Composition* 54 (December): 1–17.

VanKooten, Crystal. 2020. *Transfer across Media: Using Digital Video in the Teaching of Writing*. Logan: Computers and Composition Digital Press and Utah State University Press. https://ccdigitalpress.org/book/transfer-across-media/index.html.

Wardle, Elizabeth. 2012. "Creative Repurposing for Expansive Learning: Considering 'Problem-Exploring' and 'Answer-Getting' Dispositions in Individuals and Fields." *Composition Forum* 26. http://compositionforum.com/issue/26/creative-repurposing.php.

Yancey, Kathleen, Liane Robertson, and Kara Taczak. 2014. *Writing across Contexts: Transfer, Composition, and Sites of Writing*. Logan: Utah State University Press.

2
MAKING TRANSFER MATTER ACROSS DIGITAL MEDIA PLATFORMS
First-Year Writers' Design of Multimodal Campaigns for Social Advocacy

Jialei Jiang

A burgeoning scholarly interest in sponsoring transfer of learning across modes and media has surfaced in the field of rhetoric and composition, as suggested by increasing conversations at the intersection of transfer theories and multimodal composition.[1] The emerging body of research explores students' transfer of knowledge between print-based composition and multimodal composition (DePalma 2015; DePalma and Alexander 2015) and between digital self-sponsored writing and academic writing (Rosinski 2017; Shepherd 2018). Despite such advances, the research has not been fully extended to empirical studies comparing multiple digital media platforms and examining their affordances in facilitating writing transfer.[2] The exigency in studying different technological platforms lies in the fact that their disparate design features may facilitate or hinder the successful production of multimodal texts and transfer of rhetorical knowledge. As Jessie L. Moore and Chris M. Anson (2016, 10) make clear, "Some physical and digital space designs afford learning and transfer better than others." In this chapter, I argue that studying first-year composition (FYC) students' perceptions of a multimodal campaign assignment reveals the different affordances of three cloud-based digital platforms in transferring rhetorical knowledge. Some of the limitations include difficulties in accessing various semiotic resources, in navigating effective design choices, and in producing accessible user-friendly materials. The findings of this chapter will inform the design of more robust pedagogical approaches that enhance capacities and minimize constraints.

More specifically, I seek to build on current research by sharing the results of a mixed methods empirical study that has gathered FYC students' perceptions of various digital media platforms used to create multimodal campaigns. As a form of public rhetoric and writing pedagogy (Alexander and Rhodes 2014; Jiang 2020; Jiang and Vetter 2020; Sheridan, Ridolfo, and Michel 2012), multimodal campaign projects—such as those that focus on sexual violence, animal protection, and political activism—encourage students to address real-world social problems and confront public rhetorical situations. Through exposing students to authentic audiences in public spheres (Ball, Bowen, and Fenn 2013; Davis 2017; Moore and Anson 2016; Rosinski 2017), these multimodal projects hold potential for facilitating the transfer of rhetorical knowledge and writing process. Moreover, since multimodal campaigns usually encompass a composite of various media such as video production (Dubisar and Palmeri 2010), website design (Gries 2019; Jiang 2021), and meme creation (Warren-Riley and Hurley 2017), these projects also make it feasible to examine diverse digital platforms and their distinct capacities for promoting writing and transfer.

The arguments of this chapter proceed as follows. First, I detail the interconnected scholarship of transfer and multimodality in writing studies, with special attention given to the capacity of multimodal campaigns for teaching and studying transfer. I then provide a detailed description of the study context and research design. This IRB-approved study compares FYC students' perceptions of three cloud-based platforms used to engage in the collaborative design of multimodal advocacy campaigns: Vyond (an animation design platform), Canva (a graphic design platform), and Wix (a website design platform). Utilizing a mixed methods approach, this study draws participants from a total of eighty-five FYC students with diverse gender and racial backgrounds, who participated in the multimodal project. Ultimately, the study's dataset includes surveys completed by seventy-eight students, reflection essays solicited from seventy-three students, and individual interviews conducted with twelve students. Key findings suggest that despite their similarities, the animation, brochure, and website design platforms differ in terms of their capacities for allowing students to transfer rhetorical knowledge. Based on these findings, I conclude this chapter by offering pedagogical suggestions on ways to enhance the affordances of digital media platforms in support of writing transfer.

TRANSFER IN DIGITAL WRITING STUDIES

Writing transfer, as defined by Jessie L. Moore (2017, 2), refers to "a writer's ability to repurpose or transform prior knowledge about writing for a new audience, purpose, and context." More recently, the bulk of the research has explored students' transfer of knowledge across modes and media, such as repurposing and transforming knowledge between print-based and multimodal compositions (DePalma 2015; DePalma and Alexander 2015). Moving from print-based literacy to digital composition requires that writers rhetorically reshape, repurpose, and remediate print-based essays (DePalma 2015). Michael-John DePalma and Kara Poe Alexander (2015), for instance, demonstrate that students rely on their print-based knowledge of rhetorical constructions to approach multimodal writing tasks. While transfer of writing seems to be effective when students are able to see the commonalities between print-based and multimodal composing tasks, it is not as effective when students fail to see their multimodal assignments as connected to their print-based composing experiences. Challenges include difficulties in conceptualizing audiences, negotiating semiotic resources, and addressing rhetorical constraints.

Crucial to the current explorations is cultivating students' meta-awareness of their writing, which has the potential to facilitate writing transfer (Adler-Kassner et al. 2016; Yancey et al. 2019; Yancey, Robertson, and Taczak 2014), more specifically, writing transfer from print-based contexts to digital formats (DePalma 2015; VanKooten 2016; Yancey 2017). In DePalma's (2015, 619) study tracing transfer across print-based literacies and digital media, he places a strong emphasis on the need "to help students develop a language for talking about composing, as well as a meta-awareness of their own processes as composers." Student participants such as Noreen and Anna have developed awareness, through reflections, of the ways they remediate literacies from non-writing-related contexts, including Noreen's reworking of musical compositions and Anna's remixing of video clips. Similarly, by examining the ways FYC students create a digital video assignment, Crystal VanKooten (2016) identifies four key elements crucial for activating students' prior rhetorical knowledge and developing their meta-awareness: writing process, techniques, rhetoric, and intercomparativity. Echoing DePalma's and VanKooten's works on transfer across modes and media, Kathleen Blake Yancey and her colleagues (2019) embrace meta-awareness and reflective activities as fundamental to the teaching of transfer. The researchers analyze the extent to which a systematic approach to content-informed reflection assists in the transfer of writing and knowledge. Their findings suggest that the transfer framework, with a focus on systematic reflection, has encouraged students to engage in writing transfer in other sites of writing, from in-school contexts to out-of-school contexts.

Alongside their studies of print-based and digital forms of composition, scholars turn to students' transfer of knowledge between digital self-sponsored writing and academic writing, with a strong focus on embracing authentic writing situations and writing for public audiences (Rosinski 2017; Shepherd 2018). Multimodal projects can further serve as an empowering platform for students to engage in public rhetorical situations and produce authentic texts. Scholars increasingly recognize that multimodal projects that introduce students to authentic audiences in public spheres (Davis 2017; Moore and Anson 2016; Rosinski 2017) have the benefit of facilitating the transfer of rhetorical knowledge and writing process. The Elon Statement on Writing Transfer, for instance, calls on researchers to engage with and add to the working principle that "the transfer of rhetorical knowledge and strategies between self-sponsored and academic writing can be encouraged by designing academic writing opportunities with authentic audiences and purposes and by asking students to engage in meta-cognition" (Moore and Anson 2016, 11). Continuing the discussion initiated by Moore and Anson, Paula Rosinski (2017) further points out that when writing contexts are not authentic, teachers cannot expect students to seriously engage in rhetorical acts. Her study demonstrates that participants frequently refer to "their professors" as their audiences when producing academic texts; as a result, these students fail to address rhetorical purposes and audiences in sophisticated ways. Digital, self-sponsored writing, in contrast, opens the gateway for students to navigate audience expectations in more authentic contexts.

While there is a rich body of research exploring students' transfer of knowledge between print-based and multimodal compositions and between academic writing and digital self-sponsored writing, much of this research is not about digital platforms specifically. However, Gunther Kress (2000, 153) stresses that "semiotic modes have different potentials, so that they afford different kinds of possibilities of human expression and engagement with the world, and through this differential engagement with the world they facilitate differential possibilities of development." By keying in on the specific actions that various technological platforms allow and do not allow students to accomplish, this study carries the benefits of unraveling the different semiotic modes and resources that may potentially influence the transfer of writing knowledge from print-based media to digital media. In what follows, I seek to build on the current discussions of multimodal transfer by sharing the results of a mixed methods empirical study that gathered FYC students' perceptions of their experience using three different digital platforms. More specifically, this study turns to multimodal campaign projects that ask students to address authentic audiences in public spheres (Davis

2017; Moore and Anson 2016; Rosinski 2017) and respond to public rhetorical situations through compositions across the various platforms. By examining students' perceptions of the different digital platforms, this study will offer thoughts about the affordances—including both potentials and limitations (Kress 2010, 192)—of each platform in facilitating the transfer of rhetorical knowledge and writing process. The findings of this chapter seek to provide recommendations for pedagogical approaches that leverage the full potential of multimodal compositions across digital platforms.

METHODS

This study is an IRB-approved mixed methods project that explores FYC students' transfer of learning through different cloud-based platforms. The purpose of this study is to compare students' transfer of rhetorical knowledge across three cloud-based design platforms: Vyond, Canva, and Wix. At time of this study, the goal of the FYC course was to use writing processes to generate, develop, share, revise, proofread, and edit a multimodal project that shows genre awareness, rhetorical situations, structure, purpose, and significant content. Before starting their multimodal campaign assignment, students produced print-based problem-solution essays that asked them to identify a social problem and propose their solutions to the problem. Through this assignment, students gained rhetorical knowledge and audience awareness and demonstrated their ability to make rhetorical appeals, such as appealing to pathos, ethos, and logos. As a continuation of their problem-solution essays, the multimodal campaign assignment further allowed students to produce animated videos, brochures, and websites in response to relevant sociopolitical issues they were interested in exploring, such as poverty in education, local foods and food sustainability, revitalization of depressed areas, local waste and recycling, police force racial profiling, sexual violence among college students, and accessibility of campus space for people with disabilities.

To better understand how multimodal projects facilitate transfer, I use a grounded theory framework (Birks and Mills 2015) to collect multilayered data about the participants' perceptions of and experiences in multimodal advocacy projects. The primary source of data consisted of surveys completed by seventy-eight students, reflection essays solicited from seventy-three students, and individual interviews conducted with twelve students. Before engaging in multimodal design, students first completed a Qualtrics survey that included demographic questions about their major and gender, as well as questions about when they started having access to computers, when they started using computers regularly, and how skilled they are with computers. A total of seventy-eight students completed the survey, among whom thirty-six are female students and forty-two are male students. Commenting on their previous experience using computers, the majority of the students surveyed reported that they had always had computer access at home (58/78), that they started using computers regularly in or before middle school (72/78), and that their computer skills were average or above average (63/78). Despite students' overall familiarity with computer applications, many of them lacked experience with the particular multimodal design platforms under examination in this study. For instance, even though the majority of the students (58/78) had previous experience using graphic design and image editing software, most of these experiences involved a working knowledge of Microsoft PowerPoint; only twenty-seven students reported having used design platforms such as Canva, Adobe Photoshop, or Adobe Illustrator. In terms of their video-making experience, slightly more than half of the students (45/78) had worked with video-making or sound editing software. Of these students, thirty-four had experience with movie-making platforms such as iMovie or Windows Movie Maker, and only five had used platforms such as Vyond, Powtoon, or Animaker to produce animations. Finally, fewer than half of the students (21/78) had been exposed to website design platforms. Sixteen of those students mentioned Wix, Weebly, and Google Sites as the platforms they used for their website design projects.

After completion of their multimodal projects, seventy-three students who agreed to participate in this study submitted reflection essays by answering a list of questions, not unlike what they would do in response to focused prompts on a questionnaire. The reflection essay held the potential to assist students with cultivating meta-awareness of writing processes and transfer of rhetorical knowledge (Adler-Kassner et al. 2016; Yancey et al. 2019; Yancey, Robertson, and Taczak 2014). More specifically, the essay asked students to describe their rhetorical purposes and appeals. Students described their purposes in composing the multimodal project, the audiences they were trying to appeal to in general, their choice of mode and medium, and, most important, how these choices had an impact on the delivery of their work. Twelve of the seventy-three students also participated in thirty- to forty-five-minute semi-structured interviews after each of their multimodal products was completed. The purpose of these interviews was to learn in greater detail about the challenges the students encountered throughout the design processes as well as their perspectives on their compositional processes and final products. I analyzed the interview data in conjunction with students' reflection essays. Along with their final reflections, I collected artifacts related to their projects and processes, including brochures, animations, and websites. In an attempt to unearth specific design decisions, the final multimodal product for each of the interviews was shown to the students to first elicit general comments and then for students to reflect on their design choices. Transcripts were prepared for each semi-structured interview.

The survey and interview data were analyzed using grounded theory methods (Birks and Mills 2015). Grounded theory allowed researchers, through their data collection and analysis, to identify common themes and make generalizations about those themes. The survey data were used to report on demographic information only. To code the reflection and interview data, I first read through students' reflection texts and interview transcripts to identify common themes in the responses. At this point, I identified that much of the data pertained to students' use of rhetorical appeals and semiotic resources. I then read and coded the data again, placing emphasis on coding rhetorical appeals and semiotic resources, as well as students' sense of usability and accessibility afforded by different design platforms. Throughout the coding process, I generated secondary codes that added further detail to the primary codes; for example, rhetorical appeals were further identified as students' awareness of logos, ethos, and pathos; semiotic resources were further identified as design templates and options available on the digital platforms.

RESULTS AND DISCUSSION

Findings of this study illustrate the different affordances of three design platforms,—the animation, brochure, and website platforms—in facilitating writing transfer. Participants drew on a rich repertoire of semiotic resources when discussing their design experience related to brochures and websites and made more references to the website and brochure platforms as user-friendly and easy to navigate. Moreover, participants referred to the animation and brochure software as producing more constraints in terms of in-app purchases and limited semiotic resources. Issues with time management and content editing also hindered some participants from creating rhetorically effective designs.

Potentials: A Comparison across the Three Platforms

In their reflections, the students showed a broad range of rhetorical appeals when discussing their processes of composing multimodal texts

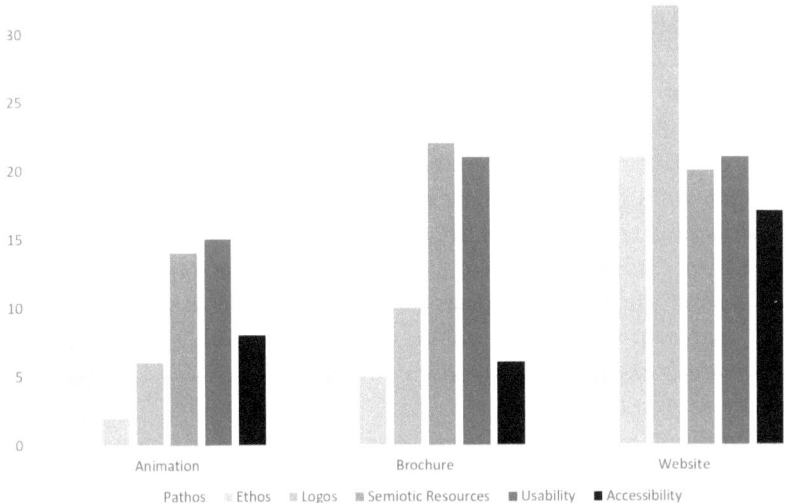

Figure 2.1. Potentials of the animation, brochure, and website for writing transfer. This figure includes a total of 292 instances of student reflections that describe the potentials of the animation, brochure, and website platforms in sponsoring writing transfer.

across multiple modes and media, as shown in figure 2.1. Students' appeals to pathos were most prominent in their animation design (32 instances) and website design (25 instances). Interestingly, students frequently referred to the animation and website platforms' storytelling features as affording them the opportunity to produce pathos. For example, one student explained in her reflection essay that "for our video[,] pathos was used because it was about a family of polar bears that lost their habitat due to climate change. It shows them having a good time and sledding with their family but then they get a drink and due to the heat from climate change the baby polar bear starts to float away from its family." Similarly, describing how website design provides the means to produce emotional appeals, another student stressed that "we tried to connect with our audience by adding heartfelt stories and real-life issues that would make people feel that they needed to do something. We added people's stories about how police brutality affected them to show people that this can happen to anyone and to show them that even after the news stops broadcasting the story, this still affects people." Compared to the animation and brochure platforms, students produced more instances of ethos (21 instances) and logos (23 instances) while mentioning their website design processes: "Ethos was used in the project by adding [a] hyperlink from the sources we got our reliable information from"; "In order to persuade readers using logos, we included facts and figures that back up our arguments and make our information much more credible." The website platform's affordances of hyperlinks and figures may have contributed to students' enhanced awareness of these rhetorical appeals. Despite the variations among the three platforms in facilitating the production of rhetorical appeals, academic writing projects that expose students to authentic audiences and situations encourage the transfer of rhetorical knowledge (Moore and Anson 2016; Rosinski 2017). Students' frequent references to the capacities of the three platforms in making rhetorical appeals demonstrate that confronted with public rhetorical situations, students may have made it easier to address their rhetorical purposes and audiences in more sophisticated ways.

In addition to rhetorical appeals, participants utilized a range of semiotic resources, or available modes for meaning making, when discussing their design experience related to brochures (22 instances) and websites (20 instances). In particular, all three cloud-based platforms provided students with the opportunities to navigate and utilize a rich repertoire of semiotic resources, including but not limited to design templates, formats, and styles. As a case in point, one student said that "with the templates in the software it made it a little easier to created [*sic*] our brochure because it already had the stuff we needed on there, we just had to find a cool and creative way to put it all together." Students' successful use of semiotic resources can also be glimpsed in their website designs: "Wix has a variety of different website formats that cater to different kinds of sites. You can make sites for blogging, selling products, and so much more. Wix also helps me to bring out my individual style in the website by providing assistance for me. The technological opportunities is [*sic*] giving people the power to create anything they want for a purpose." Students' engagement with semiotic resources using the animation software (14 instances) was mentioned less frequently, but it still demonstrates the wide range of opportunities and resources available on the platform.

When discussing their designs in terms of usability, or the ease with which they were able to make use of different design platforms, participants made more references to the website (21 instances) and brochure (21 instances) platforms as user-friendly and easy to navigate. Describing his experience with website design for this project, one student commented: "I thought it was straightforward and very easy to navigate. The thing I liked the most out of wix [*sic*] was how user friendly it was, making it very easy to complete a well-done project." Similarly, another student referred to Canva as providing guidance necessary for easing her into the brochure design process, saying that the platform "was easy to use for beginners since there was [sic] guides to help you along if you got confused on what to do next." Compared to the animation and brochure software, students more frequently referred to the website software (17 instances) as enhancing the accessibility of their multimodal campaigns: "Wix . . . allowed us to create a website where all our brochures and other information could be stored and [be] easily accessible to anyone." Students also referred to the website and brochure platforms as more accessible to audiences during face-to-face presentations: "I also learned that it seemed as if the website and brochure were the most effective when trying to communicate our thoughts to the audience while presenting." This research demonstrates that students consider the website platforms, among the three platforms, the most user-friendly and easy to navigate. As DePalma and Alexander (2015) noted, writing transfer seems to be more effective under the circumstances in which students are able to make the connections between their multimodal and print-based composing experiences. It is possible that students may have already been more familiar with the website format through their print-based composing practices. It is also possible that students may have had more resources to help with the website format and, accordingly, have had an easier time navigating it.

Limitations: A Comparison across the Three Platforms
Beyond the potentials, student reflection essays illustrate the limitations of these three platforms in allowing for writing transfer. Figure 2.2 summarizes the total number of responses for each type of challenge students encountered—constraints in regard to cost, semiotic resources, usability, and accessibility. Overall, as compared to the potentials of these design platforms (292 instances), students made fewer references to their limitations (88 instances). However, students' encounters with difficulties varied slightly according to the design platforms they utilized. While the animation and brochure platforms contained in-app purchases, students reported the website software as less restraining in this area. Given the wide range of free materials and resources available on all three platforms, in-app purchases of selected items still prevented students from choosing their preferred design elements. Describing the challenge of accessing design materials free of charge, one student shared that "a limitation of canva [sic] was that not all of the images are free, so it limited the creativity of our brochure creation." On a similar note, another student complained about the time constraint that arose

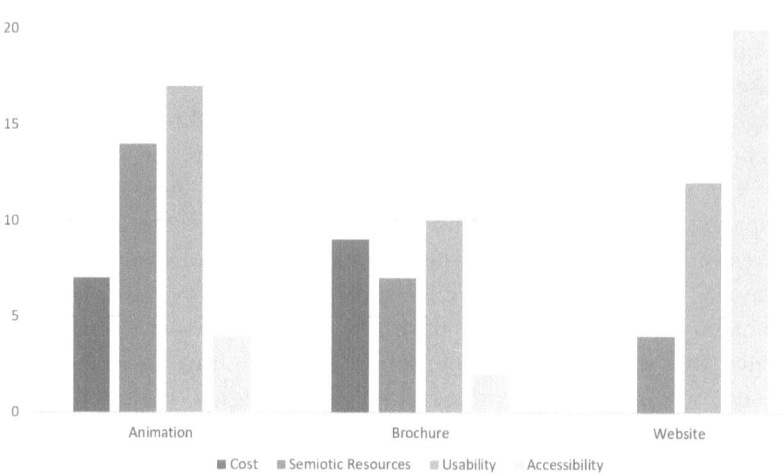

Figure 2.2. Limitations of the animation, brochure, and website for writing transfer. This figure includes a total of eighty-eight instances in student reflections that describe the limitations of the animation, brochure, and website platforms in sponsoring writing transfer.

from using the one-month trial version of Vyond: "There were some limitations in doing this project like you only had a certain time to use free trials in the video."

Among the three platforms, students mentioned the animation (14 instances) and brochure (7 instances) software as producing more constraints in terms of semiotic resources. Notwithstanding the fact that all three platforms provided students with the opportunities to navigate and utilize a rich repertoire of semiotic resources, students occasionally still found it difficult to harness the power of these resources to address the rhetorical purposes of their multimodal campaigns. In other words, some of the constraints pertain to the disconnect between students' exposure to available means of design and their need to purposefully convey meaning through these means. For example, as part of the campaign on the issue of global warming, one student sought to incorporate animal characters, such as polar bears, into the design of her animation. However, she found the animation platform limited in its capacity to create and animate animal characters. Since the platform categorized animals as props rather than characters, such a limitation prevented the student from leveraging the full potential of her animated video in addressing her rhetorical purposes: "Vyond is mainly designed for animations of people, and not animals. We were unable to animate our animals to make them talk and move, so we had to change our initial design that we created." Not unlike the animation platform, similar constraints can also be seen in students' brochure designs: "There were not many backgrounds to choose from to start out the brochure. And once someone decided the background they could not edit the color of it or replace images with something else."

All three platforms revealed issues with usability, but students seemed to have struggled the most with learning how to use the animation platform (17 instances). The variations in students' struggles with different platforms may be attributed to their previous experience with these platforms. Prior to taking the course, only five of the seventy-eight students had engaged in multimodal designs using animation platforms such as Vyond, Powtoon, and Animaker. Thus, the vast majority of the students in this study lacked relevant experience producing animations and may have experienced steeper learning curves regarding the use of the animation platform. For instance, participants noted that "I had a lot of trouble making the animation at first, I really wasn't sure how to do a lot of things on the website such as how to add animations and get the voice to line up correctly with the characters" and "there are a lot of learning curves when using new technology[,] which disabled [sic] us from going above and beyond but the more we worked with the animation website the easier it got over time." Aside from learning curves, glitches also presented challenges that prolonged students' design processes. For instance, according to one participant, "The only difficulties I encountered were the technical difficulties of saving on canva [sic] and wix [sic], and the problems with things glitching on canva [sic]. To accommodate . . . these issues, we just had to slow down our working process." Comparatively, students described far fewer instances of accessibility issues on all three design platforms but still shared concerns over the delivery of animations (4 instances) and uncertainty about the existence of their animated videos after the trial period ended: "The limitations of these technological resources are that you don't know how far your message reaches out and that these technologies are not everlasting. For example, the video will be viewed but will wear out and not be viewed like it originally had been." These findings echo Kress's (2000) assertion that semiotic modes have different potentials and limitations, opening the possibilities for differential human expression and engagement with the world.

Additional Challenges
During their interviews, participants generated a total of sixty-five instances of discussing general challenges they encountered during

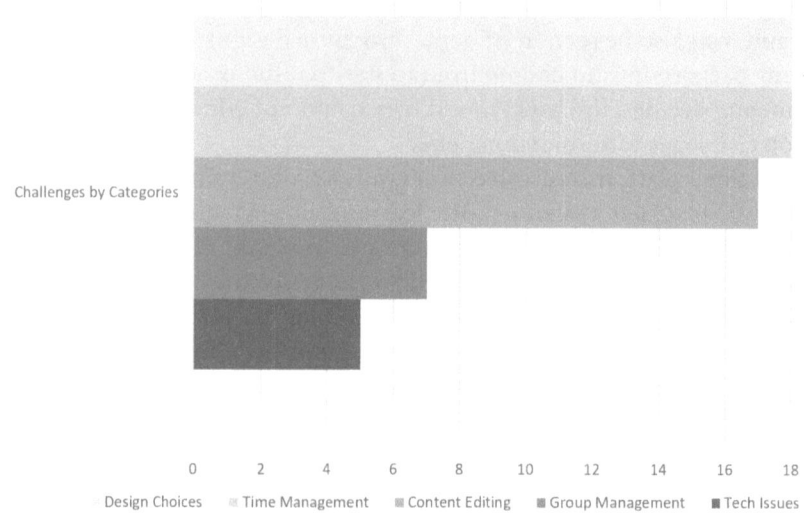

Figure 2.3. Challenges not specific to the three platforms. This figure includes a total of sixty-five instances in student interviews that describe additional challenges students encountered that are not specific to any of the three design platforms.

their design processes (figure 2.3). These additional forms of challenges ranged from more prominent challenges such as those surrounding design choices (18 instances), time management (18 instances), and content editing (17 instances) to less prominent challenges such as difficulties in group management (7 instances) and technological use (5 instances).

Regardless of the specific design platform students utilized, the task of creating a successful visual design (18 instances) posed a challenge to some participants, as they struggled with making effective design choices that would best address their rhetorical goals and purposes. The design struggle is exemplified by one participant's comment that "our brochure did not have enough space to include all that information, so we had to vary our writing and our approach." Some students found it difficult to make full use of space to convey meaning effectively: "A weakness was trying to fill up the brochure and website as there was a lot of space that needed filling"; "Even though we had the plot for our animation already, we still had to fill in some of the gaps in the plot. It'd be a challenge because we had to figure out how we want it to be shaped or basically how we wanted the plot to go along." Still others felt they could have made better choices in creating visually appealing designs that were accessible for audiences: "One of the weaknesses of our design would be the lack of attention to details in some areas of the layout.

For example, possibly changing the font in some sections or adding a graph could make the layout more appealing to the eye." Participants' encounters with design challenges confirmed previous research studies (DePalma 2015; DePalma and Alexander 2015) that revealed students' difficulty in determining how to make best use of various semiotic resources to fulfill their rhetorical purposes and objectives.

When reflecting on their design processes, students also made references to time management (18 instances) and content editing (17 instances) as particularly challenging. In terms of time management, one student pointed out that the "difficulties for us were finding times outside of class when we could meet as a group to get our work done." Indeed, ineffective time management exerted a negative impact on students' final delivery of their design products. For example, another student showed regrets about failing to "post everything on the Wix website earlier in the project so that it would had [*sic*] showed in the presentation." To manage time difficulties and to work on each other's schedules, some participants mentioned supplementing face-to-face meetings with group chat and messages: "We had to make a group chat and do a lot of the work on our own while corresponding in the messages for any questions or issues we may have had." In addition to effective time management, students found it difficult to edit content on digital platforms. Such difficulties often intersected with students' print-based literacy, as a lack of content knowledge may have hindered some students from creating rhetorically effective designs: "A few weaknesses I observed are a few gaps in our knowledge on endangered animals. I do not think that we provided enough information on specific animals." Not unlike the challenge of writing effective print-based essays, during their design processes students were also confronted with the difficulty of presenting clear arguments with well-substantiated ideas: "When adding information to either the website or [the] brochure, I had to consider what information would flow better with other information, and what should be separated. I also had to consider how to get my message across with my words efficiently enough to help my audience understand the point."

By contrast, students produced far fewer instances of challenges such as difficulties in managing group work (7 instances) and addressing technical issues (5 instances). Even though group management issues did occur, these issues were usually resolved easily after group members clearly designated each member's responsibilities: "It was also hard to agree on the color usage we had to pick to make it [the project] stand out. We managed these issues by doing majority rule; however, we did agree on most things right off the bat so there wasn't [*sic*] too many disagreements"; "I learned to just give up control of the parts of the project that I was not responsible [for]." Students also commented on occasional technical issues related to saving their files online and responding to computer crashes: "The only issues that we encountered were with technology. This included our projects not saving, which was fixed by redoing [them]." Often, these issues were fixed after students rebooted their computers or restarted the program.

CONCLUSION

This study, through a mixed methods approach, sought to explore how first-year writers perceive multiple digital media platforms and their opportunities and limitations in facilitating writing transfer. In my examination of the three datasets—student reflection essays, interviews, and surveys—I have concluded that given their similarities, the three cloud-based platforms have showcased different capacities in allowing for writing transfer. The dominant trends that emerged from the student responses are the following.

First, the animation, brochure, and website platforms differed in their capacities for facilitating writing transfer, such as producing rhetorical appeals. Participants drew on a rich repertoire of semiotic resources when discussing their design experience related to brochures and websites and made more references to the website and brochure platforms as user-friendly and easy to navigate. Moreover, participants referred to the animation and brochure software as producing more constraints in terms of in-app purchases and limited semiotic resources. Confirming similar findings of previous studies (DePalma 2015; DePalma and Alexander 2015), participants struggled with making effective design choices that would best address their rhetorical goals and purposes. Issues with time management and content editing also hindered some participants from creating rhetorically effective designs. Finally, when looking at both the potentials and the limitations, it seems clear that the website offered more connections and presented fewer problems for the students. Students may have already been more familiar with the website format, may have had more resources to help with that format, or may simply have had an easier time navigating it.

Responding to the theme of this edited book, this study contributes to the ongoing intersections of conversations about writing transfer with multimodal theories and practice. Given the increased scholarly discussions of both transfer and multimodality, there remains a lack of disciplinary attention to the overlap of these two areas of inquiry. Echoing the call of this collection, the value and significance of this study lies in the fact that it allows me to explore new paths of inquiry regarding the ways writing teachers and scholars can help facilitate writing transfer across modes and media. Extending the important research of scholars such as DePalma and Alexander (2015), Moore and Anson (2016), Rosinski (2017), and Shepherd (2018), among many others, I have sought to further compare three different digital platforms and their affordances in making space for writing transfer. This study can also be read alongside other chapters in this collection, including those by Crystal VanKooten (chapter 1, this volume) and Joseph Anthony Wilson and Josie Rose Portz (chapter 3, this volume), which centralize multimodal transfer in the context of FYC, as well as those by Anna V. Knutson (chapter 5, this volume) and Ryan P. Shepherd (chapter 6, this volume), which galvanize a critical reading of transfer across social media spaces.

As for the future of multimodal writing pedagogy, the results of this research suggest that to encourage successful transfer across digital media platforms, teachers could ask students to (1) use their rhetorical knowledge and strategies to compare the affordances of different digital platforms in fulfilling their rhetorical purposes; (2) consider the potential difficulties and challenges they might encounter while working on different digital platforms; (3) select digital platforms that may work best for addressing their rhetorical purposes and audiences; and (4) reflect on the effectiveness of their design processes and products, considering the role digital platforms play in successfully conveying meanings. These suggestions are intended to raise students' awareness of the various affordances related to digital platforms, to deepen students' reflection on a range of technological tools and their capacities, and to encourage students' successful transfer of writing knowledge across multiple modes and media. With the Covid-19 pandemic gradually shifting the realities of writing instruction, teachers are reinterpreting the ecology of multimodal writing projects and testing different tools for online and remote teaching. I hope this study presents an exigence for instructors to further leverage the potentials of cloud-based technologies in sustaining student engagement in multimodal projects and their transfer of writing knowledge.

NOTES

1. In the introduction to this collection, we learned that the term *multimodal* is used to indicate the range of modalities—printed words, still and moving images, sound, speech, music, and color—authors combine as they design texts (New London Group 1996).

2. Affordances are defined as relevant to "the question of potentials and limitations of a mode" (Kress 2010, 192). If potentials include features of a tool that facilitate the achievement of compositional purposes, then limitations are features that prevent users from easily accomplishing certain kinds of actions.

REFERENCES

Adler-Kassner, Linda, Irene Clark, Liane Robertson, Kara Taczak, and Katheleen Blake Yancey. 2016. "Assembling Knowledge: The Role of Threshold Concepts in Facilitating Transfer." In *Critical Transitions: Writing and the Question of Transfer*, edited by Chris M. Anson and Jessie L. Moore, 17–47. Logan: Utah State University Press.

Alexander, Jonathan, and Jaqueline Rhodes. 2014. *On Multimodality: New Media in Composition Studies*. Champaign, IL: National Council of Teachers of English.

Ball, Cheryl E., Tia Scoffield Bowen, and Tyrell Brent Fenn. 2013. "Genre and Transfer in a Multimodal Composition Class." In *Multimodal Literacies and Emerging Genres*, edited by Tracey Bowen and Carl Whithaus, 15–36. Pittsburgh, PA: University of Pittsburgh Press.

Birks, Melanie, and Jane Mills. 2015. *Grounded Theory: A Practical Guide*. Thousand Oaks, CA: Sage.

Davis, Rebecca Frost. 2017. "Pedagogy and Learning in a Digital Ecosystem." In *Understanding Writing Transfer: Implications for Transformative Student Learning in Higher Education*, edited by Jessie L. Moore and Randall Bass, 27–38. Sterling, VA: Stylus.

DePalma, Michael-John. 2015. "Tracing Transfer across Media: Investigating Writers' Perceptions of Cross-Contextual and Rhetorical Reshaping in Processes of Remediation." *College Composition and Communication* 66 (4): 615–642.

DePalma, Michael-John, and Kara Poe Alexander. 2015. "A Bag Full of Snakes: Negotiating the Challenges of Multimodal Composition." *Computers and Composition* 37: 182–200.

Dubisar, Abby M., and Jason Palmeri. 2010. "Palin/Pathos/Peter Griffin: Political Video Remix and Composition Pedagogy." *Computers and Composition* 27 (2): 77–93.

Gries, Laurie E. 2019. "Writing to Assemble Publics: Making Writing Activate, Making Writing Matter." *College Composition and Communication* 70 (3): 327–355.

Jiang, Jialei. 2020. "'I Never Know What to Expect': Aleatory Identity Play in *Fortnite* and Its Implications for Multimodal Composition." *Computers and Composition* 55: 1–14.

Jiang, Jialei. 2021. "Activating Multimodal Public Rhetoric in First-Year Composition: Exploring the Potential of a Social Justice Writing Project." In *Beyond the Frontiers: Innovations in First Year Composition*, edited by Jill Dahlman and Tammy Winner, 141–155. Newcastle: Cambridge Scholars Publishing.

Jiang, Jialei, and Matthew A. Vetter. 2020. "Addressing the Challenges and Opportunities of a Feminist Rhetorical Approach for Wikipedia-Based Writing Instruction in First-Year Composition." *Composition Forum* 44. http://compositionforum.com/issue/45/wikipedia.php.

Kress, Gunther. 2000. "Design and Transformation: New Theories of Meaning." In *Multiliteracies: Literacy Learning and the Design of Social Futures*, edited by Bill Cope and Mary Kalantzis, 149–157. New York: Routledge.

Kress, Gunther. 2010. *Multimodality: A Social Semiotic Approach to Contemporary Communication*. New York: Routledge.

Moore, Jessie L. 2017. "Five Essential Principles about Writing Transfer." In *Understanding Writing Transfer: Implications for Transformative Student Learning in Higher Education*, edited by Jessie L. Moore and Randall Bass, 1–12. Sterling, VA: Stylus.

Moore, Jessie L., and Chris M. Anson. 2016. "Introduction." In *Critical Transitions: Writing and the Question of Transfer*, edited by Chris M. Anson and Jessie L. Moore, 3–13. Logan: Utah State University Press.

New London Group. 1996. "A Pedagogy of Multiliteracies: Designing Social Futures." *Harvard Educational Review* 66 (1): 60–93.

Rosinski, Paula. 2017. "Students' Perceptions of the Transfer of Rhetorical Knowledge between Digital Self-Sponsored Writing and Academic Writing: The Importance of Authentic Contexts and Reflection." In *Critical Transitions: Writing and the Question of Transfer*, edited by Chris M. Anson and Jessie L. Moore, 247–271. Logan: Utah State University Press.

Shepherd, Ryan P. 2018. "Digital Writing, Multimodality, and Learning Transfer: Crafting Connections between Composition and Online Composing." *Computers and Composition* 48: 103–114.

Sheridan, David Michael, Jim Ridolfo, and Anthony Michel. 2012. *The Available Means of Persuasion: Mapping a Theory and Pedagogy of Multimodal Public Rhetoric*. Anderson, SC: Parlor Press.

VanKooten, Crystal. 2016. "Identifying Components of Meta-awareness about Composition: Toward a Theory and Methodology for Writing Studies." *Composition Forum* 33. http://compositionforum.com/issue/33/meta-awareness.php.

Warren-Riley, Sarah, and Elise Hurley. 2017. "Multimodal Pedagogical Approaches to Public Writing: Digital Media Advocacy and Mundane Texts." *Composition Forum* 36. http://compositionforum.com/issue/36/multimodal.php.

Yancey, Kathleen Blake. 2017. "Writing, Transfer, and ePortfolios: A Possible Trifecta in Supporting Student Learning." In *Understanding Writing Transfer: Implications for Transformative Student Learning in Higher Education*, edited by Jessie L. Moore and Randall Bass, 39–48. Sterling, VA: Stylus.

Yancey, Kathleen Blake, Matthew Davis, Liane Robertson, Kara Taczak, and Erin Workman. 2019. "The Teaching for Transfer Curriculum: The Role of Concurrent Transfer and Inside- and Outside-School Contexts in Supporting Students' Writing Development." *College Composition and Communication* 71 (2): 268–295.

Yancey, Kathleen Blake, Liane Robertson, and Kara Taczak. 2014. *Writing across Contexts*. Logan: Utah State University Press.

3
ON THE LABOR OF WRITING TRANSFER
Bodies and Borderlands Discourses in Translation

Joseph Anthony Wilson and Josie Rose Portz

Zhannat and her group members eagerly presented the qualitative results of their writing class's capstone project, for which they had analyzed their study participants' conflicting feelings concerning local Kazakh language reclamation programs. Her group members' motivation for this topic stemmed from their own positionalities as self-identified ethnic Kazakhs, Tatars, and Russians, respectively, in a Central Asian borderlands region where linguistic identity and ethnic identity are often considered together (Fierman 2009) and where the government has framed efforts to revitalize the Kazakh language as necessary for restoring a Kazakh people (Dave 2007). After a brief introduction in English, Zhannat began presenting her section of the group's literature review by discussing the perspectives of Russian Sign Language (RSL) literate, self-identified ethnic Kazakhs in the region, such as herself. While doing so, she oscillated between English and RSL, highlighting quoted material, arguments, and RSL community-specific vernacular and at times simultaneously translating her English speech into RSL. Following Zhannat, a groupmate engaged in similar practices by including descriptions and even entire arguments in Tatar. The group presented only the methodology section entirely in English. At a Kazakhstani institution that takes seriously the country's federal trilingual language policies, all students were encouraged to make use of whatever linguistic resources were available to them to present their research, with the goal of improving student literacies in English, Kazakh, and Russian in tandem, yet Zhannat's group ascribed alternative aims for its project.

In this chapter, we examine Zhannat's leveraging of multiple modalities as evidence of writing transfer that both resisted local language representations and cunningly engaged her peers.[1] Drawing from Laura Gonzales's (2018) rhetoric of translation, we are defining multimodality

https://doi.org/10.7330/9781646425341.c003

here as methods of conveying meaning across (linguistic, generic, technological) boundaries. While this definition differs slightly from (though overlaps with) the term's typical association with communication beyond alphabetic print, we believe it speaks to the inherent relations of multimodality, multilingualism, and transfer in part necessary for understanding Zhannat's literacy work as a borderlands student and an aspiring professional teacher and translator. Beyond a divergent approach to defining multimodality, we suggest that an understanding of how Zhannat engages multiple communities in her conference presentation consequently necessitates that we consider goals for transfer research beyond measuring students' integration into/of specific academic literacies.

We instead ask our readers to consider how to rethink common goals and contexts for transfer research, with implications for how we conceive of multimodality's relationship to transfer. Much of the present transfer literature, including that on multimodality, closely follows pedagogical aims of many writing courses—aims that treat socialization into professional and academic disciplines as the assumed goal. Christiane Donahue (2017, 2018) has called for expanding this scope across multiple publications, positing that North American writing studies' most capacious methodologies for understanding transfer still remain tethered to "optimizing integration" in which "troublesome knowledge and boundary-crossing disrupt integration . . . but the implication in the scholarship is that the disruption is useful insofar as it can enable further integration over time" (2017, 112). This is evidenced by research on multimodality and transfer. Even the most dynamic metaphors for conceiving of the adaptive remediations that occur as writers transfer across modalities, such as *literacy linking*, direct us toward how such literacies "can be transferred, integrated, and reshaped *to fit* another domain" (Alexander, DePalma, and Ringer 2016, 36, emphasis added).

Thus, while we recognize writers' abilities to both "shape and be shaped" (DePalma and Ringer 2011, 141) by transfer, a teleology of integration has not allowed us to fully account for issues of political context and power. Tessa Brown (2020, 614) recently argued that writing studies' privileging of students' adaptation into professional and disciplinary communities depends specifically on notions of linguistic diversity that do not consider broader power structures and posits instead that "we must also ask colleagues who study institutional literacies to make space for the language and the languaging that arises from pleasure, protest, reflection, and art." We posit the same of the broader transfer literature, particularly the theoretical metaphors used to conceive of multimodality and transfer; we ask specifically about moments when transfer as integration into institutional literacies occludes the ethno-political and political-historical negotiations students undergo in the process of translation. As we perceive it, Zhannat's languaging practices instead move us to consider how a focus on multimodality might help disrupt transfer literature's integration-aligned impulse in search of transformations of writing knowledge that subvert assimilation into academic discourses concatenated to specific and often violent colonial histories.

This foregrounding of relations of power in translation is imperative in borderlands contexts such as East Kazakhstan, where students may face considerable pushback from mobilizing literacies across named languages and modalities. From a linguistic perspective, Bridget A. Goodman and D. Philip Montgomery (2020) found in their research on the transfer of genre knowledge (framed as language socialization) acquired in English to Kazakh and Russian that many students perceived rhetorical strategies they learned in English as incommensurable with those taught specifically in Kazakh courses—perceptions complicated by students' self-reported differences in proficiency among the three languages. Maira Klyshbekova (2023) has similarly discussed the challenges and affordances of translanguaging in resisting English-only norms in language acquisition classrooms and in relation to Kazakhstan's trilingual language policy. In terms of multimodality, Randall Monty (2015) has similarly demonstrated how transnational students in the Texan-Mexican borderlands region perceived their multimodal communication practices as necessarily influencing their own national and local identifications and positionalities, shaping the extent to which they translated literacies across technological, institutional, and national borders.

Prior to her university studies, Zhannat had been instructed to understand translation as a neutral activity regardless of language and modality. Throughout her schooling, her relatives, administrators, and government actors had shuffled her among different academic institutions due to a combination of her ethnic identifications and home language use, frequently forcing her to segregate sociolinguistic resources in her writing in ways that belied her daily translingual practices. In the follow-up interview to her conference presentation, however, her reflections uncovered the ways her writing across modes in this WAC course resisted not only monolingual ideologies but also their ethno-linguistic attachments. We view Zhannat's efforts to transfer knowledge as primarily engaged in protest and resistance and as translations in ways for which metaphors of integration do not fully account. This is important because while participant-checking this chapter, Zhannat affirmed that she understood her translation work described here as resistance. In doing so, we echo work on writing knowledge and learning transfer external to North America that posits *translation* as a more encompassing term than *transfer*, as it implicates the rhetorical negotiations inherent but often occluded in all knowledge mobilization (Donahue 2018; Mulcahy 2013) in contexts such as the one we study in Kazakhstan. Indeed, translation studies programs were responsible for the lion's share of literacy education at universities in the borderlands city where this study takes place, making translation a more locally relevant term than transfer. We define translation here as the labor that guides all negotiations of meaning in language use (Bou Ayash 2019), including negotiations of prior knowledge as students adapt their writing across modes. In this chapter, we consequently substitute references to "transfer" for "translation" as a relational metaphor to emphasize Zhannat's multimodal languaging work as artistically engaged in protest and resistance.

This chapter's organization presents Zhannat's artistic labor as a form of embodied resistance, revealing how multiple instances of her translation work across modalities transformed not only knowledges but relations of power. Ultimately, we argue for more distributed understandings of agency in translation that allow us to both engage more fully with modalities and locate moments where translation does not lead to integration into institutional literacies. These findings draw from a larger, year-long community-engaged project in northern Kazakhstan, over the course of which Joseph volunteered with Zhannat at a local literacy hub. Neither author identifies as being from Kazakhstan, so it is important to stress that while Zhannat provided feedback on multiple iterations of this project, our findings are still subjectively shaped by our own privilege and interpretations as white teachers and researchers from the United States. Specifically, our findings draw from classroom and conference observations, textual analyses of Zhannat's and her group members' writing, and an hour-long interview with Zhannat that took place a month post-completion of the course. This interview began and ended with the question "why do issues of literacy and translation matter to you," in which Zhannat emphasized resistance as well as her RSL practices; these responses served as our point of departure for this chapter. We also made multiple revisions based on feedback from and participant-checking with Zhannat throughout the writing of this chapter, and we discussed the importance of participant anonymity in foregrounding her acts of resistance. These findings are thus relational, and we cannot offer objective or replicable pedagogical or research implications.

In what follows, we describe three phases of analysis. First, when describing the local context in which Zhannat enrolled in her WAC course, we detail how Zhannat translated her developing critical awareness of language from writing a multiliteracy autobiography for that course to composing her own interview protocol for her course's final qualitative research project. Through the language choices made in her interview protocol, we show how Zhannat conceives of the interviewer/interviewee relationship as one of distributed agency so as to resist institutional discourses that delegitimize the heritage identity of self-identifying Kazakhs through boundaries of fluency and access. Second, we illustrate how Zhannat's composition of a multiliteracy autobiography helped further transform her marketing practices when composing on social media. In these instances, she fosters engagement through strategies of collective social knowledge, allowing her to employ the affordances of multi-semiotic knowledge beyond alphabetic print. Finally, we turn to Zhannat's translation of her qualitative research paper to a conference presentation for a public audience, revealing how she leverages embodied and digital translation practices to distribute the labor of translation and cunningly engage her peers. We conclude our chapter by reflecting on the relationship between multimodality and translation and offering considerations for future research.

TRANSLATING LOCAL LITERACIES: FROM MULTILITERACY AUTOBIOGRAPHY TO INTERVIEW PROTOCOL

Universities in East Kazakhstan have historically undergone and continue to undergo considerable linguistic and demographic changes. Although Kazakhstan witnessed a mass exodus of self-identifying ethnic Russian residents to Siberia post-independence, a large Russian presence remains in this borderlands province. Since the mid-twentieth century, the Russian language has also served as the lingua franca in eastern cities despite the Kazakh language's growing prominence in the country's southern and western regions. Language policies since the early 2000s have openly called for increasing the status of Kazakh, a Kipchak Turkic language, as a Kazakh rights project; many Kazakh language speakers feel they are correcting nearly a century of Soviet Russian oppression by reclaiming Kazakh as the language of all Kazakhs. In the borderlands region that includes East Kazakhstan, where Kazakh language use is much less common, many local Russian speakers conversely lament federally funded migration and educational programs that require Kazakh language proficiency and provide either repatriation or scholarships to Kazakh speakers willing to settle in East Kazakhstan specifically. Several minority groups, including Koreans, Tatars, Uighurs, and Volga Germans, also were displaced to or historically resided in the region and generally speak Russian in addition to their heritage languages, while Mongolian Kazakhstani residents—many of whom can trace kinship ties to Kazakhs and historically engaged in nomadic pastoralism throughout the oblast—speak Mongol and often Kazakh. Against this diverse linguistic backdrop, federal trilingual language policies promote learning of English, Kazakh, and Russian; public and private institutions alike group students by the medium of education (MoE) through which they will receive the majority of their instruction, typically Kazakh or Russian.

Zhannat identifies ethnically as Kazakh, and she and many of her local Kazakh classmates were placed by their university into the Russian group, as they had matriculated from Russian-medium local secondary schools. In many ways, the MoE divide at this institution was more cultural and geographic than linguistic: those enrolled in Kazakh sections mostly identified as either southern Kazakhs or Mongolian and had traveled to East Kazakhstan on scholarship to attend the university, while those in the Russian-medium section were local students. Majoring in "two foreign languages" (English and Korean), Zhannat enrolled in the WAC course as one of the few classes on her schedule offered in English. Following Guillaume Gentil (2018), this class adopted an academic biliteracy approach, centering translation as content. Zhannat completed three major course assignments: a multiliteracy autobiography; a terminology assignment through which she had contributed various meanings of the term *gender* across Russian, Kazakh, and English to a class multilingual glossary; and a final, collaborative, qualitative research project on some aspect of translation, the results of which were submitted as a single academic essay and presented at an undergraduate research conference at a neighboring university designed to showcase students' work to the local community.

Although Zhannat felt highly skilled in navigating local language politics as a young adult, in her multiliteracy autobiography she described the dissonance she perceived between her own linguistic and ethnic identities and those of her relatives and later institutions:

> When I was born in my parents' family, my grandparents decided that they were going to live with us: with my deaf mom, deaf father, and me. My Kazakh grandparents were afraid that I would never speak in my life and that I should know Kazakh even though my parents don't speak Kazakh. Kazakh is the language of Kazakhstan now. While my parents spoke in Russian Sign Language to me. My parents had taken me to a Russian

Kindergarten, and my grandparents moved me to a Kazakh school at the age of 5 or 6. Then I messed and mixed the languages and spoke them mostly at the same time, but amazingly I did speak.

From a young age, Zhannat learned to move confidently through different institutional spaces in ways that eventually conformed to communities' expectations for her language use, and (with the exception of her relatives) she described her languaging practices in reference to the ethnicity of those with whom she communicated. She reported that through the multiliteracy autobiography, she cultivated a deeper understanding of these literacy identities, expanding the class's discussion of "discourse community" to frame her Russian and Kazakh usage in reference to those languages' situated histories of ethnic identification in the country. By contrast, she associated her Korean and RSL practices in reference to "K-pop lovers" and her town's tight-knit RSL-speaking community.

Critically considering how her different languaging practices signaled community membership helped Zhannat conceptualize participant interaction in the WAC course's subsequent qualitative research project as she developed her own discourse surrounding literacy, which she described in her post-course completion interview:

> The first thought I had was I never thought of my languages in this way like I never had to explain each language that I spoke like how it happened why and stuff like nobody asks that people say how many languages do you speak I say 5 and they're like wow you're so smart you're a genius of course from the USA especially and when we were writing that paper I thought that's good now I kinda appreciate the languages I speak I put like frames in my head like I'll use this language this way that's good . . . I think [the multiliteracy autobiography] helped me to understand the languages that I speak and explain to the interviewee for example as for me, I know that I speak Korean this much but for example if I didn't speak Kazakh but I understood it I would know it I would know what this person felt here and what this person is trying to explain to me.

Zhannat here juxtaposes Korean and Kazakh both to link her linguistic identities to her affective experiences as an ethnic Kazakh in the region and to help her interview participant describe their own practices. By suggesting that "if I didn't speak Kazakh but I understood it I would know it," she seeks to ameliorate any embarrassment her interview participant might feel toward perceived limitations in Kazakh language use. She instead suggests that lived experiences as an ethnic Kazakh offer a perfectly acceptable substitute for perceived gaps in proficiency, seeking to affirm her participant's daily translanguaging practices. In the construction of interview questions with her qualitative research group and her individual interactions with study participants, she began to translate her own developing critical understanding of language use from the multiliteracy autobiography into her qualitative research design to tap into her participants' conceptions of their own literacies. By reframing her interview protocol and leveraging its dialogic and thus multimodal affordances, she also tacitly resisted institutional discourses she felt delegitimized the heritage identity of those identifying as Kazakhs with less fluency and access to quality Kazakh literacy programs.

PUTTING MULTIMODAL GENRES TO WORK: TRANSLATION FROM MULTILITERACY AUTOBIOGRAPHY TO SOCIAL MEDIA MARKETING

Reflecting on her daily language use through the multiliteracy autobiography enabled Zhannat to cultivate critical awareness of language such that she could articulate her rhetorical choices concerning translation across digital modalities in addition to spoken ones, which she often framed in terms of discourse community—a term introduced in her WAC class. When speaking about marketing through social media for her work at a local library, Zhannat revealed her thought process when posting videos on Instagram. For her, language choices across modes determine who will engage and how, and Zhannat wanted peak engagement with all her posts. Pointing to a Kazakh hashtag associated with older Kazakh әжелер (grandmothers), she laughingly said: "In Instagram when I'm trying to make like a funny video I'm thinking who will watch this if it's in Kazakh some people can't relate like people who speak Russian but they can understand Kazakh even if they can't speak it they can understand Kazakh because they see it because they say oh Zhannat is behaving like my grandma hahahaha it's funny so that's how I use discourse community."

Thinking through the affordances of Kazakh and Russian, Zhannat started to conceptualize both nuanced and broad target audiences as she considered which literacies each might possess and in what languages, exhibiting the kinds of situational awareness on social media demonstrated by the borderlands students in Monty's (2015) study. She noted that for some time she had only posted in Russian with the exception of some English terms on her profile, stating that Russian and English "are trending right now," especially among her co-workers at the library. While participant-checking, Zhannat asked that we include her frustration that these languages, rather than Kazakh, were trending. She also framed her recent use of some Kazakh terms, such as *әжелер* here, as indicative of her growing understanding of discourse community knowledge and values specifically because they further circulated popular Kazakh imagery her Russian-speaking friends would find accessible. This accessibility stemmed in part from its brief circulation as a hashtag that allowed curious peers encountering her profile to easily locate more examples of how the term is used.

From a translingual perspective, we understand Zhannat's articulation of her own translation practices testifies to labor she performs in both maintaining and resisting language representations through her writing (Horner and Alvarez 2019). Beyond her individual labor, however, her efforts to revise such language practices depended on the work conducted by and through multimodal genres—such as the mobility and didactic affordances of a hashtag—beyond her own conscious promotion of her writing to further open up a Kazakh lexis toward more cosmopolitan audiences (You 2016). Zhannat elaborates on flexible and transferable strategies dependent on embodied, multi-semiotic knowledge and circumstance. She refines these strategies through engagement with contingent situations, exemplifying her strategies of intervention, as when she appeals to collective social knowledge of Kazakh *әжелер* beyond the boundaries of alphabetic print. Further, she mobilizes strategies of translation to affect particular results, such as gaining Instagram traffic and followers by calculated use of discourse and transition between named languages. Most significant, Zhannat's recognition and legitimization of diverse literacy identities reflect the potential of translation to transform and blur lines marking social categories as she translates discourse about language ideologies from her multiliteracy autobiography to her qualitative interview protocol to resist constructions of what might constitute legitimate Kazakh language practice. Similar to the perspectives of Kazakh language users in other studies in the region, such as Juldyz Smagulova's (2019) research on Kazakh language socialization, Zhannat recognizes key places and times to reclaim Kazakh language resources; further, she does not believe she must circumscribe her Kazakh literacies to completely assimilate into the Russian-speaking academic communities she studies alongside. As she moves between different professional and institutional spaces, she instead leverages the labor and affordances of modes—including the spoken interview and Instagram posts—to position herself in such a way as to complicate generalizing discourses surrounding Kazakh and Russian ethnic and linguistic positionalities.

DISTRIBUTING ARTISTIC LABOR: FROM QUALITATIVE RESEARCH PAPER TO MULTIMODAL CONFERENCE PRESENTATION

Zhannat's positioning in relation to local language representations shaped her rhetorical translation practices when presenting her research. After completing the WAC course, Zhannat and her group presented their qualitative project's results at an undergraduate research conference hosted by a nearby university. This presentation required translation on multiple fronts. As the research was initially composed for academic audiences in an English-medium class, Zhannat and her classmates needed to consider languaging choices that accounted for the diverse sociolinguistic landscape represented by their East Kazakhstani peers, faculty, and community members attending the conference. The presentation also translated across modes: from research paper genre to a conference presentation heavily utilizing data analysis charts and participant quotations and analyses on a PowerPoint, as well as embodied multimodal strategies (Gonzales 2018) such as gestures and targeted eye contact. In each of these translation processes, Zhannat further transformed her own knowledge of writing in light of the contingencies of the conference presentation.

While most students presenting at the conference relied on either Russian or a combination of Russian and English to present their research, Zhannat's group stood out for its strategic and considerable use of Tatar, Kazakh, and RSL. Zhannat specifically translated into RSL all directly quoted material from her interview participants, terminology and phrases describing her town's RSL-speaking community, and her entire closing final argument. These choices certainly drew the attention of her audience members, particularly when Zhannat's use of RSL gave the appearance of silence in the large conference room. She and her classmates knew that many of the audience members would not understand RSL, Tatar, or perhaps even Kazakh; yet she was adamant in her interview that she wanted attention from everyone in the room. She cited the presence of Russian on every slide of the PowerPoint as a way to ensure understanding, while all presenters were also able to represent their own languages in delivering the presentation.

Zhannat recalled standing before the screen, displaying information from her project that she had translated into Russian while she physically communicated in part by drawing from a diverse range of literacies she sought to legitimize. In the follow-up interview with one of the authors a month later, she argued that this positioning served her own purposes in multiple ways. Concerning the majority of her peers and faculty in the audience, she recalled: "We got the attention we wanted to get the goal was accomplished they were paying attention to us and they were also looking at the presentation like what is it she's translating what is it she said when you don't understand something you need to understand right you try to see the view you want to know." In projecting Russian literacies using a non-human agent while communicating RSL through embodied translation strategies (Gonzales 2018), Zhannat demanded active engagement from her audience members with her research and with the perspectives of her interview participants. She also felt she could only authentically represent quoted perspectives of RSL speakers using RSL, reorganizing her presentation to front this quoted material. Her group's study's more quantitative information and summative results thus appeared toward the end of the conference presentation (as opposed to beginning paragraphs of the results section of her research paper).

Zhannat felt these translation decisions encouraged continual engagement with the research presented beyond an arbitrary use of RSL and Tatar. She framed her choices with the following metaphor: "We used our languages as Easter eggs well not exactly Easter eggs but we didn't give it all at the beginning we didn't just slap people with the facts that we had we just started showing something different that you don't understand but to understand that you have to look at [the graphics on the screen] active[ly] look at the research and actively engage with it." As she explained her group members' choices to include their own individual languages, she indicated a conscious decision to orchestrate audience interaction. By refusing to "just slap people with the facts," she also contrasts her group's presentation with "more boring" presentations that her group felt followed the "template" of the qualitative research paper too closely. Her group's negotiations of the conventions of the conference presentation genre instead worked to highlight presenters' heterogeneously languaged deliveries, diverging from the other groups' integrative attempts to conform to institutional literacies and monolingualist language policies. She contrasted these appeals with peers' and even her own past writing that used unnecessarily dense vernacular in English or Russian, recalling that she told her group members "if we're trying to make people understand this, we don't need to make it that hard." Instead, she agonized over the clarity of her translation work across literacies. Her delivery through RSL further made concrete the embodiment of these appeals through gesture as a central rather than supplemental form of communication.

Beyond conceptions of a general conference audience, Zhannat's group sought to speak directly to and legitimize the practices of individual communities with whom they identified. In her interview, she spoke about her group's decision to utilize RSL and Tatar literacies specifically, as these respective communities might especially appreciate their research's findings:

> ZHANNAT: We were speaking to people who speak Tatar, or people who have some Tatar heritage people who have some relatives who are deaf in Kazakhstan they could also relate and they could be like oh this person kinda knows what I know it relates to what I know or I kinda know what she knows.
>
> JOSEPH: Did you think of that before you began your presentation?
>
> ZHANNAT: Well I thought . . . we're gonna like get in there like in their hearts . . . not like exactly hearts but yeah but now when I said about discourse community now I'm thinking like yeah that was about discourse community.

Rather than communicate exclusively to a generally conceived local audience, Zhannat also focused on communities with shared literacies: communities she felt language policies, specifically MoE programs, had excluded. In efforts to relate to her multiply conceived audience, Zhannat sought to make richer affective appeals by connecting to audience members on an experiential level located in her own body, a move she retroactively recognized as her growing awareness of the boundaries of particular literacy communities.

We view Zhannat's translation practices in this presentation as interventional in the production of critique and the expectation of justice.[2] Through this lens, knowledge transformation is productive insofar as it upends (rather than balances) bodies of knowledge perceived as discrete and stable. Zhannat's presentation is notable from this perspective for its attention to juxtaposing recognition of individual and collective bodies in ways resistant to broad ethno-linguistic generalizations. This dual purpose significantly departs from Zhannat's prior understanding of translation work as politically neutral movement between two discrete languages and thus from her prior efforts to integrate into her translation studies program by treating languages as discrete entities attached to particular populations. Instead, she does not simply refuse to occlude the rhetorical negotiations inherent in her translation process from the qualitative paper in English to the conference presentation: she also uses multiple modes to distribute the labor of translation.

In this case, we are suggesting that translation becomes actualized when transforming the particular social boundaries demarcating language representations. In posing modal (digital, generic, linguistic) boundaries to her audience, Zhannat seeks to introduce them to the same negotiation work she regularly engages in when translating. Through layered performance, she guides her audience to grapple with indeterminacies through translation alongside her own fraught languaging work, moving everyone in the room to rethink how they understood, for example, RSL's potential as a productive mode in a self-identifying Kazakh person's cosmopolitan and academic linguistic repertoire. In short, Zhannat demonstrates not only the agency required to negotiate boundaries but the agency of modalities and boundaries themselves to trigger moments of rhetorically fraught translation. Through targeted use of RSL, Zhannat anticipates that the supposed untranslatability of her communication through the embodied mode of gestured speech will form an impenetrable boundary to understanding such that her audience members must both turn toward the projected graphics she has composed to make sense of her project and, more important by her telling, renegotiate their own assumptions concerning the conflations of ethnicity, language, and ability in ways that fail to account for Zhannat's understanding of her own multiple positionalities in the uptake of that speech. In other words, we are suggesting that Zhannat's labor in translating the qualitative research paper into a translingual conference presentation worked in concert with both the labor of the modes incorporated into her presentation and the labor of her audience members who were forced to recognize their own role in meaning making.

This is not to say that Zhannat lacks pride in her own Kazakh language use. In her interview and in giving feedback on this chapter, she described her Kazakh language proficiency as an extension of her Kazakh identity, both defending the language as similar to but more beautiful than French and lamenting that some Russian and international peers had mocked local Kazakh speech practices. For her presentation, she explained to us that she determined that expressing her and her interview participants' own struggles with navigating competing positionalities would not intervene productively enough to challenge her peers' deeply held meso-political beliefs about language; instead, her audience members needed to personally experience the work of both boundary negotiation (of language representations) and feelings of stasis (in reference to their own inabilities to immediately translate her gestured speech).

When Zhannat and her group members translate their research into their respective languages for the sake of identifying more deeply with the Tatar- and RSL-speaking communities, we suggest that they further invoke an appeal to justice rooted in respect for the boundary-demarcating practices of regional language groups. They take up this posture through their desire to center RSL and Tatar community literacies and maintain their participants' exact quotations. These practices parallel Kazakh researcher Juldyz Smagulova's (2018) findings in research on Kazakh language reclamation practices in multigenerational households. In her observations near Almaty, many self-identifying ethnic Kazakhs treated Kazakh as "an object" (750), a discrete and stable language, somewhat belying daily translingual practices to augment Kazakh's status as an educational language. Distant (a twenty-six-hour train ride) from any Kazakhstani metropolitan area, Zhannat's group takes up and complicates this practice through the use of RSL and Tatar as a way of demanding intersectionality, situating anti-imperialist practices of Kazakh ethnic and language reclamation efforts alongside those of the RSL- and Tatar-speaking communities—many of whom were also disproportionately impacted by Soviet policies (Dave 2007).

At the same time, this labor depends on the agency of the body as distributed, reshaping boundary-making practices. Critical feminist research as early as Donna Haraway (1988) has argued for the treatment of bodies also as "objects" and "genres" that draw situated agencies from the perspectives of their own mapped boundaries, and this view understands the dissonance "between bodily self and representation as a productive space for critique" that might lead to the "formation of an ethical stance" (Alexander and Rhodes 2014, 116). Zhannat explained to us while participant-checking how her body, read as female and ethnically Kazakh, placed in an institutional space that designated her as primarily a Russian speaker, and positioned in front of—yet importantly separated from—technologies displaying conventional institutional literacies, acts to help foment this space of critique. Such a space is shaped by Zhannat's efforts to transform relationships to institutional contexts and blur ethnic attachments to both elevate the status and legitimize the practices of her audiences' few yet present RSL and Tatar community members. Just as she aspires for her group to "get in" the hearts of these audiences, her group's own hearts and bodies remain actively postured toward the expectation of mutual respect.

IMPLICATIONS FOR RESEARCH AND PEDAGOGY

By conceiving of writing knowledge transfer as translation, we have sought to reorient our approach to multimodality and transfer by considering the highly relational, political-rhetorical languaging work Zhannat conducts as she translates her knowledge across different modalities. We are particularly impressed by Zhannat's translation from her qualitative paper to the conference presentation, specifically the ways she leverages digital and embodied modes to resist occluding the contingent and ethno-political negotiations of her speech acts. Often, these negotiations prove elusive to transfer researchers attempting to uncover them after the fact; as Elizabeth Wardle (2007, 69) memorably wrote, "We are looking for apples when those apples are now part of an apple pie." Instead of attempting to retroactively recall the recipe, Zhannat makes space for her audience members to join her in the actual baking of the pie. She becomes an ally with different modes to resist offering the illusion of equivalence in translation and instead cunningly intervenes in her conference presentation, inviting her participants to engage in the fraught negotiations of languaging work alongside her.

We argue that centering translation beyond integration in academic discourses about transfer might illuminate the positionalities writers negotiate and occlude in this process of remediating prior knowledge, contributing to conversations about transformation already present in the literature on transfer, multilingualism, and multimodality in Kazakhstan. This includes previously cited work on language socialization by Smagulova (2019), who describes how Kazakh-speaking parents challenge the dominance of Russian in metropolitan areas as the language of education through code mixing. Zhannat's experiences offer moments of resistance to notions of dominant linguistic practices by drawing from multimodal affordances as well as linguistic resources from her RSL community. As transparent as Zhannat made her resistant translation practices in the final conference presentation, an observer with an eye for integration alone might mistake her efforts for linguistic tourism (Matsuda 2014) rather than artistic labor. A positionality toward translation that considers resistance might instead clue teachers and researchers in to the gendered, hetero-normative, ableist, and ethnic discourses (to name a few) that writers negotiate, even in the production of texts appearing in line with institutional and pedagogical objectives. Moreover, this understanding of translation begins to account for the embodied memories that help demarcate the discursive contextual boundaries for transfer as well as writers' abilities to leverage modalities to resist and redraw such boundaries. In attuning to the labor of modes specifically—including semantic and embodied modes—in acts of translation, we seek to foreground a more political-rhetorical approach to translation that recognizes the agency of language representations, language policies, and modes *as distributed and transformative* as that of the individual translator in the historical and ongoing maintenance and revision of language.

Future research would benefit from recognizing acts of resistance in translation, as well as the agency of boundaries drawn around languages by individual translators, communities, and technologies such as translation software. How those boundaries are revised moment by moment toward cosmopolitan relations could serve as a methodological point of departure (as opposed to how successfully students' translations integrated into institutional norms). Toward this aim, we hope to have contributed participatory research from a context in Kazakhstan outside the major metropolitan areas of Almaty and Astana. We see much opportunity for future research in continuing to engage language socialization work (Goodman and Montgomery 2020; Smagulova 2019) and translanguaging scholarship (Kyshbekova 2023; Tuskeyeva 2022) in Central Asia, as well as transfer methodologies of "interdependence" (VanKooten, chapter 1, this volume) and transfer and translingualism (Donahue 2018; Lorimer Leonard and Nowacek 2016), as these lines of research have considered the agency of bodies and places, semantic agency, the agency of researchers investigating transfer and translanguaging, and the labor of individual language users, respectively. Such synthesis seems generative toward the goal of supporting borderlands students in cultivating a critical awareness of language, intervening in local language representations, and productively negotiating their positioning in relation to their institutions and their communities.

NOTES

1. By *language representations*, we mean "ideas, perceptions, images, and metaphors language users entertain about their own . . . language resources and the value they grant to the way they (or others) utilize them" (Bou Ayash 2019, 21).
2. Some of our thinking here was influenced by *techne* theory's conceptions of art (see Atwill 2006; Pender 2011).

REFERENCES

Alexander, Jonathan, and Jacqueline Rhodes. 2014. *On Multimodality: New Media in Composition Studies*. Champaign, IL: Conference on College Composition and Communication and National Council of Teachers of English.

Alexander, Kara Poe, Michael-John DePalma, and Jeffrey Ringer. 2016. "Adaptive Remediation and the Facilitation of Transfer in Multiliteracy Center Contexts." *Computers and Composition* 41: 32–45.

Atwill, Janet. 2006. "Bodies and Art." *Rhetoric Society Quarterly* 36 (2): 165–170.

Bou Ayash, Nancy. 2019. *Toward Translingual Realities in Composition: (Re)working Local Language Representations and Practices*. Logan: Utah State University Press.

Brown, Tessa. 2020. "What Else Do We Know? Translingualism and the History of SRTOL as Threshold Concepts in Our Field." *College Composition and Communication* 71 (4): 591–619.

Dave, Bhavna. 2007. *Kazakhstan: Ethnicity, Language, and Power*. New York: Routledge.
DePalma, Michael-John, and Jeffrey Ringer. 2011. "Toward a Theory of Adaptive Transfer: Expanding Disciplinary Definitions of 'Transfer' in Second-Language Writing and Composition Studies." *Journal of Second Language Writing* 20: 134–147.
Donahue, Christiane. 2017. "Writing and Global Transfer Narratives: Situating the Knowledge Transformation Conversation." In *Critical Transitions: Writing and the Question of Transfer*, edited by Chris M. Anson and Jessie. L. Moore, 107–136. Logan: Utah State University Press.
Donahue, Christiane. 2018. "Writing, English, and a Translingual Model for Composition." In *Composition, Rhetoric, and Disciplinarity*, edited by Rita Malenczyk, Susan Miller-Cochran, Elizabeth Wardle, and Kathleen Blake Yancey, 206–224. Logan: Utah State University Press.
Fierman, William. 2009. "Identity, Symbolism, and the Politics of Language in Central Asia." *Europe-Asia Studies* 61 (7): 1207–1228.
Gentil, Guillaume. 2018. "Modern Languages, Bilingual Education, and Translation Studies: The Next Frontiers in WAC/WID Research and Instruction?" *Bilingual Education* 15 (3): 114–129.
Gonzales, Laura. 2018. *Sites of Translation: What Multilinguals Can Teach Us about Digital Writing and Rhetoric*. Ann Arbor: University of Michigan Press.
Goodman, Bridget A., and D. Philip Montgomery. 2020. " 'Now I Always Try to Stick to the Point': Socialization to and from Genre Knowledge in an English-Medium University in Kazakhstan." *Journal of English for Academic Purposes* 48: 1–13.
Haraway, Donna. 1988. "Situated Knowledges—the Science Question in Feminism and the Privilege of Partial Perspective." *Feminist Studies* 14 (3): 575–599.
Horner, Bruce, and Sara Alvarez. 2019. "Defining Translinguality." *Literacy in Composition Studies* 7 (2): 1–30.
Klyshbekova, Maira. 2023. "The View from Here: A Kazakhstani English Language Teacher's Perspective on Multilingual Practices." *ELT Journal* ccado30: 1–4.
Lorimer Leonard, Rebecca, and Rebecca Nowacek. 2016. "Transfer and Translingualism." *College English* 78 (3): 258–264.
Matsuda, Paul Kei. 2014. "The Lure of Translingual Writing." *PMLA* 129 (3): 478–483.
Monty, Randall. 2015. "Everyday Borders of Transnational Students: Composing Place and Space with Mobile Technology, Social Media, and Multimodality." *Computers and Composition* 38 (1): 126–139.
Mulcahy, Monica. 2013. "Turning around the Question of 'Transfer' in Education: Tracing the Sociomaterial." *Educational Philosophy and Theory* 45 (12): 1276–1289.
Pender, Kelly. 2011. *Techne, from Neoclassicism to Postmodernism: Understanding Writing as a Useful, Teachable Art*. Anderson, SC: Parlor.
Smagulova, Juldyz. 2019. "Ideologies of Language Revival: Kazakh as School Talk." *International Journal of Bilingualism* 23 (3): 740–756.
Tuskeyeva, Aliya. 2022. "Perceptions of Translanguaging from EFL Teachers with Different Linguistic Backgrounds in Kazakhstan." Master's thesis, Nazarbayev University, Astana, Kazakhstan.
Wardle, Elizabeth. 2007. "Understanding Transfer from FYC: Preliminary Results of a Longitudinal Study." *WPA: Writing Program Administration* 31 (1–2): 65–85.
You, Xiaoye. 2016. *Cosmopolitan English and Transliteracy*. Carbondale: Southern Illinois University Press.

PART II

Multimodality and Transfer in the Vertical Curriculum

4
EQUIPPING TUTORS TO TRANSFER MULTIMODAL WRITING KNOWLEDGE TO WRITING CENTER CONTEXTS

Kara Poe Alexander, Becca Cassady, and Michael-John DePalma

Scholarship on transfer in writing center (WC) contexts has emerged as a vital area of research in rhetoric and writing studies. Ever since Rebecca S. Nowacek (2011, 136) contended that tutors in WC settings are well situated to be "handlers" who serve to "facilitate transfer of writing-related knowledge for student writers," research focused on WCs as generative sites for facilitating writing transfer has abounded (Bromley, Northway, and Schonberg 2016; DeFeo and Caparas 2014; Driscoll 2015; Driscoll and Harcourt 2012; Hahn and Stahr 2018; Nowacek et al. 2019; Weaver 2018). For instance, in her primer for WC directors on transfer research, Bonnie Devet (2015) maps the kinds of transfer that occur on a regular basis among writing consultants. Likewise, Heather N. Hill (2016) demonstrates the value of extensive tutor education in transfer theory for tutors, writers, and WCs. The recent collection by Devet and Dana Lynn Driscoll (2020), *Transfer of Learning in the Writing Center*, offers insight into the ways transfer theory can animate conceptions, structures, dispositions, and practices of WCs.

While scholars have theorized transfer in relation to WCs, qualitative research is only beginning to consider transfer in relation to multimodal composition and WCs (e.g., Alexander, DePalma, and Ringer 2016; Bowen and Davis 2020). Lauren Marshall Bowen and Matthew Davis (2020), for example, emphasize the importance of equipping tutors with the knowledge and strategies required for tutoring writers with multimodal texts. Although not their primary focus, they articulate the need for consultants to be educated to tutor writers who compose multimodal texts. They thus invite future research in this area of inquiry: "How might tutors and writers develop and transfer what they know about composing in multiple modes during their mutual work in the writing center" (n.p.).

Our chapter engages this exigent question by examining the extent to which WC consultants transfer—adapt, apply, and remediate—their prior writing knowledge and experience when working with writers on multimodal compositions. We define transfer in the context of our study as consultants' "conscious or intuitive process of applying or reshaping learned writing knowledge" as they tutor (DePalma and Ringer 2011, 141). The line of inquiry we take up in this chapter is important because it showcases the rich knowledge and experience consultants bring with them to WC work and highlights how these experiences shape (or fail to shape) their sessions with writers. Moreover, it can help WC professionals better equip consultants to mobilize and adapt their writing knowledge and experience in the context of tutoring.

In what follows, we first contextualize our research study and explain our methods. Then, we examine the prior multimodal writing knowledge and experience consultants draw from when tutoring writers on multimodal texts. We also demonstrate that although consultants have a rich array of multimodal composing experiences, they have difficulty adapting and mobilizing these experiences when tutoring, or considering how they would tutor, multimodal texts. We close by reflecting on strategies for WC practitioners to help consultants better harness their knowledge and experience when tutoring writers on multimodal texts.

METHODS

Thirteen writing consultants working in the University Writing Center (UWC) and one consultant working in the Graduate Writing Center (GWC) at Baylor University participated in this study. Five consultants were graduate students, and nine were undergraduate students (seven seniors and two juniors). Thirteen of the participants were female, and one was male. Nine were white, three were Asian American, one was Hispanic, and one was Chinese.

The UWC was founded in 1983 and at the time of this study had a staff of twenty-five consultants, including both undergraduate and graduate students from a variety of disciplines. The GWC was founded in 2012 and at the time of this study had a staff of five graduate consultants from across disciplines. Although the UWC and the GWC state that they consult on a range of texts, neither is a multiliteracy center, and in both centers consulting on multimodal texts is rare. In preparation for tutoring, consultants undergo initial and ongoing tutor education that encompasses writing and rhetorical concepts, tutoring strategies, genre analysis, multimodal writing, and tutoring English language learners, among other topics.

Participants in our study completed an online survey and a follow-up interview that sought information on the extent to which consultants draw upon and adapt their prior writing knowledge and experience to tutoring sessions with multimodal texts. The interviews were transcribed and the data were analyzed using grounded theory, where we individually and collaboratively coded for emergent themes. In our coding, we identified moments in which participants shared and failed to share the ways their prior multimodal writing knowledge and experience inflected their tutoring practice. This study was approved by the Baylor University IRB, and all names used here are pseudonyms.

PRIOR MULTIMODAL COMPOSING EXPERIENCES

Results show that the writing consultants in our study draw primarily from their own multimodal writing experiences when tutoring writers on multimodal texts. These experiences are abundant, wide-ranging, and diverse—from both inside and outside the classroom and in multiple genres, media, and modes. In this section, we outline consultants' varied composing experiences in both the academic and professional settings, which they access in multimodal tutoring sessions.

Academic and Class Experiences

Consultants utilize the knowledge they have gained from reading and writing in class, including participating in peer reviews, in-class presentations, design work, and project work. From consuming podcasts, social media posts, and television shows to composing Instagram posts, flyers, reports, and other class assignments, the consultants gained writing insights and skills that impact the approaches they take as WC consultants. These past experiences are formative in helping them understand what makes good writing and how to give effective feedback.

Lexey's experiences with composing multimodal texts as an undergraduate writing major, for example, inform her tutoring as a PhD student in the UWC. As a student, Lexey composed numerous multimodal texts—including brochures, posters, reports with charts and graphics, and a Pecha Kucha—which proved to be significant experiences for her. When she tutors someone on a multimodal presentation, she looks to see how the text comes together as a whole. She states, "I would definitely be, like, 'okay, let's look at what your visual elements are and when they're matching or not matching with the text that you're speaking.'

Or if, like, the reader is supposed to be reading at the same time, like, how those are interacting to make sure they're on time with each other." Although Lexey believes her "graphic design knowledge is very low," when tutoring, she tries to emphasize how the verbal and visual should work together, lessons she learned from her own composing experiences: "I think from that [design] knowledge, just making sure that things look crisp and clean and organized. So if someone came in, and they were using, like, ten different texts and five different colors, I'd be, like, 'hey, maybe we should tone this down, make it more accessible to the viewer in the same way that we would want just a purely written text to be accessible?' . . . Emphasizing what we want to emphasize and using multimodal elements to our advantage."

Students also connect their in-class experiences of analyzing and responding to texts to their tutoring of multimodal texts. For instance, students like Anna, Emily, Mo, and Amy draw from their experiences as Professional Writing and Rhetoric (PWR) majors who have learned about visual rhetoric and page design to assist writers with multimodal texts. In her work with writers, Emily utilizes what she learned in her upper-division writing courses about how to meet client expectations and determine the rhetorical purpose of a piece. She has also composed a flyer and a technical report with visuals, which enable her to understand how the visual and textual components of a piece work together. Similarly, Amy, though she "forget[s] the acronym" (Robin Williams's CRAP), names principles related to conciseness, consistency, and effectively incorporating graphics when dealing with multimodal texts like brochures. The knowledge Amy and other students gain through their classroom experiences helps them as multimodal composers and consultants. They try to recall this knowledge, even if they can't remember the terms, and help writers understand how various elements of a text work together.

Other consultants draw from the knowledge gained through their experiences in non-writing courses. LF, for instance, applies what she learned from composing posters and research reports in her science classes to her work as a consultant. She remarks: "For multimodal genres, we were always taught that the most important information fits on the poster . . . You're not going to be able to put all of it on the page. So a lot of that is [asking], 'What do I prioritize? What's actually important?' Does it really matter that I spent twenty hours sifting through specimens? Not really. I just need to communicate these results." LF has learned that the message or "bottom line" is more important than explaining the data collection methods. She understands, through coursework, that readers want to know what the significance is, and she seeks to communicate that to the writers she works with on multimodal texts.

Savannah, a senior in her third year as a consultant, outlines several prior multimodal writing experiences she views as relevant to her approach to tutoring writers with multimodal texts. As a business student, Savannah sees her immersion as a reader in texts that utilize a range of charts and graphs as important to her multimodal writing knowledge. She states, "I get a lot of my experience from working . . . in the business school and having to read a lot of papers with, like, graphs and charts and things like that." For her thesis, she's writing an economics paper: "So I have, like, kind of all these charts and I'm having to build the charts myself, like in statistical software. And so . . . part of that is like the data science work, but then part of that is like this English work where I have to format it in a way where the results are obvious and make sense so I'm thinking about those kinds of rhetorical purpose things."

Professional and Workplace Experience

In addition to drawing from their classroom experiences, several consultants remarked that their professional experiences help them tutor multimodal texts. For instance, Gabbie's knowledge of multimodal composition comes primarily from her teaching experiences, first as a middle school English teacher and later as a teaching assistant in her MA program. Gabbie, a doctoral student from China in her first year as a tutor, discusses both composing PowerPoint presentations to better engage her middle school students and assigning multimodal projects, such as writing songs, shooting videos, or designing posters. These assignments required her to be well versed in such media. Later in her MA program, Gabbie taught a multimodal composition unit that asked students to choose among a variety of multimodal genres for their final project such as podcasts, video essays, magazine articles, or posters. From these experiences, Gabbie gained the "formal knowledge" she has about multimodal composition and genre. More specifically, those experiences helped her understand the importance of "taking advantage of the particular ability a genre affords," a concept that was emphasized throughout that curriculum. Through the act of teaching, she gained familiarity with multimodal composition and the affordances of various modes and genres. While she has not had the opportunity to tutor someone on multimodal pieces, she hypothesizes that this knowledge would, in fact, inform her approaches to such sessions.

Like Gabbie, Baruch also has a vast array of professional experiences that help him as he consults. Baruch, a current doctoral student in the social sciences, worked as a professional layout artist for two magazines before returning to graduate school. There he spent time laying out copy and graphics for the magazine. He notes that his approach is traditional: "When you're creating something, these are the rules of kind of how it's supposed to work out, line up, the design principles of contrast, repetition, alignment, proximity . . . So, knowing those sort of basic principles, I can bring those to bear." In addition, Baruch draws from his experience teaching where he utilized PowerPoint heavily (he won an award from his community college for a PowerPoint presentation he gave). He considers good presentations to be those that are affirmed by the audience when people "come up afterward and say 'wow, that was great.'" Ultimately, Baruch draws from his "practical experience" with composing multimodal texts and his "professional experience with layout and formatting of texts" to shape his work with multimodal writing.

In sum, consultants are well versed in composing and reading multimodal texts in both classroom and professional settings. These experiences are rich, diverse, and varied. Consultants recognize how these experiences have shaped their understanding of multimodal texts and have added to their knowledge about multimodal composing. Ultimately, our data suggest that these experiences inevitably inform their approaches to tutoring multimodal texts.

HARNESSING PRIOR KNOWLEDGE AND EXPERIENCE

In theory, consultants' wealth of multimodal knowledge and experience should allow for more informed and effective approaches to tutoring sessions with multimodal texts. Yet, as their responses reveal, consultants' perceptions of the helpfulness of their past multimodal writing experience are wide-ranging. While consultants' diverse experiences no doubt inform their approaches to tutoring multimodal texts, our results show that they are not always able to convey how their rich prior composing experiences actually have bearing on their tutoring. Some students were able to articulate ways their specific knowledge of and experiences with multimodal texts would shape their approaches to those sessions, but most were unable to describe how they would mobilize those experiences.

Some consultants, like Baruch, can describe extensively how their past work with multimodal texts enables them to help students with these sessions. While other consultants nod to the idea that aspects like audience and purpose play across all writing types, Baruch discusses their rhetorical effect in more depth. He tells us that the biggest difference between tutoring students with multimodal texts and those with print-based alphabetic texts is understanding the change in rhetorical situation ("what the audience expects and desires"). To help students navigate these new expectations, he must change his recommendations. Primarily, he anticipates that while students understand "basic forms of writing" in terms of formatting and conventions, they "don't have the same amount of training for multimodal texts in terms of what should this look like when it's finished." As a result, he sees himself as able to provide more "objective rules of writing" that he has learned through his own multimodal composition experience. He lists design principles such as "contrast, repetition, alignment, [and] proximity." Although he has never tutored someone on a video, he speculates that he would bring up "technical components": "You could get into things like, 'Hey, your audio is clipping at this point, or your transitions are too long. You shouldn't have black frames between these two scenes that you'd either have a fade-in or go directly into.'" Baruch points to specific knowledge of particular modes and conventions when assisting students with multimodal texts, and that knowledge is distinct from that which he typically utilizes in sessions with print-based alphabetic texts.

While Baruch does focus on conventions or "rules," he also articulates a more nuanced understanding of multimodal composition. The new rhetorical expectations have much to do with what is ultimately presented through that specific genre. He discusses what he would say to a writer composing a PowerPoint presentation: "'You wrote a forty-page paper . . . When you are presenting this at a conference, you need to create a PowerPoint. You need to have these basic details. It needs to end up being about twenty minutes long, about this much time focused on this information, this much time focused on this information.' So sort of changing in that way to help with the specifics of the new genre that they're working in." The type and amount of information conveyed as well as the time spent working on the text are important features of PowerPoints that would shape Baruch's priorities in tutoring a student with a multimodal text. While there are many multimodal genres, Baruch's assumption here is that students are likely less familiar with most of them. As a consultant, then, his focus would be helping familiarize his tutees with these rhetorical expectations using his own knowledge and experience of composing and consuming these multimodal genres.

Savannah also effectively articulates how her prior experiences might influence her tutoring sessions with multimodal texts. Savannah is highly confident in her ability to tutor students with multimodal texts, giving herself a 9 on our 1 (extremely unconfident) to 10 (extremely confident) scale. She cites her formal WC training as having prepared her but also credits the knowledge she has gained through tutoring:

> Over the years I have learned to adapt to a lot of different prompts and students' needs, and that has helped me to think about writing more broadly in terms of its rhetorical situation, rather than something specific. Even if I haven't written many multimodal texts, I know what to look for when tutoring them. Overall, while it might take me a minute to adjust to a new rhetorical situation, by thinking about the essence of good writing and the elements that make it up, I feel confident that I can at least provide some direction to writers that will help them accomplish their own purpose.

As a writing tutor, Savannah rightly sees rhetorical situation as vital to understanding a text and feels capable of thinking through a piece in such terms—multimodal or otherwise. While she knows of specific knowledge she would be able to apply, she can also successfully fulfill her role as a consultant should she be unfamiliar with particular modes or genres. In fact, she implies an understanding of what types of questions she should be asking: while "good writing" is a nebulous term at best, her language of "adjust[ing]" to new scenarios indicates an understanding that the definition will change depending on the text.

Savannah no doubt shows an ability to apply more general rhetorical knowledge to multimodal texts, but she also identifies how specific skills from one of her English courses, like analyzing film, would enable her to better understand the complexity of a multimodal text:

> While I've never had someone bring in a film, I realized from analyzing things like visuals, diegetic and non-diegetic sound, and the expressions of actors in film that multimodal texts are more complicated because they have more moving parts—but this also means there are more opportunities to reinforce a message. With that in mind, I like to apply this kind of analysis even to things like résumés, where the visual elements like font, color, and white space can reinforce an impression of the candidate conveyed by the text, in the same way that the score of a movie might reinforce an actor's performance.

In this example, Savannah names specific concepts relevant to multimodality and design that she could utilize in a tutoring session. Like others in the study, she recognizes the potential advantages "more moving parts" afford the writer. She even sees how things she learned about these types of texts in her English course would be applied to other types of multimodal texts. She draws parallels between her analysis of film and an analysis of a visual text, using not just static knowledge of terms but a deeper understanding of the rhetorical moves a multimodal composer must make to successfully convey their message. Savannah is thus able to access and name the tools and technical vocabulary needed to help a multimodal composer.

Although Baruch and Savannah could successfully articulate how they would transfer their multimodal composing knowledge to multimodal tutoring, far more consultants admitted to being hesitant when tutoring students with multimodal texts. Jane is an MA student in English who double-majored in biology and English as an undergraduate. Her scientific background gave her experiences in composing technical reports with graphics, which she calls "less creative multimodal texts," while her marketing background gave her experience with more visually driven documents. When asked in the survey what she would use when helping students with multimodal texts, she notes that she would draw on both experiences depending on the type of text: "If something was more on the creative side, I would draw on my marketing experience, and if it was more on the technical side, I would draw on my biology instructor experience." Jane recognizes that her background has given her relevant knowledge about composing and teaching multimodal texts that could potentially transfer to a tutoring situation. However, when asked about her confidence in tutoring a student with a multimodal text on our 1 to 10 scale, Jane selects only a 4. She explains: "I feel that I could create a multimodal text effectively myself, but I'm not sure how to translate that knowledge into something useful to the student. I also am not sure how to ask questions specifically in the context of multimodal texts, so I would probably fall back on the questions about rhetorical situation (audience, purpose, goals, assignment requirements, genre, etc.) that I typically use." Jane is confident in her own multimodal composing abilities, but she lacks knowledge of how to successfully "translate" that knowledge to the tutee, seemingly because of an insufficient vocabulary. As a result, she cannot mobilize her multimodal composing experience in her tutoring sessions even as she acknowledges its potential.

In addition, Jane's survey response implies a need for specific multimodal-related questions in these types of appointments. The differences she names between alphabetic and multimodal texts in her interview—that the latter leave room for "more interpretation" and "look a little different"—do not seem to affect how she would approach her tutoring. Rather, her inability to ask context-specific questions about multimodal texts forces her, in a sense, to rely on the same strategies she would use in a session with a print-based alphabetic text. Her language of "falling back" on general rhetorical questions during sessions with multimodal texts is important. While Jane correctly understands that these rhetorical aspects still apply to multimodal composition, she implies that there is potential for a richer, more nuanced approach to multimodal writing that she feels she cannot deliver despite her relevant experiences.

Anna also rated herself as unconfident (4) in her ability to tutor students with multimodal texts. Throughout her interview, she names various principles related to multimodal composition and design that could, in fact, come to bear on her sessions, such as questions of alignment, size, and amount of text; design; color scheme; voiceover and audio placement; and audience reception of various modes. When describing in the survey what she would employ in multimodal tutoring sessions, she responds that she could use the video and website knowledge she gained from her PWR classes and other composition experiences, but she notes that her knowledge is still limited: "It would take a lot of trial and error for me myself to create a good video or website, so the student would have to be incredibly patient with me." In addition, when asked about how her tutoring strategies would change when encountering a multimodal text in a session, she only briefly references her wealth of multimodal knowledge:

> I think you have to change the perspective a little bit that it's not so much working on, like, a paper, a solid paper; it usually has video or audio aspects to it as well. So kind of thinking about it almost more well-rounded than just focusing on "Does this paper have a thesis?" In thinking about "Does this multimodal text tell me what it needs to tell me through different audio and visuals? Does it complete what the assignment says?" . . . I don't have a ton of experience working with this kind of session, so honestly, I think a lot of the strategies could remain the same. But it just is kind of like, okay, we're working on a video or a PowerPoint instead of a paper, so that would be like [a] change of mind-set a little bit. But . . . it kind of remains the same in my opinion.

Anna does suggest that writers of multimodal texts are accomplishing their purposes through diverse modes that must be addressed differently than print-based alphabetic texts. Whereas in a print-based alphabetic text she would focus primarily on the thesis, a multimodal text would cause her to think more specifically about how that thesis or argument is conveyed. The "change of mind-set" she mentions is presumably related to recognizing that various modes ("video or audio aspects") or genres ("a PowerPoint [presentation] or something") have particular affordances she would want the student to take advantage of. Such thinking echoes her earlier explanations of what multimodal composition knowledge she has previously gained.

However, Anna's overall emphasis is on the perceived similarities of these texts rather than their differences. Anna's tutoring "kind of remains the same." This sentiment is echoed in her survey response: "I would use my general knowledge about writing and design to help the best I could just like in any other session." Despite her lengthy explanations of her video and document design knowledge, she does not articulate an attempt to intentionally leverage those specific experiences when working with students on multimodal texts. Whether this is an issue of not recognizing that potential or having trouble articulating those connections is not clear. What is evident is that Anna struggles to see how she can harness her valuable experiences and knowledge as a multimodal composer in the context of tutoring multimodal texts.

Like Anna, Jennie is unable to articulate how her rich knowledge and experience as a multimodal composer will help her as a consultant. Jennie's interview revealed a very strong background in composing multimodal texts, most prominently for the "University Scholar" Instagram account she runs through Baylor. Jennie explains how she addresses issues of audience and purpose through very intentional design choices when choosing "posts" versus "stories"—engaging the audience, creating patterns through images, and crafting the overall appearance of the profile. Yet when asked in the survey what experiences she would draw from to tutor multimodal texts, she makes no explicit mention of her vast social media experience. In fact, she brings up her Instagram knowledge in the interview only when prompted by one of our authors who knew of her involvement. This omission implies that Jennie might not immediately see her multimodal composing experience in non-academic areas as applicable or relevant to her tutoring sessions or at least that she does not have the vocabulary to explicitly connect them. In fact, when asked to explain her high confidence (an 8) in her tutoring of multimodal texts, she asserts only that many "elements of writing in general," along with the strategies she uses in a "normal" session, could be applied.

Although this general approach seems to characterize Jennie's multimodal tutoring, when asked what experiences she would assemble in such sessions, she briefly nods to more specific multimodal concerns: "I think I would probably try to draw on my knowledge of rhetorical situation because that is an element of writing that most definitely applies to multimodal texts. I might ask the writer about their purpose/audience and then talk with them about how they can best reach their audience and achieve their purpose given the different elements of their multimodal text." Like others in the study, Jennie acknowledges that rhetorical concerns must be attended to across all types of writing. She specifies, though, that she would address questions about audience and purpose using "the different elements" of the text. Jennie begins to take her response beyond print-based alphabetic writing and understands that different modes offer different affordances for the writer, something she has demonstrated previously in her own composition of social media content. This understanding would shape, she imagines, the questions she would ask in those sessions. While Jennie's experience of multimodal composition appears to inform her ability to tutor multimodal writing, she is unable to fully articulate those connections.

We see among these consultants a spectrum of ability to harness their prior knowledge and experience when tutoring students on multimodal texts. Some recognize the potential for transfer—a feat in and of itself—but do not know how to mobilize it. Others focus on the commonalities across alphabetic texts and multimodal texts, giving less attention to specific ways their experiences could better inform multimodal sessions. Still others are able to name ways their specific experiences would allow them to better read and tutor for multimodal texts. These responses, however, do not noticeably correspond to specific types of prior knowledge or levels of experience. These findings beg two consequential questions: (1) What factors inhibit consultants from mobilizing and adapting their multimodal experiences in the context of tutoring? (2) How might WC directors design tutor education that will help facilitate the transfer of consultants' prior multimodal writing knowledge and experience to tutoring contexts?

FACTORS INHIBITING THE TRANSFER OF CONSULTANTS' MULTIMODAL WRITING KNOWLEDGE

Our study suggests several factors that inhibit writing consultants' ability to mobilize and adapt their knowledge of multimodal writing in the context of their WC work. One important constraining factor is the limited experience consultants have had tutoring writers with multimodal texts. Every participant in our study noted that the vast majority of their tutoring experiences involved working with writers of print-based alphabetic essays or "research papers." Every consultant also made a point to say they had few opportunities to tutor writers who were composing multimodal texts. With few occasions for tutoring writers with multimodal texts and thus few opportunities to think metacognitively about the potential for transfer, it makes sense that consultants would have difficulty articulating the ways they use or adapt their multimodal writing knowledge in the context of their tutoring. Some consultants even state, "I do not feel extremely equipped because I lack experience working with multimodal texts" (Jennie).

Another crucial factor that is apt to hinder consultants' ability to transfer their knowledge of multimodal writing to tutoring is the enduring perception that multimodal writing isn't quite "*real* writing"—a category reserved for print-based alphabetic texts, a finding that is resonant with our previous research on transfer and multimodal composition (DePalma and Alexander 2015; see also Shepherd, chapter 6, this volume). This perception perpetuates the view that WCs are sites that engage exclusively with print-based alphabetic writing rather than ones that engage with writing in all its various iterations—posters, brochures, podcasts, digital stories, and websites. Although the directors of Baylor's UWC, GWC, First-Year Writing Program, and PWR Program have been intentional about working to expand student and faculty perceptions of writing to include multimodal texts, the long-standing conception of writing as limited to print-based alphabetic texts is slow to change. Part of the reason this notion endures is that print-based alphabetic writing remains the predominant kind of high-stakes writing many undergraduate and graduate-level students are composing in their university courses. Even though multimodal writing is occurring far and wide across disciplines in the academy, it is still the case that an overwhelming number of assessment practices give uneven weight to print-based alphabetic texts. This emphasis on alphabetic texts communicates to students that such writing requires more intellectual heft, while multimodal writing is assigned as a mere presentation of the substantive content that was written in the form of the print-based alphabetic text. When WC consultants' encounters with multimodal texts in their coursework and in the WC are contextualized in these ways, the significance, rhetorical complexity, and substance of multimodal writing are diminished.

Repeated encounters of this kind can lead to the internalization of misconceptions about the nature and value of multimodal composition, as indicated in our interviews. When asked about the kinds of writing knowledge and expertise they deemed as essential for writing consultants, consultants responded with in-depth answers about knowledge of rhetorical purpose, genre, context, and audience; not a single consultant mentioned multimodal composition specifically, and they did not mention considerations related to media, modes, affordances, or design. While we recognize that these rhetorical and design considerations are not exclusively limited to either print-based alphabetic texts or multimodal texts, our point is that print-based alphabetic writing functions as the default when consultants think of writing.

A third key factor inhibiting consultants' ability to utilize and reshape their multimodal writing knowledge is the lack of a robust critical vocabulary for articulating that knowledge. As work by Kathleen Blake Yancey, Liane Robertson, and Kara Taczak (2014) and Yancey and her colleagues (2018) on Teaching for Transfer (TFT) has insightfully demonstrated, learning and internalizing key terms about writing are crucial for promoting the transfer of writing knowledge and practices. As our data illustrate, however, many consultants struggled to come to terms with concepts and frameworks that would allow them to effectively tutor writers composing multimodal texts. Even when students suggested concepts important to multimodal composing (e.g., affordances, exigence, modalities, and remediation), they were unable to name them explicitly. Further, their ability to articulate their in-depth knowledge about concepts such as genre, audience, and rhetorical situation in relationship to print-based alphabetic writing far exceeds their ability to discuss rhetorical concepts related to multimodal composing. Despite their rich backgrounds composing multimodal texts, consultants' incomplete critical vocabularies for articulating conceptual knowledge related to multimodal composing limit their possibilities for transferring that knowledge to tutoring contexts.

Recognizing these constraints and acknowledging that experience with multimodal texts does not easily transfer to a tutoring scenario, many consultants expressed their desire for more guidance and strategies related to tutoring multimodal texts so they can transfer their prior knowledge more successfully. Lexey, Allison, and LF rated their confidence in tutoring multimodal texts a 7, 8, and 8, respectively, but they all see the value in more direct multimodal tutor education. Lexey, for example, states, "We have not focused on multimodal texts in tutor training, so I am not prepared with tutoring strategies for multimodal texts." Lexey suggests that while she has knowledge of multimodal texts, specific strategies of communicating about them with tutees would boost her effectiveness.[1] Similarly, Allison explains, "I have trust in my own experience, but having more professional or academic insight could definitely bolster my knowledge on the topic and my ability to tutor it effectively." LF, too, values her "general training" from the UWC along with her multimodal experience but notes, "I would feel better equipped if I received specific multimodal training." These consultants hedge their comments about the value of their multimodal knowledge with caveats about a lack of specific training. While Allison, LF, and Lexey all have backgrounds they could draw from in sessions, they desire more "insight" into how to better leverage their own knowledge and experience with multimodal texts as they tutor. Providing this insight through tutor education, it seems, would increase their sense of self-efficacy—a dispositional factor shown to increase the likelihood of successful transfer (Driscoll and Wells 2012)—and give them more confidence to boldly leverage the multimodal knowledge they *do* have. Moreover, our study suggests that these consultants' intuitions about the helpfulness of training focused on multimodal texts are spot-on.

FACILITATING THE TRANSFER OF CONSULTANTS' MULTIMODAL WRITING IN WRITING CENTER CONTEXTS

Our study demonstrates that writing consultants have gained generative knowledge about multimodal writing through their various and ongoing experiences as multimodal composers. Results also show that this knowledge remains siloed in many ways and thus has little bearing on consultants' writing knowledge and practices in WC contexts. Several inhibiting factors contribute to the lack of transfer between consultants' multimodal writing knowledge and their work as consultants, some of which include few opportunities to tutor writers with multimodal texts, the ubiquitous perception that multimodal writing is not *really* "writing," and a limited critical vocabulary for articulating multimodal writing knowledge. These findings suggest that consultants in WC contexts could benefit from tutor education that addresses these concerns. We thus conclude our chapter with strategies WC directors can employ in tutor education that can enable them to better facilitate the transfer of writing consultants' multimodal knowledge to their work as writing consultants.

Addressing Misconceptions about Multimodal Tutoring: WC directors have ample opportunity in tutor education to shape consultants' understanding of what writing is and how it functions in various contexts. While consultants might enter the WC having conceived of writing only as print-based alphabetic texts, there is room to combat this misconception through more explicit definition and scaffolding. For example, directors might make a habit of consistently using multimodal examples alongside print-based alphabetic texts when teaching more "general" rhetorical considerations such as purpose, audience, and context to normalize the idea that both types of texts are indeed "writing." They might also demonstrate how some design concepts associated with multimodal texts also apply to print-based alphabetic texts. By not relegating multimodal texts to a single training unit, directors can teach consultants to think in more nuanced and inclusive ways when talking about and tutoring writing.

Prompting Reflection about Multimodal Experiences through Literacy Linking: Transfer research has shown the benefit of reflection and metacognition in encouraging successful writing transfer (DePalma 2015; Taczak 2015; Taczak and Robertson 2016; see also Roozen, chapter 7, and Knutson, chapter 5, this volume). While not always *necessary* for transfer, reflection allows students to intentionally think through their past writing experiences, what knowledge they gained from those experiences, why they make specific rhetorical choices, and how those considerations might apply to new scenarios (Adler-Kassner et al. 2017; Nowacek 2011; Robertson, Taczak, and Yancey 2012; Yancey 2017). To facilitate this kind of meta-awareness, directors might assign short reflections at staff meetings or through online platforms such as Canvas or Blackboard specifically related to multimodal composition, beginning with reflections on what their multimodal knowledge is and where it comes from and building up to more nuanced reflections about how their own knowledge might be relevant to tutoring multimodal texts. Specifically, we recommend that WC directors utilize literacy linking, a "strategy [that] provides composers opportunities to reflect on how their network of literacies (e.g., academic, community, professional, visual, linguistic, functional, critical, multimodal, rhetorical) might inform one another" in the context of tutoring multimodal writers (Alexander, DePalma, and Ringer 2016, 35). By intentionally guiding this type of reflection, directors invite consultants to make connections among their various domains of literacy and prompt them to consider how they might mobilize and reshape their multimodal writing knowledge in the context of their WC work.

Equipping Consultants with a Critical Vocabulary about Multimodal Composition: To successfully leverage their prior multimodal writing knowledge and experience so they can work effectively with writers on multimodal texts, consultants must do more than attend to "general" rhetorical considerations: they must be able to name and explain key concepts and theories related to multimodal writing (see also Bearden, chapter 8, this volume). WC directors can more directly equip consultants with key terms related to multimodal composition—such as multiliteracy, multimodality, remediation, design, remix, and affordances—and then demonstrate how those terms can be used when tutoring multimodal texts. Through reflective activities, writing center directors can also help consultants identify their tacit multimodal writing knowledge. Consultants in our study mentioned "different elements" of texts (modes) and "specific tools" that writers have at their disposal (affordances), but they did not have the terms to discuss these ideas in an in-depth way. In such cases, directors could help connect consultants' vernacular terminologies for discussing multimodal writing concepts to theoretical frameworks in the field of rhetoric and writing studies. While offering a fully fleshed-out pedagogical strategy for naming and distilling such terms falls beyond the scope of this chapter, writing transfer scholarship makes clear that knowledge about writing, meta-awareness about writing, and a critical vocabulary for articulating that knowledge are significant factors that impact the transfer of writing knowledge across contexts (Yancey, Robertson, and Taczak 2014; Yancey et al. 2018). In the case of the consultants in our study, structured opportunities to expand their knowledge and critical vocabularies about multimodal composition could enhance their ability to draw from and adapt their rich prior writing experiences when tutoring writers with multimodal compositions.

Securing More Opportunities for Tutoring of Multimodal Texts: Consultants in our study had limited opportunities to attempt to transfer their multimodal knowledge in real, substantive ways in the context of their WC work. In WCs with few multimodal texts coming through, directors must find ways to allow consultants to practice transferring multimodal knowledge into their tutoring sessions in real time. First, WC directors can be intentional about communicating to the broader academic community (e.g., through advertising campaigns, social media, emails) that multimodal texts are welcome at the WC and that consultants are trained to help with them. By framing the WC as a site for supporting multimodal writers, WC directors can also help expand narrow definitions of "writing" in their broader university communities and potentially generate increased traffic by multimodal composers. A second way to expand multimodal tutoring opportunities is to invite consultants to bring their own multimodal pieces into training sessions. These strategic practices would allow WC directors to emphasize that multimodal writing is pervasive, consequential, and a valued form of writing, both in the WC and beyond.

In sharing these strategies, it is our hope that consultants will be well equipped to mobilize and reshape the rich knowledge they have gained as multimodal writers in the context of their WC work.

NOTE

1. UWC tutor education does, in fact, focus on multimodal writing each year. However, while consultants are exposed to multimodal genres, such as résumés, reports, and posters, they do not explicitly connect them to terms like affordances or modes or even call them multimodal composition. In addition, as a first-year tutor during the Covid-19 pandemic, Lexey has had more limited exposure to multimodal tutor education than have more experienced consultants.

REFERENCES

Adler-Kassner, Linda, Irene Clark, Liane Robertson, Kara Taczak, and Kathleen Blake Yancey. 2017. "Assembling Knowledge: The Role of Threshold Concepts in Facilitating Transfer." In *Critical Transitions: Writing and the Question of Transfer*, edited by Chris M. Anson and Jessie L. Moore, 17–47. Logan: Utah State University Press.

Alexander, Kara Poe, Michael-John DePalma, and Jeffrey M. Ringer. 2016. "Adaptive Remediation and the Facilitation of Transfer in Multiliteracy Center Contexts." *Computers and Composition* 41 (6): 32–45.

Bowen, Lauren Marshall, and Matthew Davis. 2020. "Teaching for Transfer and the Design of a Writing Center Education Program." In *Transfer of Learning in the Writing Center: A WLN Digital Edited Collection*, edited by Bonnie Devet and Dana Lynn Driscoll. https://wlnjournal.org/digitaleditedcollection2/.

Bromley, Pam, Kara Northway, and Eliana Schonberg. 2016. "Transfer and Disposition in Writing Centers: A Cross-Institutional, Mixed-Methods Study." *Across the Disciplines* 13 (1): 1–16. wac.colostate.edu/atd/articles/bromleyetal2016.cfm.

DeFeo, Dayna Jean, and Fawn Caparas. 2014. "Tutoring as Transformative Work: A Phenomenological Case Study of Tutors' Experiences." *Journal of College Reading and Learning* 44 (2): 141–163.

DePalma, Michael-John. 2015. "Tracing Transfer across Media: Writers' Perceptions of Cross-Contextual and Rhetorical Reshaping in Processes of Remediation." *College Composition and Communication* 67 (1): 615–642.

DePalma, Michael-John, and Kara Poe Alexander. 2015. "A Bag Full of Snakes: Negotiating the Challenges of Multimodal Composition." *Computers and Composition* 37: 182–200.

DePalma, Michael-John, and Jeffrey M. Ringer. 2011. "Toward a Theory of Adaptive Transfer: Expanding Disciplinary Discussions of 'Transfer' in Second-Language Writing and Composition Studies." *Journal of Second Language Writing* 20 (2): 134–147.

Devet, Bonnie. 2015. "The Writing Center and Transfer of Learning: A Primer for Directors." *Writing Center Journal* 35 (1): 119–151.

Devet, Bonnie, and Dana Lynn Driscoll. 2020. *Transfer of Learning in the Writing Center: A WLN Digital Edited Collection*. wlnjournal.org/digitaleditedcollection2/index.html.

Driscoll, Dana Lynn. 2015. "Building Connections and Transferring Knowledge: The Benefits of a Peer Writing Course beyond the Writing Center." *Writing Center Journal* 35 (1): 153–181.

Driscoll, Dana Lynn, and Jennifer Wells. 2012. "Beyond Knowledge and Skills: Writing Transfer and the Role of Student Dispositions." *Composition Forum* 26. https://compositionforum.com/issue/26/beyond-knowledge-skills.php.

Driscoll, Dana Lynn, and Sarah Harcourt. 2012. "Training vs. Learning: Transfer of Learning in a Peer Tutoring Course and Beyond." *Writing Lab Newsletter* 36 (7–8): 1–6.

Hahn, Susan, and Margaret Stahr. 2018. "Some of These Things ARE Like the Others: Lessons Learned from Tutor-Inspired Research about Transfer in the Writing Center." *WLN: A Journal of Writing Center Scholarship* 43 (1–2): 10–17.

Hill, Heather N. 2016. "Tutoring for Transfer: The Benefits of Teaching Writing Center Tutors about Transfer." *Writing Center Journal* 35 (3): 77–102.

Nowacek, Rebecca. 2011. *Agents of Integration: Understanding Transfer as a Rhetorical Act.* Carbondale: Southern Illinois University Press.

Nowacek, Rebecca, Andrew Hoffmann, Carolyne Hurlburt, Lisa Lamson, Sareene Proodian, and Anna Scanlon. 2019. "Everyday Reflective Writing: What Conference Records Tell Us about Building a Culture of Reflection." *Writing Center Journal* 37 (2): 93–126.

Robertson, Liane, Kara Taczak, and Kathleen Blake Yancey. 2012 "Notes toward a Theory of Prior Knowledge and Its Role in College Composers' Transfer of Knowledge and Practice." *Composition Forum* 26. https://www.compositionforum.com/issue/26/prior-knowledge-transfer.php.

Taczak, Kara. 2015. "Reflection Is Critical in the Development of Writers." In *Naming What We Know: Threshold Concepts of Writing Studies*, Classroom Edition, edited by Linda Adler-Kassner and Elizabeth Wardle, 78–79. Logan: Utah State University Press.

Taczak, Kara, and Liane Robertson. 2016. "Reiterative Reflection in the Twenty-First Century Writing Classroom: An Integrated Approach to Teaching for Transfer." In *A Rhetoric of Reflection*, edited by Kathleen Blake Yancey, 42–63. Logan: Utah State University Press.

Weaver, Brent. 2018. "Is Knowledge Repurposed from Tutoring to Teaching? A Qualitative Study of Transfer from the Writing Center." *WLN: A Journal of Writing Center Scholarship* 43 (1–2): 18–24.

Yancey, Kathleen Blake. 2017. "Mapping the Prior: A Beginning Typology and Its Impact on Writing." In *Contemporary Perspectives on Cognition and Writing*, edited by Patricia Portanova, J. Michael Rifenburg, and Duane Roen, 313–330. Logan: Utah State University Press.

Yancey, Kathleen Blake, Matthew Davis, Liane Robertson, Kara Taczak, and Erin Workman. 2018. "Writing across College: Key Terms and Multiple Contexts as Factors Promoting Students' Transfer of Writing Knowledge and Practice." *WAC Journal* 29: 42–63.

Yancey, Kathleen Blake, Liane Robertson, and Kara Taczak. 2014. *Writing across Contexts: Transfer, Composition, and Sites of Writing.* Logan: Utah State University Press.

5
"IT'S NOT LIKE I CAN PUT A PICTURE OF A PAPER ON INSTAGRAM, YOU KNOW?"
Genre and Multimodality in Writing Knowledge Transfer across Contexts

Anna V. Knutson

GENRE, MULTIMODALITY, AND PRIOR KNOWLEDGE

Both genre and media play a role in writing knowledge transfer but are seldom analyzed in tandem in the transfer literature. The extant scholarship has explored the relationship between genre and transfer (e.g., Beaufort 2007; Nowacek 2011; Reiff and Bawarshi 2011; Rounsaville 2012; Rounsaville, Goldberg, and Bawarshi 2008; Wardle 2009), and an emerging body of scholarship has considered the relationship between media and transfer (Alexander, DePalma, and Ringer 2016; DePalma 2015; DePalma and Alexander 2015; Shepherd 2018). While writing studies has made significant strides in mapping the relationship between genre and multimodality (e.g., Ball 2012; Ball, Bowen, and Fenn 2013; Bowen and Whithaus 2013; Gonzales 2015), more research is needed that explores the connections between the two phenomena and their combined implications for transfer. In that spirit, in this chapter I set out to explore the complex interplay between genre and media in the case of one feminist college student's efforts to transfer her academic genre knowledge while creating a blog post. By exploring this intersection in more detail, we may be better prepared to welcome a diverse group of students (and their prior language, literacy, and writing knowledge) into our classrooms and institutions.

This chapter, which sets out to map this terrain, rests on two related premises: (1) that education is a public good, and (2) that when provided with adequate resources,[1] college writing instructors have the unique privilege of welcoming all students into our institutions and helping them value their prior knowledge alongside the knowledge they seek to develop as students, professionals, and global citizens. Informed by writing studies scholars like Angela Rounsaville (2017), Juan Guerra (2008), and Kevin Roozen (2008, 2009), as well as education and critical race theory scholars like Tara J. Yosso (2005), I contend that social justice–informed research on writing knowledge transfer can support faculty in honoring students' prior knowledge about language and writing from their home communities. Genre and multimodal pedagogy are key here: through flexible assignment design, writing teachers create what Rebecca S. Nowacek (2011) terms *genred discursive spaces* in which students can engage with transfer and enact agency (see also Bawarshi 2003). The agentive stances enabled by thoughtfully designed writing assignments can be further enhanced with opportunities for multimodal composition. By inviting students to engage with multimodal rhetorics, writing faculty can create flexible and capacious genred discursive spaces where students can harness a wide range of prior knowledges from their home communities (see, e.g., Fraiberg 2010; Gonzales 2015; Lotherington and Jenson 2011; Martín, Hirsu, Gonzales, and Alvarez 2019; Nelson 2006; Selfe 2009; Shin and Cimasko 2008; Tardy 2005).

In the pages that follow, I analyze the complex interplay between genre and multimodality in one writer's process of transferring writing knowledge across contexts through a case study of a first-year student majoring in art history at a large midwestern public university. Drawn from a qualitative longitudinal study of eight feminist college students' writing across contexts over the course of two years, this case study provides insights into how we might support student writers in their efforts to transfer knowledge between academic and non-academic contexts, such as home literacies and digital civic writing. Drawing on the frameworks of *adaptive remediation* (Alexander, DePalma, and Ringer 2016), *uptake* (Rounsaville 2012), and *antecedent genre knowledge* (Jamieson 1975), I build on the extant scholarship by highlighting the critical roles of genre and multimodality in writing knowledge transfer while exploring how one participant in this study searched for, located, and adapted prior academic genre knowledge to respond to a new and ill-defined online writing challenge. After discussing the interactions between genre and multimodality in this writer's efforts to adapt her prior knowledge to a new context, I call for:

1. More sustained attention to the intersection(s) between genre, multimodality, and transfer;
2. Further investigation into the role of *text length* in genre knowledge; and
3. Pedagogies that reverse the direction of transfer demonstrated in this case study by encouraging the transfer of students' prior knowledge *into* the writing classroom, particularly in terms of inviting knowledge from extracurricular, civic, and home contexts.

By creating assignments that are capacious enough to welcome the breadth of prior knowledge student writers bring from their home communities, writing teachers can leverage the complex interactions among genre, multimodality, and transfer to create more inclusive learning environments that position a wide range of student writers as multifaceted, agentive rhetors.

METHODS

While social media is certainly no rhetorical utopia, many students engage in sophisticated reading, writing, and rhetorical activities online (Anson 2017; Buck 2015; Gold, Garcia, and Knutson 2019; Rosinski 2016; Shepherd 2018; Vie 2008). However, it appears that writers tend to struggle to perceive connections between academic and digital self-sponsored writing (Keller 2013; Lenhart, Arafeh, Smith, and Macgill 2008; Shepherd 2015). This may be further complicated by differences among genres in both domains, especially when it comes to *medium*. Since transfer across modes may be especially difficult (Alexander, DePalma, and Ringer 2016; DePalma 2015; DePalma and Alexander 2015; Shepherd 2018), students might face challenges when attempting to transfer writing knowledge across academic and online contexts; similarities between multimodal, digital genres and more alphabetic, print-based academic genres may not be readily discernible to students.

When designing a study to explore the challenges of transfer between online and academic domains, I recruited eight undergraduate students from feminist student organizations at a large, public midwestern research university. Given my own background in gender studies, the substantial body of research on gender, feminism, and technology in writing studies (see, e.g., Blair 2012; Blair, Gajjalaand, and Tulley 2009; Blair and Takayoshi 1999; Haas, Tulley, and Blair 2002; LeCourt and Barnes 1999; Takayoshi 1994), and the tendency for young feminists to read and write frequently online (see, e.g., Jackson 2018; Keller 2012; Keller 2016; Kim and Ringrose 2018), I determined that intersectional feminist college students would serve as an ideal student population to provide insight into transfer between academic and self-sponsored contexts.

The participants in my study wrote for a wide range of co-curricular and self-sponsored contexts, including student organizations, activist groups, and student journalism, as well as online writing on multiple platforms. Participants represented a range of majors, with roughly equal representation from STEM fields, social sciences, and humanities.

Participants skewed toward the upper-division levels, with one first-year student, one sophomore, and the remaining six in the upper levels: three juniors and three seniors. They also were relatively diverse compared to the university's general student population: half of the participants were people of color (one African American woman, two Chinese American women, and one Indian American man), and the remaining participants were white women; of the four white participants, three were Jewish.

I interviewed each participant four times in total: three times over the course of one academic year and one time a year after the initial data collection period. In the fourth interview, I invited participants to review my initial findings for the purposes of member checking, and I also asked questions about their continued writing development. Throughout the study, I collected a wide range of writing samples from academic, self-sponsored, co-curricular, and professional contexts. I analyzed interview data using grounded theory coding (Charmaz 2006), turning to writing samples for triangulation when applicable. When selecting a case for this chapter, I turned to the three participants who had described adapting their academic genre knowledge of "the essay" when composing longer online genres because these cases illuminated the relationship between genre and multimodality in transfer most clearly. These three cases were:

1. Emmanuelle, a senior majoring in an interdisciplinary program in biopsychology, cognition, and neuroscience, who drew on the essay to guide her composition of an unusually long Facebook status about #sayhername and the role of women in the Black Lives Matter movement

2. Nora, a senior majoring in English who leveraged her knowledge of the essay to help her compose articles for a book blog

3. Kate, a first-year student majoring in art history who drew on her academic genre knowledge to help her write a blog about her first year of college.

While all three participants significantly adapted their prior knowledge to meet the demands of online writing, Kate's blog was the most multimodal in nature; as a result, she serves as the focal case for this chapter.

"SKILLS FROM MY ENGLISH CLASSES AREN'T ALWAYS AS EFFECTIVE ON SOCIAL MEDIA, EITHER": ADAPTING PRIOR ACADEMIC GENRE KNOWLEDGE TO ONLINE CONTEXTS

The eight participants in my study affirmed the growing body of scholarship suggesting that like genre, *media* can play a significant role in transfer. For example, when asked how social media platforms shape her online writing, one participant, Ava, a junior majoring in English and film, commented on the complex role of visuals in social media writing: "On Twitter you have to be short and concise . . . that's why we are relying more on GIFs and pictures and stuff, because we can't say everything we want to say in words; [Twitter's platform] just doesn't allow for that. On Instagram . . . some things just are not going to photograph well . . . It's not like I can put a picture of a paper on Instagram, you know? . . . You need an interesting, captivating, moving subject."

Baked into this statement are multiple insights about the complex relationship between visual and textual composition, as well as the relationship between genre and media expectations on specific social media platforms. In Ava's view, the length constraints imposed by Twitter's interface urge writers to create meaning beyond the written word by harnessing visual rhetorics ("GIFs and pictures and stuff") to fully express themselves. Similarly, the inherently visual nature of Instagram's platform renders textual content inappropriate in the genre of the Instagram post; an alphabetic paper written for school doesn't count as an "interesting, captivating, moving subject" on this visual platform. Clearly, Ava is thinking in sophisticated ways about the relationship between genre and multimodality in online writing, even if she is not using the same language writing studies researchers would use to describe these phenomena.

Ava's statement also (correctly) suggests that it would be challenging to import an academic genre into an online self-sponsored context without altering or adapting it. Although these writers saw a great deal of overlap between their reading and writing online and in school in terms of subject matter and content, the genre expectations of social media (e.g., concise prose, multimodal elements, personal tone) typically render academic genre knowledge inappropriate in the context of online writing. As Nora suggested, the genre expectations in the two contexts vary dramatically due to academic writing's emphasis on textuality: "Skills from my English classes . . . aren't always as effective on social media . . . [on social media] it's all about getting things that are shareable. So, people don't necessarily want to see you analyze a quotation to death or even really cite your sources, they kind of want to take you at your word, and either agree or disagree . . . In some cases, I've had to actively go against my English major instincts."

Nora sees one of the main distinctions between academic and online literacies as a difference in modes. "Shareability," a construct Nora learned while working in online journalism, is all about multimodality.

Nora reiterated a past employer's guidelines for shareability: "Write a headline that will get clicks . . . break up text with pictures or GIFs, write in lists whenever possible." As a result of differences in terms of modes, genre knowledge transfer across the two contexts can be challenging. Nora described the uneasy and compartmentalized relationship between her academic writing and her online writing in no uncertain terms: "That's just a different brain."

Despite this tendency toward compartmentalization across the two contexts, three participants in the study—including Nora—did report drawing on academic genre knowledge to aid their attempts at writing new online genres. Emmanuelle drew on her academic genre knowledge when writing an unusually long Facebook status update, and Nora drew on the genre of the essay when writing online articles for a book blog. Finally, as I'll discuss in more detail shortly, while documenting her first year of college on her blog, Kate drew on her knowledge of the academic essay to guide her early attempts at blogging.

Across these three cases, it appeared that text *length* seemed to cue the uptake of prior genre knowledge: when composing new genres in the online context that were longer than a tweet or a caption, these writers turned to their knowledge of the "essay," an academic genre that bore similarities to their target genre in terms of length and sometimes structure. Kate even directly references length when explaining how her academic genre knowledge informed her early blog posts: "All the ways of constructing an argument and the ways of constructing a *longer* writing . . . the idea of like, college writing has definitely gone to that" (emphasis added).

It is unsurprising that a study exploring online writing illuminated the importance of text *length* in genre knowledge transfer; in most online contexts, rhetorical efficacy is tied to brevity, which may hinder the transfer of academic genre knowledge into digital self-sponsored contexts. As Ava stated, "I don't really care when someone posts like a super long status, being like, 'These are all my political thoughts from forever.' I'm like, 'Congratulations.'" Similarly, Quinn, a sophomore majoring in women's studies and sociology, said, "Social media caters to shorter, more impactful paragraphs." Emmanuelle echoed these sentiments, stating, "Well, if [the argument is] almost made like, 'Here is the intro, abstract, whatever' on Facebook, I'm like, 'Okay, bro. I'm not reading that' . . . I don't need a whole research paper." This genre expectation of online writing—conciseness—runs counter to the genre knowledge cultivated in school, as Emmanuelle's listing of academic genre conventions that are unwelcome on social media suggests. Below, I showcase

Kate's efforts to compose a new online genre that is longer than a tweet or a caption; the similarity between this new genre—the blog post—and academic essays in terms of length appeared to cue the uptake that enabled her to remediate her prior academic genre knowledge.

These writers shed light on the role of uptake in transfer, which Angela Rounsaville (2012, under "Transfer and Uptake") describes as "a space of intergeneric and intertextual memory" that "not only translates new genres from memories and repertoires of genre knowledge, but also folds that translation into what is meaningful within that current repertoire through active knowledge construction." While uptake as a framework has been used to explore the relationships between multimodal genres (Ray 2013), there have been fewer explorations of how uptake might guide the transfer of alphabetic genre knowledge into multimodal environments. Michael-John DePalma (2015, 618) notes, for example, the "dearth of empirical work on the ways writers perceive the transfer of their print-based writing knowledge and literacies when remediating written texts to suit a digital medium." In response to this gap, Kara Poe Alexander, DePalma, and Jeffrey M. Ringer (2016) synthesize Jay David Bolter and Richard Grusin's theory of remediation (1999) with DePalma and Ringer's (2011) notion of adaptive transfer to account for how writers "reshape prior knowledge to fit novel writing tasks" (Alexander, DePalma, and Ringer 2016, 34) across media, a process they term *adaptive remediation*. Bolter and Grusin's theory of *remediation*, which informs Alexander and colleagues' framework, is particularly useful for the study of genre, multimodality, and transfer because it traces the way older media (such as alphabetic texts) can be translated into new media (such as blog posts, online articles, and Facebook status updates). As Kate's case suggests, blogs may be a particularly fruitful space for exploring adaptive remediation. Carolyn R. Miller and Dawn Shepherd (2009, 283) invoke Kathleen M. Jamieson's exploration of *antecedent genres* when highlighting the fact that the blog bears the traces of earlier genres, many of which are alphabetic texts. By infusing the "chromosomal imprint of ancestral genres" (Jamieson 1975, 406) with multimodal elements, bloggers transform genre knowledge as they move across contexts, platforms, and media.

My findings build on Alexander, DePalma, and Ringer's work by showcasing how adaptive remediation can work organically, outside of a formal writing assignment. The writers in my study engaged in adaptive remediation: when lacking the expert writing knowledge required by an unprecedented rhetorical challenge, they searched for similar genres with which they *were* familiar and infused their prior genre knowledge with the conventions of online writing to meet the new rhetorical demands. Specifically, when faced with the challenge of writing online genres longer than a tweet or a caption—such as an article or a blog post—participants like Kate drew on their knowledge of "the essay," a genre they perceived as largely academic. By infusing their prior genre knowledge with more multimodal and personal elements than would be typical in an academic essay, these writers transformed not only the genre but the presentations of self that are permitted within the boundaries of a traditional "essay."

"THE IDEA OF LIKE, COLLEGE WRITING HAS DEFINITELY GONE TO THAT": UPTAKE AND ADAPTIVE REMEDIATION IN KATE'S BLOGGING PRACTICE

Although she had "hated writing for pretty much all of [her] life," Kate, a first-year student majoring in art history, had "develop[ed] a love for writing" while reading about feminism online. Her newfound passion for writing extended into multiple contexts—academic, co-curricular, and self-sponsored—and prompted her to experiment with a range of new genres, including multimodal ones such as speeches and comics. As part of this dispositional shift *toward* writing, Kate started a blog during her first year of college. In it, she wrote about many topics, including her college experiences, social issues, politics, mental health, and modeling. While the topics addressed in her posts varied greatly, the posts were unified by visuals. Given her background and interest in art, Kate dexterously integrated images in all of her blog posts. "I make a bunch of different kinds of blog posts, which is maybe a problem," Kate said, adding, "I don't really have like one thing I specifically write about on my blog . . . I incorporate visuals a lot of different ways." Despite her apparent anxiety about the wide range of topics covered in her blog, she did note that in addition to visual elements, her posts were unified by passion and self-expression: "My blog is always stuff I'm really passionate about. I'm posting about the rallies, the clubs that I'm going to. I'm posting about these photo shoots, or my art, or my photography . . . they're all ways of expressing myself." The visual components supported by the blog's interface—photo shoots, art, photography—allowed her to express herself and to simultaneously showcase a range of presentations of self: the student, the woman, the activist, the model, the artist, the photographer, and more.

The different "kinds" of blog posts described by Kate are likely a byproduct of the somewhat flexible, unstructured nature of blogs; as

Miller and Shepherd (2009) suggest, the blog bears the mark of so many different antecedent genres that it almost makes more sense to categorize it as a medium instead of a genre. As a result of their generic instability, blogs may be somewhat difficult for new composers, like Kate, to navigate. These challenges render blogs a particularly fruitful site for investigating the relationship between genre and media: while many bloggers write about their political beliefs and personal experiences, thus invoking the print genres of journalism and the diary, the interface also permits writers to enhance or transform this antecedent genre knowledge to suit the multimodal context of online writing. Kate described her blog posts, which blended personal and informational purposes, as guided by a third print-based genre—the essay—which she remediated to incorporate visual elements, such as images, color, and layout.

Although she demonstrated considerable flexibility by exploring a range of topics and leveraging multiple media in her early blog posts, Kate expressed some uncertainty about her performance in this new genre. In short, it seemed that she expected herself to write in a more formal tone on her blog: "I'm kind of bummed out with some of my recent blog posts . . . Every one is, like, just photo shoots . . . Or like, I posted my comics . . . It's hard to combine like a really formal style of writing or really interesting post just with photo shoots and art . . . Because I have a lot of ideas, so I just have to figure out how to word them, really sit down and find the time to do it."

Kate's emphasis on formal prose is, at first glance, somewhat curious given the informality of the blog genre, but she seemed to aspire to adopt a more professional or academic tone in her blogging: "My last blog post was very casual. I used a lot of curse words. I used a lot of slang, 'cause it was supposed to be about my experiences, and just like, my raw emotions, so I didn't want to keep it academic, but I'm guessing that in the future, my writings on social media will be more professionally written." For Kate, more formal or "professional" prose (meaning less casual language, which she defined as curse words and slang) was aligned with the construct of writing she aspired to enact in this domain.

Although Kate had begun to adopt and develop an approach to blogging that fulfilled many of the genre expectations of blog posts by writing about her experiences in an informal voice, complemented by visual aids, it seems as though the capaciousness of the blog post as a genre left her wondering whether she could further elevate her posts as a means of establishing her ethos as an activist and a writer. Kate struggled with reconciling the visual and personal elements native to the blog with a more formal prose style, which she associated with academic and professional contexts. She perceived a mismatch between genres from self-sponsored and formal contexts, which resulted in her own internal conflict about the quality of her blog posts.

To respond to these uncertainties, Kate turned to her antecedent genre knowledge of the essay—an academic genre—to guide her composition of the blog post, an unfamiliar and ill-defined genre: "Taking the philosophy course, and in my writing seminar . . . that applies to my blog posts now. Like, in the beginning I usually have the anecdote or what I'm talking about . . . and then expanding on that idea, and then again coming back to the original message . . . All the ways of constructing an argument and the ways of constructing a longer writing . . . the idea of like, college writing has definitely gone to that."

Kate adapted an approach to writing that she had learned in her dual-enrollment college philosophy course and in her writing seminar to the composition of a new type of a "longer writing" (a phrase that, in itself, signals a bit of uncertainty in terms of genre knowledge): a blog post. In listing the rhetorical strategies she had previously learned while writing print-based essays in academic contexts, Kate engaged in what Alexander, DePalma, and Ringer (2016, 34) refer to as "charting," where composers who seek to remediate an alphabetic essay into a multimodal text create "action-oriented descriptions that accurately describe the kinds of work each portion of the text performs." This practice, they suggest, may help facilitate the type of meta-awareness that supports transfer across media. The approach Kate described for composing a "longer writing"—introducing a text with an anecdote before "expanding on that idea" (e.g., providing additional complicating claims) and returning to the "original message"—was evocative of the five-paragraph essay as well as argument-driven writing taught in the early years of college, especially considering that she identified her philosophy course and first-year writing seminar as the origins of this academic genre knowledge. Although Kate's description of the elements in her prior academic genre knowledge was primarily linguistic and textual—for example, "anecdote," "expanding," "message"—she ultimately infused this genre knowledge with multimodal elements.

Extended argumentation over the course of multiple paragraphs would not have been possible in a shorter, micro-blogging platform like Twitter. Because of its flexibility, the blog interface supports the composition of longer texts, offering users more room to engage with complex, extended forms of argumentation that are more akin to the academic genres Kate had learned in her philosophy course and her first-year writing seminar. As Rounsaville (2012, under "Implications") suggests,

"Being able to locate what about a new genre or new writing task connects with prior experience provides a starting point for understanding how prior knowledge is being used in a new situation." For Kate, the recognition that both college writing and blog posts call for an extended argument over the course of multiple paragraphs seemed to prompt her to engage in adaptive transfer (and subsequent remediation) of the rhetorical strategies she had previously associated with academic genres.

The blog interface also provides more flexibility in terms of the integration of visuals, which Kate fully utilized. By enhancing her posts with images, such as photographs and comics, she remediated the genre of the alphabetic essay into the multimodal genre of the personal blog post, enhancing her narrative arguments with complementary visual evidence and providing the audience with more insight into her personality and multifaceted identities. In doing so, she engaged in what Alexander, DePalma, and Ringer (2016, 35) refer to as "inventorying," wherein writers "take stock of the range of semiotic resources at their disposal in various modes" as they remediate a text.

In her final blog post of her first year in college, titled "Last Photo Shoot of First Year and Reflections," Kate seized on the three rhetorical features of academic writing that she had listed (providing an anecdote or a hook, expanding on her main idea, and returning to her original message) to reflect on her first year of college while simultaneously engaging the reader with hyper-mediated elements such as visual design, photographs, and a personal, inviting tone. Although the majority of the post seems to be addressed to a general audience, in her conclusion she addresses a more specific audience—high school students—to whom she offers advice about college.

She starts by explaining the visuals accompanying the text—modeling photos of her taken by her friend (whose Facebook photography page was included as a hyperlink attached to her friend's name in the text) from her last photo shoot of the academic year—in which she posed against the backdrop of her college campus. Kate describes the photo shoot, which had resulted from her friend reaching out before leaving town for the summer, as "a lovely way to wrap up the year." In doing so, she provides context for the images woven throughout the reflective, end-of-year post. After contextualizing the visuals, Kate begins the reflective segment of her post with an anecdote: "When people asked me how my first year of college went, I often did not know how to respond. I knew I was supposed to say 'I've had the best year of my life!' 'Everything is amazing!' 'I've never been happier!' And sure, I feel that way sometimes to some extent. But battling through final exams, struggling with mental health, and going through the biggest transition of my life: how am I supposed to say it's that simple, that easy?" Here, Kate sets up the central tension of the narrative argument she had set out to convey with the post: while she knows she is expected to present her first year in college as "the best year of [her] life," her experiences have not all been positive, thus contradicting cultural narratives of the college experience and the societal pressure to adopt a generally positive tone when writing online.

In her post, Kate then "expand[s] . . . on that idea" by developing the conflict in the next paragraph, where she contrasts some downsides of her college experience with her friends' positive experiences in their first year of college: "And seeing everyone around me talk about how perfect they claim to be doing combined with my older friends saying 'Oh, I wish I could be a freshman again . . . those were the days,' didn't help much either." She continues to build this idea in the following paragraph, where she acknowledges her positive experiences in her first year of college, such as participating in activism, publishing and showing her art, and learning about art and activism. She ultimately "come[s] . . . back to the original message" in her conclusion by reemphasizing her main point: that her first-year experience was not perfect but that it was still worth it:

> It's complicated, and I don't want to stand here and tell you it's all been perfect. But overall, today I am able to say I am proud of myself and for what I've done during my first year of college, and yes, I would take it over high school any day. So high schoolers, don't worry.
> With Love,
> Kate Kane[2]

In this passage, she connects with her audience, giving the sense that she is directly accessible. She "[doesn't] want to *stand here* and *tell you* it's been perfect," suggesting her physical proximity to her audience—invoking Bolter and Grusin's (1999) concept of *immediacy*—whom she addresses directly in this instance: high schoolers. This sense of closeness is further emphasized by Kate's use of direct address and her choice to drive her final point home before signing off: "So high schoolers, don't worry."

Over the course of four paragraphs, the first introducing the photo shoot and the three expanding on her reflections on her first year of college, Kate crafts a narrative argument for a targeted audience with the intention of sharing the wisdom she has obtained through her college experiences. Clocking in at 423 words, this post is considerably shorter than a typical essay in a first-year writing course; however, Kate does adapt the rhetorical structure of academic genres she described as influencing her blog posts.

Beyond the textual elements of the post, Kate harnessed the multimodal affordances of the interface. In doing so, she demonstrated her engagement with adaptive remediation. She did not merely trans*port* genre knowledge across domains, she trans*formed* her antecedent genre knowledge across modes and media. The hashtags Kate selected are displayed to the right of the post, rendering the content of her blog as a whole more immediately accessible. The hashtags categorizing the post are based on visual, aesthetic content showcased in the photographs ("art," "fairy," "model," "modeling," "photo," "photo shoot," "photography," "spring," "style," "summer") as well as in themes discussed in the text of the post ("college life," "mental health," "personal"). Upon clicking a hashtag, the reader is directed to other posts on Kate's blog tagged with the same descriptors. These carefully curated hashtags, then, network and connect Kate's blog posts by theme, allowing users to seamlessly flip between posts labeled "art" to see her other posts tagged as such.

Similarly, the minimalist template Kate selected for the blog is primarily pink, teal, and seafoam—a color palette that is consonant with the colors showcased by her physical appearance, wardrobe, and props selected for her photo shoot. In the photographs showcased in this post, the template's colors are mirrored by Kate's long pink hair, pink flowers blooming on the tree behind her, and flower petals surrounding her as she poses on the ground. In aligning the color palette of the template with the colors showcased in her images, Kate's design choices for the blog harmonize with the content of her post.

Kate's *immediacy* (Bolter and Grusin) is perhaps most viscerally communicated through the photos woven throughout the post. In them, she is depicted posing in outdoor settings on campus, among various props: trees, fallen flower petals on the ground, and LED string lights. These photos render the author (and her argument) immediately present, not only through her written voice but represented in her physical form. Using the university's campus as a backdrop, Kate collaborated with her friend to produce eight images of herself interacting with the natural and built environment of the campus, conveying a range of emotions and reinforcing the post's rhetorical aims. Through the affordances of the interface, Kate reinforces and echoes her argument—that her relationship with college has been complicated but ultimately worth showcasing and celebrating, just as she showcases her modeling photos.

At its core, her post follows the rhetorical structure she learned in her philosophy course and her writing seminar. By infusing the textual content with visual elements reinforcing her argument, she adapts, enhances, and remediates her antecedent genre knowledge of the academic essay to guide her efforts to write for this new, unfamiliar, and multimodal rhetorical context.

IMPLICATIONS

(Locally) Theorizing the Relationship between Genre and Multimodality

Kate's experiences highlight the close relationship between genre and multimodality in transfer. While Kate noted similarities in terms of genre (i.e., length) across contexts as a cue for transfer, she also engaged in uptake and remediation to support and enable the transfer of genre knowledge across disparate domains. Writing studies scholars like Christiane Donahue (2012) have called for more sustained attention to the role of multimodality in transfer. Indeed, a body of literature authored by this collection's editors and authors has begun to map that territory (Alexander, DePalma, and Ringer 2016; DePalma and Alexander 2015; Shepherd 2018). However, to date, genre, multimodality, and transfer have remained relatively distinct theoretical phenomena. This is particularly challenging when it comes to the relationship between genre and multimodality: although genre and multimodality are typically theorized as separate phenomena, when engaging in adaptive remediation in organic contexts, writers reveal how the transfer of genre knowledge may be slowed or even obscured by differences across contexts in terms of medium.

Rounsaville (2012) makes a compelling case for situating scholarship on writing transfer in the theories of our own discipline: "Without fully contextualizing writing-related transfer within terms, theories, and intellectual traditions intrinsic to composition studies we struggle to see what is uniquely exciting and uniquely difficult about writing-related transfer." Nowacek (2011, 29) notes that genres can cue transfer, but they can also obscure opportunities for transfer. Kate's recognition of the similarities between academic and digital self-sponsored genres enabled her to make connections across domains. For many writers, however, these connections may remain obscured by superficial differences. More robust theories of multimodality and genre forged within the tradition of writing studies research might illuminate how *media* can both cue and obscure opportunities for transfer across contexts.

Genre and Text Length

Kate's experiences shed light on *length* as a genre convention, which is discussed frequently in curricular materials but seldom in theory. There are very few discussions of the relationship between genre and document length in the literature on genre—neither in rhetorical genre studies nor in linguistics. In contrast, in our classrooms and in the documents that guide and support our teaching (e.g., learning outcomes statements, course descriptions, syllabi, assignment prompts), page-length requirements are a pressing concern with great consequences for students and, in some cases, for administrators and instructors. Length requirements, too, are often one of the first concerns instructors bring up when encouraged to assign multimodal assignments. Nowacek (2011, 103) notes that when students are asked to discuss academic genres, length comes up frequently, a finding that was reinforced by my study.

The importance student writers place on length is understandable, as "length" is commonly discussed in pedagogical guides and curricular materials; it is a commonplace topic in teaching artifacts such as popular teacher-training textbooks (e.g., Bean 2011), writing textbooks (e.g., Devitt, Bawarshi, and Reiff 2004), first-year composition rubrics (Dryer 2013), and academic writing assignments (Melzer 2014). Formatting issues are typically framed as critically important in formal writing curricula; as Dylan B. Dryer (2008, 524) notes, writing syllabi are often riddled with "severely worded proscriptions about placement of staples, width of margins, location of titles, number of pages, or size of fonts." In the first-year writing program at the institution where this research was conducted, for example, quantity was emphasized frequently; instructors were advised to assign "no fewer than three, no more than five formal essays," culminating in "25–30 pages of polished, peer-reviewed prose" over the course of the semester.

Like their instructors,[3] students feel pressure about length requirements in writing assignments, as participants in this study discussed at length. This makes sense, as length is often tied to very real consequences in terms of assessment. For example, Dryer's (2013, 21–22) corpus analysis of rubrics from eighty-three writing programs suggests that document length is only explicitly named when it is insufficient: while the descriptor "short" is applied to failing papers, the corresponding terms for *successful* papers, terms such as "thoughtfully," "thoroughly," "beyond . . . requirements," focus on quality rather than quantity. In other words, not meeting page-length requirements (quantity) is often viewed as a mark of failure, while meeting or exceeding them is a mark of excellence (quality). It is understandable, then, that students tend to place so much value on how *much* they write as an indicator of how *well* they write.[4]

Despite the inordinate attention paid to document length in teaching, less attention has been paid in research and theory; there is scant research in rhetorical genre studies or linguistics that considers the relationship between genre and document length. This could be the case for a number of reasons. On the rhetorical genre studies side, for example, it is likely that researchers resist exploring facets of genres that could be construed as formulaic or, in Peter Medway's (2002, 141) terms, "ossified," opting instead for conceptions of genre that are sufficiently "fuzzy."[5] Researchers may also worry that attention to document length implies that "length" is more rhetorical than it actually is; concerns about *quantity* of writing seem rather superficial and associated with "answer-getting dispositions" (Wardle 2012) and the curriculum structured around them (e.g., standardized tests).

However, as any technical writer will tell you, rhetorical efficacy often hinges on understanding what constitutes an appropriate length for a given document. Social media also troubles the dichotomy between quantity and rhetorical quality of writing; in this context, length and rhetorical efficacy are inextricably bound (see, e.g., Shepherd 2018; Takayoshi 2015). Even in the academic context, specific disciplines tend to value genres of specified lengths (e.g., the sciences generally favor shorter articles). High-stakes academic genres such as personal statements and grant applications further demonstrate the rhetorical weight of document length in many situations.

At any rate, a disproportionate amount of attention is paid to document length in pedagogical materials as compared to research and genre theory. This disconnect suggests that our pedagogical emphasis on quantity of writing may lack grounding in empirical evidence, especially given that writing contributes to gains in learning when writing pedagogy emphasizes *quality* over quantity (Anderson, Anson, Gonyea, and Paine 2015). Since length can shape a text's rhetorical effects, we might productively consider the rhetoricity of document length by positioning *chronos* (quantity of time) as a twin rhetorical concept to *kairos* (quality of time). Future research on the relationship between genre and document length in teaching and research could potentially emulate recent efforts to consider whether and how teaching artifacts such as textbooks (Knoblauch 2011; Schiavone 2017) and rubrics (Dryer 2013) map onto the research and theories of our discipline.

ASSIGNMENT DESIGN

Writing assignments shape what writing can occur in a given environment. As Anis S. Bawarshi (2003, 127, original emphasis) states: "To treat the writing prompt merely as a conduit for communicating a subject matter from the teacher to the student, a way of 'giving' students something to write about, however, is to overlook the extent to which the prompt situates student writers within a genred site of action in which students acquire and negotiate desires, subjectivities, commitments, and relations before they begin to write. The writing prompt not only *moves* the student writer to action, it also *cues* the student writer to enact a certain kind of action." While writing assignments create conditions for students to make meaning, express their identities, and enact agency, they also impose constraints that less advanced or flexible writers (see, e.g., Reiff and Bawarshi's [2011] discussion of "boundary crossers" versus "boundary guarders") may struggle to work within.

Ultimately, Kate's experiences suggest that when writing environments allow for a range of languages and modes, writers may have access to more tools to express their identities, showcase prior knowledge, and make meaning. Kate's engagement with the blog post, an ill-defined genre, reveals how flexible generic spaces may invite writers to enact a range of identities and draw on a range of knowledge—in terms of both genre and media—when taking on new writing challenges.

Given the value typically placed on academic writing knowledge, it makes sense that Kate drew on the knowledge of the essay when composing her blog post; students are more likely to transfer knowledge they value (Bergmann and Zepernick 2007; Driscoll and Wells 2012), and young people tend to view informal online communication as distinct from "writing" (Lenhart, Arafeh, Smith, and Macgill 2008). This may prevent students from drawing on prior knowledge from environments outside of school, which may prevent them from drawing on valuable resources. To encourage transfer from home or self-sponsored contexts into the writing classroom, instructors might create more flexible assignments—possibly leveraging ePortfolios—in which student writers are invited to draw on their prior knowledge from a range of contexts, genres, and media from *out*side academic contexts.

By creating flexible assignments that invite students to draw and reflect on multiple modes, writing faculty may create more hospitable learning environments where students can showcase their prior knowledge and embrace the range of identities they bring *in*to the university alongside the academic and professional identities that too often take precedence in higher education.

NOTES

1. Namely, fully funded graduate training in writing studies, access to ongoing professional development in writing studies, full-time work, access to support

networks (i.e., geographical flexibility), healthcare and other benefits, a reasonable teaching load, reasonable pay, engagement with writing studies scholarship, authorial agency, and academic freedom (particularly when authoring antiracist scholarship—we should not be censored when advocating for inclusion of diverse students).
2. I invited all participants to select their own pseudonyms. Kate selected "Kate Kane," also known as Batwoman.
3. Researchers too. While revising this chapter, I was asked to move content from the implications section into the introduction. When I asked for the rationale behind this recommendation, I was advised that the introduction should be longer to match the length of introductions in other chapters.
4. Furthermore, as Les Perelman (2008) suggests, to even initially gain access to universities that require the SAT Writing section, students may be asked to master a writing task that highly rewards quantity (length) over quality (in terms of honesty and accuracy).
5. I do not mean to undercut the field's tendency to view genres as "fuzzy"; in fact, this study suggests that ill-defined genres and rhetorical situations can prompt and enable students to transfer writing knowledge across disparate contexts.

REFERENCES

Alexander, Kara Poe, Micheal-John DePalma, and Jeffrey M. Ringer. 2016. "Adaptive Remediation and the Facilitation of Transfer in Multiliteracy Center Contexts." *Computers and Composition* 41: 32–45.

Anderson, Paul, Chris Anson, Robert M. Gonyea, and Charles Paine. 2015. "The Contributions of Writing to Learning and Development: Results from a Large-Scale Multi-institutional Study." *Research in the Teaching of English* 50 (2): 199–234.

Anson, Chris M. 2017. "Intellectual, Argumentative, and Informational Affordances of Public Forums: Potential Contributions to Academic Learning." In *Social Writing / Social Media: Publics, Presentations, and Pedagogies*, edited by Douglas M. Walls and Stephanie Vie, 309–330. Fort Collins, CO: WAC Clearinghouse.

Ball, Cheryl. 2012. "Assessing Scholarly Multimedia: A Rhetorical Genre Studies Approach." *Technical Communication Quarterly* 21: 61–77.

Ball, Cheryl, Tia Scoffield Bowen, and Tyrell Brent Fenn. 2013. "Genre and Transfer in a Multimodal Composition Class." In *Multimodal Literacies and Emerging Genres*, edited by Tracey Bowen and Carl Whithaus, 15–36. Pittsburgh, PA: University of Pittsburgh Press.

Bawarshi, Anis S. 2003. *Genre and the Invention of the Writer*. Logan: Utah State University Press.

Bean, John. 2011. *Engaging Ideas: The Professor's Guide to Integrating Writing, Critical Thinking, and Active Learning in the Classroom*. San Francisco, CA: Jossey-Bass.

Beaufort, Anne. 2007. *College Writing and Beyond: A New Framework for University Writing Instruction*. Logan: Utah State University Press.

Bergmann, Linda S., and Janet Zepernick. 2007. "Disciplinarity and Transfer: Students' Perceptions of Learning to Write." *WPA: Writing Program Administration* 31 (1–2): 124–149.

Blair, Kristine L. 2012. "A Complicated Geometry: Triangulating Feminism, Activism, and Technological Literacy." In *Writing Studies Research in Practice*, edited by Lee Nickoson, Mary P. Sheridan, and Gesa E. Kirsch, 63–72. Carbondale: Southern Illinois University Press.

Blair, Kristine L., Radhika Gajjalaand, and Christine Tulley. 2009. *Webbing Cyberfeminist Practice: Communities, Pedagogies, and Social Action*. Cresskill, NJ: Hampton.

Blair, Kristine L., and Pamela Takayoshi. 1999. *Feminist Cyberscapes: Mapping Gendered Academic Spaces.* Westport, CT: Greenwood.

Bolter, Jay David, and Richard Grusin. 1999. *Remediation: Understanding New Media.* Cambridge: MIT Press.

Bowen, Tracey, and Carl Whithaus. 2013. *Multimodal Literacies and Emerging Genres.* Pittsburgh, PA: University of Pittsburgh Press.

Buck, Elizabeth H. 2015. "Facebook, Instagram, and Twitter—Oh My: Assessing the Efficacy of the Rhetorical Composing Situation with FYC Students as Advanced Social Media Practitioners." *Kairos: A Journal of Rhetoric, Technology, and Pedagogy* 19 (3). http://kairos.technorhetoric.net/19.3/praxis/buck/index.html.

Charmaz, Kathy. 2006. *Constructing Grounded Theory: A Practical Guide through Qualitative Analysis.* Los Angeles: Sage.

DePalma, Michael-John. 2015. "Tracing Transfer across Media: Investigating Writers' Perceptions of Cross-Contextual and Rhetorical Reshaping of Processes of Remediation." *College Composition and Communication* 66 (4): 615–642.

DePalma, Michael-John, and Kara Poe Alexander. 2015. "A Bag Full of Snakes: Negotiating the Challenges of Multimodal Composition." *Computers and Composition* 37: 182–200.

DePalma, Michael-John, and Jeffrey M. Ringer. 2011. "Toward a Theory of Adaptive Transfer: Expanding Disciplinary Discussions of 'Transfer' in Second-Language Writing and Composition Studies." *Journal of Second Language Writing* 20: 134–147.

Devitt, Amy, Anis Bawarshi, and Mary Jo Reiff. 2004. *Scenes of Writing: Strategies for Composing with Genres.* New York: Pearson.

Donahue, Christiane. 2012. "Transfer, Portability, Generalization: (How) Does Composition Expertise 'Carry?'" In *Exploring Composition Studies: Sites, Issues, Perspectives*, edited by Kelly Ritter and Paul Kei Matsuda, 145–166. Logan: Utah State University Press.

Driscoll, Dana L., and Jennifer Wells. 2012. "Beyond Knowledge and Skills: Writing Transfer and the Role of Student Dispositions." *Composition Forum* 26. http://compositionforum.com/issue/26/beyond-knowledge-skills.php.

Dryer, Dylan B. 2008. "Taking up Space: On Genre Systems as Geographies of the Possible." *Journal of Advanced Composition* 28 (3–4): 503–543.

Dryer, Dylan B. 2013. "Scaling Writing Ability: A Corpus-Driven Inquiry." *Written Communication* 30 (1): 3–35.

Fraiberg, Steven. 2010. "Composition 2.0: Toward a Multilingual and Multimodal Framework." *College Composition and Communication* 62 (1): 100–126.

Gold, David, Merideth Garcia, and Anna V. Knutson. 2019. "Going Public in an Age of Digital Anxiety: How Students Negotiate the Topoi of Online Writing Environments." *Composition Forum* 41. https://compositionforum.com/issue/41/going-public.php.

Gonzales, Laura. 2015. "Multimodality, Translingualism, and Rhetorical Genre Studies." *Composition Forum* 31. http://compositionforum.com/issue/31/multimodality.php.

Guerra, Juan. 2008. "Cultivating Transcultural Citizenship: A Writing across Communities Model." *Language Arts* 85 (4): 296–304.

Haas, Angela, Christine Tulley, and Kristine Blair. 2002. "Mentors versus Masters: Women's and Girls' Narratives of (Re)negotiation in Web-Based Writing Spaces." *Computers and Composition* 19: 231–249.

Jackson, Sue. 2018. "Young Feminists, Feminism, and Digital Media." *Feminism and Psychology* 28 (1): 32–49.

Jamieson, Kathleen M. 1975. "Antecedent Genre as Rhetorical Constraint." *Quarterly Journal of Speech* 61: 406–415.

Keller, Daniel. 2013. *Chasing Literacy: Reading and Writing in an Age of Acceleration.* Logan: Utah State University Press.

Keller, Jessalynn Marie. 2012. "Virtual Feminisms: Girls' Blogging Communities, Feminist Activism, and Participatory Politics." *Information, Communication, and Society* 15 (3): 429–447.

Keller, Jessica. 2016. *Girls' Feminist Blogging in a Postfeminist Age*. New York: Routledge.
Kim, Crystal, and Jessica Ringrose. 2018. "'Stumbling upon Feminism': Teenage Girls' Forays into Digital and School-Based Feminisms." *Girlhood Studies* 11 (2): 46–63.
Knoblauch, Abby A. 2011. "A Textbook Argument: Definitions of Argument in Leading Composition Textbooks." *College Composition and Communication* 63 (2): 244–268.
LeCourt, Donna, and Luann Barnes. 1999. "Writing Multiplicity: Hypertext and Feminist Textual Politics." *Computers and Composition* 16: 55–71.
Lenhart, Amanda, Sousan Arafeh, Aaron Smith, and Alexandra Rankin Macgill. 2008. "Writing, Technology, and Teens." *Pew Internet and American Life Project*. https://www.pewresearch.org/internet/wp-content/uploads/sites/9/media/Files/Reports/2008/PIP_Writing_Report_FINAL3.pdf.pdf.
Lotherington, Heather, and Jennifer Jenson. 2011. "Teaching Multimodal and Digital Literacy in L2 Settings: New Literacies, New Basics, New Pedagogies." *Annual Review of Applied Linguistics* 31: 226–246.
Martín, Cristina Sánchez, Lavinia Hirsu, Laura Gonzales, and Sara P. Alvarez. 2019. "Pedagogies of Digital Composing through a Translingual Approach." *Computers and Composition* 52: 142–157.
Medway, Peter. 2002. "Fuzzy Genres and Community Identities: The Case of Architecture Students' Sketchbooks." In *The Rhetoric and Ideology of Genre: Strategies for Stability and Change*, edited by Richard M. Coe, Lorelai Lingard, and Tatiana Teslenko, 123–151. Creskill, NJ: Hampton.
Melzer, Dan. 2014. *Assignments across the Curriculum: A National Study of College Writing*. Logan: Utah State University Press.
Miller, Carolyn R., and Dawn Shepherd. 2009. "Questions for Genre Theory from the Blogosphere." In *Genres in the Internet: Issues in the Theory of Genre*, edited by Janet Giltrow and Dieter Stein, 263–290. Philadelphia: John Benjamins.
Nelson, Mark Evan. 2006. "Mode, Meaning, and Synaesthesia in Multimedia L2 Writing." *Language Learning and Technology* 2: 56–76.
Nowacek, Rebecca S. 2011. *Agents of Integration: Understanding Transfer as a Rhetorical Act*. Carbondale: National Council of Teachers of English and Southern Illinois University Press.
Perelman, Les. 2008. "Information Illiteracy and Mass Market Writing Assessments." *College Composition and Communication* 60 (1): 128–141.
Ray, Brian. 2013. "More Than Just Remixing: Uptake and New Media Composition." *Computers and Composition* 30: 183–196.
Reiff, Mary Jo, and Anis Bawarshi. 2011. "Tracing Discursive Resources: How Students Use Prior Genre Knowledge to Negotiate New Writing Contexts in First-Year Composition." *Written Communication* 28 (3): 312–337.
Roozen, Kevin. 2008. "Journalism, Poetry, Stand-up Comedy, and Academic Literacy: Mapping the Interplay of Curricular and Extracurricular Literate Activities." *Journal of Basic Writing* 27 (1): 5–34.
Roozen, Kevin. 2009. "From Journals to Journalism: Tracing Trajectories of Literate Development." *College Composition and Communication* 60 (3): 541–572.
Rosinski, Paula. 2016. "Students' Perceptions of the Transfer of Rhetorical Knowledge between Digital Self-Sponsored Writing and Academic Writing: The Importance of Authentic Contexts and Reflection." In *Critical Transitions: Writing and the Question of Transfer*, edited by Jessie L. Moore and Chris M. Anson, 247–272. Fort Collins, CO: WAC Clearinghouse.
Rounsaville, Angela. 2012. "Selecting Genres for Transfer: The Role of Uptake in Students' Antecedent Genre Knowledge." *Composition Forum* 26. http://compositionforum.com/issue/26/selecting-genres-uptake.php.

Rounsaville, Angela. 2017. "Genre Repertoires from Below: How One Writer Built and Moved a Writing Life across Generations, Borders, and Communities." *Research in the Teaching of English* 51 (3): 317–340.

Rounsaville, Angela, Rachel Goldberg, and Anis Bawarshi. 2008. "From Incomes to Outcomes: FYW Students' Prior Genre Knowledge, Meta-cognition, and the Question of Transfer." *WPA: Writing Program Administration* 32 (1–2): 97–112.

Schiavone, Aubrey. 2017. "Consumption, Production, and Rhetorical Knowledge in Visual and Multimodal Textbooks." *College English* 79 (4): 358–380.

Selfe, Cynthia L. 2009. "The Movement of Air, the Breath of Meaning: Aurality and Multimodal Composing." *College Composition and Communication* 60 (4): 616–663.

Shepherd, Ryan P. 2015. "FB in FYC: Facebook Use among First-Year Composition Students." *Computers and Composition* 35: 86–107.

Shepherd, Ryan P. 2018. "Digital Writing, Multimodality, and Learning Transfer: Crafting Connections between Composition and Online Composing." *Computers and Composition* 48: 103–114.

Shin, Dong-shin, and Tony Cimasko. 2008. "Multimodal Composition in a College ESL Class: New Tools, Traditional Norms." *Computers and Composition* 25: 376–395.

Takayoshi, Pamela. 1994. "Building New Networks from the Old: Women's Experiences with Electronic Communications." *Computers and Composition* 11: 21–35.

Takayoshi, Pamela. 2015. "Short-Form Writing: Studying Process in the Context of Contemporary Composing Technologies." *Computers and Composition* 37: 1–13.

Tardy, Christine M. 2005. "Expressions of Disciplinarity and Individuality in a Multimodal Genre." *Computers and Composition* 22: 319–336.

Vie, Stephanie. 2008. "Digital Divide 2.0: 'Generation M' and Online Social Networking Sites in the Composition Classroom." *Computers and Composition* 25: 9–23.

Wardle, Elizabeth. 2009. "'Mutt Genres' and the Goal of FYC: Can We Help Students Write the Genres of the University?" *College Composition and Communication* 60 (4): 765–789.

Wardle, Elizabeth. 2012. "Creative Repurposing for Expansive Learning: Considering 'Problem-Exploring' and 'Answer-Getting' Dispositions in Individuals and Fields." *Composition Forum* 26. http://compositionforum.com/issue/26/creative-repurposing.php.

Yosso, Tara J. 2005. "Whose Culture Has Capital? A Critical Race Theory Discussion of Community Cultural Wealth." *Race Ethnicity and Education* 8 (1): 69–91.

6

THE OTHER CURRICULUM
Social Media and Its Connection to University Writing

Ryan P. Shepherd

In Korean, if someone asks what you do in your free time, you might respond with the equivalent Korean phrase to "I like to read books." When I taught English in Korea, I would sometimes correct students if they used this phrase in English, telling them they did not need to use the word *books* in this sentence because it was implied. Adding *books* sounded redundant to me. What else would you read? Once, a student pointed out to me the problem with my thinking. He said he liked to read books, but he did not like to do other types of reading. I told him he could just say "I like to read." He asked what he would say if he liked to read magazines or online articles instead, and I told him he would have to say that explicitly.

At the time, it did not occur to me what this exchange illustrates about literacy. To me, the word *books* in the sentence was invisible or unnecessary: reading *was* books. It was the unspoken part of reading. Books could be left off, but the speaker would have to mention comics, newspapers, journal articles, blog posts, or tweets.

Similarly, if I were to say "I like to write," I imagine many people will picture a very specific and narrow kind of writing. Perhaps this kind of writing would be creative writing, personal writing, or school writing. But it is unlikely that the listener would imagine writing emails, expense reports, Facebook posts, text messages, image captions, or video scripts. People do these kinds of writing every day but may overlook them *as writing*. In essence, many people have decided to subconsciously define what literacy means in a very narrow way. I demonstrated my own narrow view when I suggested leaving off *books* in the sentence above, and we all demonstrate this narrow view when we define writing that excludes the writing of everyday life. Teachers may inadvertently help students define writing as *only* what is done in school and may overlook the broader constellation of writing practices that take place outside of school.

In this chapter, I focus on one small piece of the constellation of writing practices: the writing on social media. I followed six university students as they moved from first-year students through graduation, and I explore how their perceptions of social media changed. During that time, these students made fewer connections between the writing they were doing on social media and the other parts of their writing lives. Because of that, they may have missed important opportunities for learning and for writing transfer—particularly for understanding multimodal composing. I argue that students engage in two separate curricula when learning to write. They are learning to write both in school classes and in extracurricular writing that takes place outside of school, such as writing for social media. By actively including students' experiences on social media in our writing classes, teachers may help students to define writing more broadly and to make connections more easily across their myriad writing experiences. Teachers may help expose the "other curriculum" in students' writing lives so they can apply lessons learned from those experiences.

WRITING TRANSFER AND THE OTHER CURRICULUM

The idea of the "other curriculum" builds on the concept of the "extracurriculum" presented by Anne Ruggles Gere (2001) in her article "Kitchen Tables and Rented Rooms." The extracurriculum includes "the multiple contexts in which persons seek to improve their own writing" (279). The "other curriculum" is writing students do concurrently with their learning in school but that is left out of the writing class. Unlike the extracurriculum, students are often not *intentionally* "seek[ing] to improve" their writing in the other curriculum. Instead, they may be tacitly learning about writing through writing-based practices. These may include any writing students are doing that is not a focal point of the writing curriculum, such as writing for part-time jobs, for clubs and organizations, or for social media (or other "literate activity," see Roozen, chapter 7, this volume). The other curriculum is parallel to the school curriculum, but it is often hidden from both students and teachers. Even so, the other curriculum is valuable: it can serve as a means of supporting ideas students are learning in those classes and introduce ideas not covered in class at all, perhaps even bridging across languages (see Wilson and Portz, chapter 3, this volume). Each extracurricular experience may teach students lessons about writing that could be useful elsewhere in their writing lives. For example, Lilian W. Mina (2017, 270) says that exploring writing on social media in writing classes

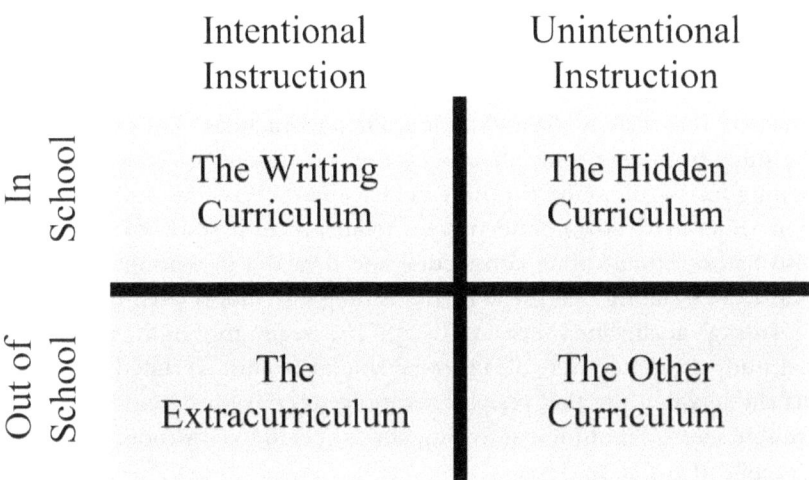

Figure 6.1. Relationship of the other curriculum to the writing curriculum, the hidden curriculum, and the extracurriculum

is a means of "helping students understand rhetorical choices, enhancing learners' analytical and reflective thinking skills, developing student writing skills, and building communities and student engagement." Students may be unconsciously learning these lessons as they engage with the other curriculum.

Some readers may see parallels here between the other curriculum and the "hidden curriculum." This term has been defined numerous ways, but it is often expressed in critical pedagogy works, such as Paulo Freire (2000), Ira Shor (1992), and bell hooks (1994), as socializing lessons taught unintentionally. While the other curriculum is also taught unintentionally, it takes place outside of school and usually without formal instruction. In figure 6.1, I offer some clarity about what differentiates the curricula described above. The regular writing curriculum, including first-year writing and any formal writing instruction that takes places in any classes, is both in school and involves intentional instruction. The hidden curriculum is in school, but the instruction is unintentional—often invisible. The extracurriculum involves intentional instruction but takes place outside of formal learning contexts. And the other curriculum is both outside of school and without intentional instruction.

Unfortunately, because the other curriculum is taking place outside of writing classes, many students may not be seeing this writing as "real writing" (Alexander, Cassady, and DePalma, chapter 4, this volume;

Cunningham 2018, 67; Roozen 2012, 100), as "worthwhile" (Keller 2014, 52), or as *writing* at all (Shepherd 2015, 2018a, 2018b). Mina (2017, 277) sees a "new digital divide" that has formed between "students' everyday practices on social media and their academic practices." For example, in my study from 2015, only about a quarter of students surveyed thought writing for social media (in this case, Facebook) was a kind of composition (Shepherd 2015). Interviewees from my 2018 study of Facebook also had a difficult time connecting social media to writing, with one interviewee stating that social media writing was "not related to the skill of writing" at all (Shepherd 2018b, 75). The beginnings of the longitudinal study presented here also showed similar results. As stated in a 2018 article detailing the first year of this study, interviewees seemed to have trouble seeing "multimodal writing as connected to classroom practice" (Shepherd 2018a, 103).[1]

Because students sometimes struggle to see connections between writing that takes place in their lives on social media (and other out-of-school contexts) and writing that takes place in writing classes (and other school contexts), it may be difficult for them to apply writing knowledge acquired in one context to the other (DePalma and Alexander 2015; James 2008; Shepherd 2018a). Students may perceive the context of social media writing and school writing as dissimilar, and this may make it is unlikely for them to engage in the "mindful abstraction" necessary to connect the contexts effectively.

Mindful abstraction is a phrase I borrow from Gavriel Salomon and David N. Perkins (1989), which they expand upon in a later article (Perkins and Salomon 2012). The idea of mindful abstraction draws attention to students' need to reflect mindfully on what has been learned and to generalize beyond the context in which the learning took place. Mindful abstraction is associated with "high-road transfer," which is the kind of learning transfer associated with "deliberate reflective processing" (251). It allows learners to expand beyond the learning context and make learning more easily connected to new learning contexts. High-road transfer is in opposition to "low-road transfer," which is associated with "pattern recognition and the reflexive triggering of routines" (251). This is the kind of learning application that happens automatically, out of habit. It is reflexive, and it generally only happens when learners immediately recognize the similarity between the learning situation and the situation in which they might apply the learning.

For example, let us imagine that a student is learning to write a thesis statement. Often, teachers treat this as a low-road transfer situation. A teacher might show the student examples of various thesis statements.

They might have the student look at examples of possible thesis statements for a situation and choose the best option. They might have the student practice writing thesis statements for various situations. Finally, they might have a student draft a thesis statement for a specific project the student is writing. The thinking behind this is that students will recognize the situation in the future and be able to repeat this process easily when they encounter a writing situation that requires a thesis statement.

However, there is a problem with this approach: it defines a thesis statement as a narrow set of skills that looks largely the same across all writing contexts. Rarely do writers encounter situations that require a thesis statement in writing for part-time jobs, for clubs, or in their free time. *But* students might encounter situations that require types of writing that do similar work. They might be called on to clearly define the purpose of a piece of writing in a short phrase. Perhaps they will need to make a claim about the results on their lab report or write a subject line for a memo. Even writing on social media often requires us to succinctly state the purpose of our post, such as when captioning an image, writing a video description, or making a meme.

In other words, when engaging in class activities that would encourage low-road transfer, teachers are discouraging students from seeing broader connections to other types of writing they may encounter that *are not* the same but that might in some ways *resemble* what they have learned. Often, teachers operate under the impression that students will automatically connect classroom content to writing they are doing in the other curriculum: of course, students will connect these ideas to other similar contexts. Unfortunately, this does not seem to happen so easily (Russell 1995; Smit 2004). So-called "general writing skills instruction" (Russell 1995, 51) does not "easily lead to transfer" (Haskell 2001, 79). Teachers need to actively encourage students to mindfully abstract what they are learning and apply it to other contexts. The vast majority of what students learn about writing—concepts such as audience, organization, genre, purpose, tone, style, and others—are practices that are best served when engaging in mindful abstraction. Students do not necessarily need a narrow set of contexts in which these practices can be directly applied. Instead, they need to reflect on these concepts and generalize them beyond the classroom for application across multiple, sometimes not-yet-encountered, contexts.

In what follows, I offer insights into the interviewees I worked with for this study. As they moved through their college careers, their perceptions of connections across writing contexts narrowed instead of broadened. This may be an impediment for high-road transfer and has broader implications for the development of effective writing pedagogy. It may be helping to keep the other curriculum separate from what we do in writing classes.

THE INTERVIEWEES AND THEIR PERCEPTIONS OF SOCIAL MEDIA WRITING

The purpose of this study was initially to understand how students' perceptions of writing for school and outside of school connected. With that in mind, I began the study with a survey of 151 students from across the United States in the fall of 2015. From the initial survey, I chose 10 students to interview more extensively about their experiences writing for school and outside of school. Interview participants were chosen to get the maximum diversity in terms of cultural background, educational background, and institution type (table 6.1).

The interviewees were followed from their first year at a university through graduation, with future interviews planned for their experiences in the workforce. During the four-year study, some of the interviewees declined to continue, meaning that only six of the original ten interviewees were interviewed for all four years of the study. The survey and all interviews were conducted with IRB approval. Initial survey and interview questions were published in a previous study (Shepherd 2018a). Questions in subsequent years followed the same pattern but included additional questions about the interviewees' writing experiences in different classes and additional out-of-school contexts.

In the interviews, I asked students to define the word *writing*, to tell me about their experiences with writing both in school and out of school, and to explain any connection they saw between the various writing contexts. As the interviews went on, I added questions about the interviews themselves, such as whether the annual check-ins changed the ways they thought about writing. Among the topics discussed were writing online music reviews, writing business proposals, translating comic books from Mandarin to English, coding as writing, running communication for a sorority, writing for part-time jobs (such as managing a Starbucks), and, of course, writing for social media. Students were engaging in writing a great deal outside of school.

One interesting takeaway from the interviews was that students' definitions of writing remained relatively stable across the four years of the study. For example, Enrique defined writing as "making an argument through written words like as compared to oral" in 2015 and as "expressing your arguments to an audience without being able to speak" in 2018.

Table 6.1. Interviewees

Pseudonym	Age[a]	Gender[b]	Race	High School	University	Major[c]
Enrique	18	Non-binary	Latino and white	Large public HS	Southwestern public R1	Computer science
Evan	18	Male	Hispanic	Small public "test-in" HS	Southwestern public R1	Political science
Jessica	19	Female	White	Home schooled	Midwestern public R2	Photojournalism
Lily	19	Female	Asian	Large public HS	Southwestern public R1	Communication
Michael	18	Male	White	Large public HS	Midwestern public R2	Meteorology
Samuel	18	Male	Asian	Large public HS	East Coast public R2[d]	Electrical computer engineering

a. Age at time of first interview.
b. Race and gender are reported exactly as stated by the interviewee.
c. Major at graduation. Enrique, Evan, Jessica, and Lily changed majors during the course of the interviews.
d. Samuel changed institutions over the course of the interviews from an M1 to an R2 institution.

But some of the interviewees' definitions contracted a bit. Samuel, for instance, defined writing as working "to process information or . . . to convey information" in 2015 but shifted to "trying to put together words to kind of communicate ideas" in 2018. He seemed to keep the idea of conveying information or communicating ideas but entirely dropped the idea of processing information. Other interviewees followed a similar pattern: either their definitions stayed very similar to their original in the first interviews, or the definitions contracted a bit as time went on. The suggestion seems to be that the definition of writing was already coalesced by the time they entered the university and that the definition may have been able to contract but rarely expanded. Stuart Blythe and Laura Gonzales (2016) found a similar pattern when looking at the metagenre of research: students often believe they learned the metagenre *before* university writing.

These definitions of writing were focused exclusively on traditional definitions of writing that center alphabetic literacy. None of the six participants include anything that would hint at multimodal literacy in any of their interviews; in fact, some expressly seem to limit their definition to exclude multimodal writing, such as Jessica, who says writing is "a way to put your thoughts on paper." Three of the six interviewees use the word *words* in their definitions, but none mentions images, charts, graphs, links, or anything digital. These participants' definitions of writing do not seem to be multimodal. The findings mirror the results of the initial study (Shepherd 2018a).

These limited definitions of writing are somewhat surprising when we consider that five of the six interviewees had engaged in at least one multimodal writing assignment at some point in high school or early in university. Jessica included images and wrote captions for them in photojournalism, both Enrique and Michael did rhetorical analyses of images, Lily used charts in writing for an economics class, and Samuel used images and charts in several pieces of writing both before and early in his college career. Perhaps the problem lies in the fact that this writing was not often seen as writing or put in a central place in the students' writing classes. Samuel, for example, said he used images in a first-year writing class but that the instruction "tended to be very text centered." This was echoed by other interviewees who had used multimodal writing but had not really reflected on its importance. This could also be because, as in John-Michael DePalma and Kara Poe Alexander (2015, 186), students "viewed multimodal composition as oppositional to 'academic' writing."

The participants also steered away from social media and multimodal writing elsewhere in the interviews. I asked students in both 2015 and 2018 if writing they had done on social media helped with university writing. In 2015, five of the six interviewees said they thought social media writing helped with writing in the university. Interviewees mentioned connections with engaging an audience, writing more concisely, developing research questions, and helping with writing for presentations. Michael even made a broad, sweeping connection when he said "you're still writing, and you still got your mind going" when writing in either context. In 2018, only three of the six interviewees said social media writing helped in the university. The idea of engaging an audience still came up for one interviewee, but even the interviewees who answered "yes" did so much more tenuously. For example, Lily said there was a connection but that it only helped "for the classes that are talking about digital marketing."

When I flipped the question and asked if university writing would help with writing on social media, the results were quite different. In 2015, three of the six interviewees said writing for university would help with writing on social media, but in 2018, five of the six said university writing helped. This is exactly the reverse of the results when the question was asked the other way around. In both interview years, respondents focused largely on formal elements of writing education helping with writing on social media, things such as grammar and tone.

The social media writing students were doing was decidedly multimodal. All six mentioned that images were included with their social media writing in 2015; four mentioned including video, and four mentioned linking to media on other sites through social media. In 2018, the results were even starker: all six interviewees had made written posts that used images, video, and links to other media off-site. The students were creating multimodal posts extensively on social media. This is perhaps one reason students separated the two writing contexts. Because one situation was more multimodal, it may have led the students to consider it more "oppositional" (DePalma and Alexander 2015, 186). In other words, the other curriculum was just too "other."

I cannot be certain why the change in the interviewees' thinking about social media happened or why multimodal elements were absent from their descriptions of writing, but I do think some factors likely contributed. One reason might be a devaluing of writing outside of school taking place in the interviewees. The writing curriculum in school took a more central role in their definition of writing, and the other curriculum just became more hidden. In other words, to them, there may have been nothing to learn on social media. In 2015, they saw a value in both social media writing and in writing for the university. In 2018, they saw less value in social media writing. This seems to be supported by the interviewees' responses elsewhere in the interviews as well: as the interviews went along from 2015 into 2018, the discussion of their writing lives focused more and more on the writing they were doing for school—specifically on the writing they were doing in the classes for their majors. Students seemed to define writing more and more within the narrow confines of how writing was done in their field—therefore, they saw social media writing as less important to their writing lives and less *as writing*. Students were still learning lessons as they wrote on social media, but those lessons were becoming hidden to them. They continued to develop the writing practices from multimodal writing as suggested by Mina (2017), but they no longer were consciously aware of it.

The biggest support for this conclusion comes from the interviewees' answers to a question about out-of-school writing in 2018. When I asked what writing they had done outside of school in the last year, four of the six interviewees did not mention social media at all during that discussion or during follow-up questions about it. Instead, most discussed writing that was focused on work-related contexts: part-time jobs, internships, applications, and so forth. But when I asked them about writing on social media directly, all six had done such writing in the previous year—some of them fairly regularly. This seems to suggest that while students were engaging in writing practices on social media, they were not thinking about what they were doing *as writing*. It did not occur to them to include writing on social media when I asked about writing outside of school. This is even more telling when we consider that I had been asking them about writing and social media for four years at the time of the interview: they *still* were not making that connection unprompted.

Interviewees were making some connections between writing contexts, however. For example, Lily mentioned using content from her business writing classes in her other business courses, and another respondent mentioned using writing knowledge learned in one political science class in another, similar class. A few interviewees mentioned citation practices, but only to the extent that learning APA helped in future situations where APA was called for. This seems to be an indication that low-road writing transfer may have been happening but that it is somewhat limited to *very* similar writing situations. More general writing practices were mentioned as well, but they were also limited. Grammar and audience connections across contexts were mentioned, but only in very general ways. Lessons taken from writing classes were—unfortunately—minimal according to the interviewees. Similar conclusions have been drawn elsewhere (Russell 1995; Smit 2004; Wardle 2009).

THE BROAD CONSTELLATION FADES AWAY

These data seem to suggest that as the interviewees moved further into their university careers, they begin to focus more narrowly for university classes. This may not be surprising and, in some ways, may even be positive. However, as they focused in on that university writing, they also seemed to be leaving behind connections to other types of writing—including, among other things, connections to writing on social media and multimodal writing. In essence, these interviews suggest that students may define writing in a very narrow way by the end of their university careers. They may leave behind the broad constellation of writing that takes place in their lives—in organizations, in part-time jobs, and, of course, on social media. The other curriculum loses its connection to students' university writing experiences. If students no longer see connections between writing they are doing for school and extracurricular writing, they may struggle to use lessons from one writing context in another. They may leave behind important writing lessons they have learned on social media and struggle to apply lessons from school to social media.

Building a robust connection across writing contexts may mean also building in a broader constellation of writing practices in writing courses. But it may also mean—and I think this may be the more important point—that writing instructors need to build in transparency regarding what they hope students are learning about writing. In other words, students may not be making connections across writing contexts because teachers are not asking them to do so. If teachers want students to engage in the mindful abstraction necessary for them to connect writing across contexts more easily, they will have to ask them to engage in it directly (Driscoll 2011, among many others).

Transparency in what writing teachers want their students to learn seems to be a common refrain in writing transfer literature. We see this explicitly in Teaching for Transfer pedagogies, in which scholars such as Kathleen Blake Yancey, Liane Robertson, and Kara Taczak (2014, 33, original emphasis) say "students need to *participate* with us in creating their own frameworks for facilitating transfer." But we also see this more generally when we ask students specifically to reflect on what they are learning and how they might use it (Adler-Kassner et al. 2017; Alexander, DePalma, and Ringer 2016; Andrus, Mitchler, and Tinberg 2019; DePalma 2015; Downs and Wardle 2007; Nelms and Dively 2007; Nowacek 2011; Reiff and Bawarshi 2011; Yancey et al. 2019). These commonly suggested reflective activities not only get students to place their learning into broader contexts, but they also offer a second benefit of creating more transparency about what teachers want students to learn and why. Reflective practice seems to be particularly important in terms of creating positive student dispositions toward writing content, which can be a tremendous boon to facilitating transfer as well (Driscoll 2011, 2013; Driscoll and Powell 2016; Driscoll and Wells 2012; Driscoll et al. 2017; Gorzelsky, Driscoll et al. 2017; Gorzelsky, Hayes et al. 2017; Hayes et al. 2018; Anson, foreword, this volume; Naftzinger, chapter 10, this volume). Reflection, transparency, and positive disposition seem to be lacking among the interviewees in this study. They may be struggling to see connections across contexts—at least in part because they have not been asked to look for connections—and negative dispositions may be impeding connections from being made as well. For example, most of the interviewees had negative perceptions of their first-year writing experiences. A poor perception of experiences in writing courses may ensure that connections are not made or that connections do not persist beyond the class. One of the biggest questions writing teachers should ask themselves is how they can keep connections across writing contexts after the class has finished.

KEEPING THE CONSTELLATION ALIVE

Each year during the interviews, I asked the interviewees to tell me about what they remembered from their classes. Certain things stuck with them, and those things were different for each student. For example, Jessica focused exclusively on help with research when recalling her first-year writing experience as a senior, whereas Michael focused on rhetorical appeals and Samuel focused on audience awareness. Both Lily and Evan stated that did not remember anything from their experiences in their writing classes. None of the interviewees mentioned experiences with social media or multimodal composing. Even when asked directly, the interviewees said they did not compose using images, charts, graphs, or links; they also said social media was rarely mentioned in their writing classes.[2]

And yet, social media was a very big part of these students' lives. All of them used social media during all four years of the interviews. Many of the interviewees posted on social media regularly, even multiple times a day. They were making comments, posting pictures, sharing videos and gifs, and engaging in a wealth of multimodal practices through their experiences on Instagram, Snapchat, Twitter, and Reddit—among many other spaces. Early in the interview process, students were making connections between these experiences and university writing. Recall that five of the six interviewees said they saw a connection between social media writing and university writing during the 2015 interviews. Unfortunately, this was down to just three interviewees by 2018.

While I can only speculate as to why these connections disappeared as students went through the university, I do have several theories that make sense based on the evidence available. It seems that social media and multimodal writing were not valued in these interviewees' experiences in first-year writing or in subsequent writing-intensive classes in their majors. Multimodal composition and social media writing were rarely included in class content. Because social media and multimodal writing were sidelined in the classes, teachers were sending an implicit message that these kinds of writing are not valued in the university. Students may have picked up on that message—even subconsciously—and may have chosen to focus on more traditional forms of writing instead.

These messages seemed to be reinforced as students moved through other university classes: writing in their major was presented as the primary focus—perhaps even just as *what writing is* to the interviewees. I do not mean to suggest that this is a problem: having students explore the purposes, audiences, contexts, and genres of writing in their major and in their future field is a helpful approach. But at the same time, these lessons may be connected to the other writing students may be doing outside of class as well. Students should engage both the low-road approach of connecting to specific writing contexts and the high-road approach of thinking abstractly about how those lessons may apply to other writing contexts as well. In other words, the other curriculum should be included alongside the traditional writing curriculum.

Building these connections needs to start in first-year writing courses and be reinforced throughout students' writing experiences in college. While it is important to explore writing for the university, this should not be done at the exclusion of other writing practices. Instead, university writing should be put into conversation with those practices. How does university writing overlap with and differ from writing they did in high school, writing they do on social media, and writing they will do in their future careers? Writing in the university is not isolated from other types of writing. It is part of a broad constellation of writing practices that writing teachers should be working to help students build connections between. Writing teachers need to encourage students to consider how what they learn on social media might inform university and job writing. This is particularly important when it comes to multimodal writing. If the interviews in this chapter are representative, students will likely have far more experience writing multimodally on social media than they will in other contexts.

CONCLUSIONS AND THE FUTURE

The interviewees in this study seemed to narrow their definition of writing as they moved through the university. Early on, they seemed much more inclined to make positive connections between writing on social media and writing in university classes, but those connections appeared to wither as they moved through their university careers. My suggestion is that by actively attempting to help students hold on to those connections, we will help them be able to tap into a greater wealth of writing experiences and put their writing for school into the much broader constellation of writing that takes place outside of school. The main mechanisms teachers should use to maintain those connections need to take place during their writing classes. Teachers need to connect university writing to writing in out-of-school contexts, to explore multimodal writing, and to be transparent in their efforts to facilitate connections between writing contexts (for example, see Shepherd 2020; Yancey, afterword, this volume). Furthermore, these mechanisms for facilitating transfer can be used to develop writing curricula with multimodality and transfer in mind (see Bearden, chapter 8, this volume) or to work with writing majors (Maynard, chapter 9, this volume).

As the field moves forward with these endeavors, it is important that scholars continue to analyze the efficacy of these approaches. The study I describe here is only a starting point for discussions about connections across writing contexts. In the future, additional longitudinal studies are necessary to understand connections students make and how those connections are maintained. One of the main things missing from my design is simply a mechanism for verification: what I have in this study is an in-depth look at what students *perceived* and *remembered* about writing in the university and their first-year writing experience. One drawback of this study is that I do not know for certain what students were *actually* taught in first-year writing or what assignments they did. So, for example, I cannot say for certain whether students rarely discussed multimodality and social media in their first-year writing class or if they simply did not remember those discussions. While the first interviews in this study happened concurrently with their first-year writing course, there is still a chance that students had forgotten discussions that happened in the class. In future longitudinal studies, syllabi, assignment sheets, course schedules, and students' completed projects could also be collected to compare the teachers' approaches to the course with the way the course was remembered. Additional materials could be collected from other courses as students continued through their university careers, and perhaps other methods for collecting data on transfer and multimodality could be used (for example, see VanKooten, chapter 1, and Jiang, chapter 2, both this volume).

Furthermore, while I think a more mindful and reflective approach to teaching writing may help students make connections to their broader writing lives after the course, I do not have verification that that is the case. In future studies, following students after they leave class and seeing if their perceptions of connections across writing contexts persisted better than those of students in other writing contexts would help teachers to see whether this approach was helpful. I encourage teachers to both create alternate pedagogies designed to build connections and to test those connections after the students have left the course. In other words, directly make the other curriculum part of your writing curriculum.

I hope this chapter begins a conversation that other scholars and I can complete elsewhere. Connecting writing across modes and actively encouraging students to build a perception of writing as more than simply university writing may help students conceive of broader writing lives and make it easier for them to build bridges between those contexts and use what they are learning in one context in various others. At the beginning of this chapter, I presented my misperception when I conflated reading books with all reading and put reading of other types in a separate category. Teachers should actively encourage writing students not to limit their understanding of writing as just school writing. The writing for school should be one piece in a much broader constellation that includes writing for university clubs, religious organizations, part-time jobs, careers, hobbies, and—among many other things—multimodality and social media.

NOTES

1. Knutson (chapter 5, this volume) suggests that one reason students may have trouble making connections is because of length.
2. Some students *did* do multimodal writing or social media assignments in FYC and mentioned these experiences in earlier interviews. They just did not recall these experiences when they were seniors.

REFERENCES

Adler-Kassner, Linda, Irene Clark, Liane Robertson, Kara Taczak, and Kathleen Blake Yancey. 2017. "Assembling Knowledge: The Role of Threshold Concepts in Facilitating Transfer." In *Critical Transitions: Writing and the Question of Transfer*, edited by Chris M. Anson and Jessie L. Moore, 17–47. Fort Collins, CO: WAC Clearinghouse.

Alexander, Kara Poe, Michael-John DePalma, and Jeffrey M. Ringer. 2016. "Adaptive Remediation and the Facilitation of Transfer in Multiliteracy Center Contexts." *Computers and Composition* 41: 32–45.

Andrus, Sonja, Sharon Mitchler, and Howard Tinberg. 2019. "Teaching for Writing Transfer: A Practical Guide for Teachers." *Teaching English in the Two-Year College* 47 (1): 76–89.

Blythe, Stuart, and Laura Gonzales. 2016. "Coordination and Transfer across the Metagenre of Secondary Research." *College Composition and Communication* 67 (4): 607–633.

Cunningham, Jennifer M. 2018. "'Wuz Good Wit U Bro': Patterns of Digital African American Language Use in Two Modes of Communication." *Computers and Composition* 48: 67–84.

DePalma, Michael-John. 2015. "Tracing Transfer across Media: Investigating Writers' Perceptions of Cross-Contextual and Rhetorical Reshaping in Processes of Remediation." *College Composition and Communication* 66 (4): 615–642.

DePalma, Michael-John, and Kara Poe Alexander. 2015. "A Bag Full of Snakes: Negotiating the Challenges of Multimodal Composition." *Computers and Composition* 37: 182–200.

Downs, Douglas, and Elizabeth Wardle. 2007. "Teaching about Writing, Righting Misconceptions: (Re)envisioning 'First-Year Composition' as 'Introduction to Writing Studies.'" *College Composition and Communication* 58 (4): 552–584.

Driscoll, Dana Lynn. 2011. "Connected, Disconnected, and Uncertain: Student Attitudes about Future Writing Contexts and Perceptions of Transfer from First Year Writing to the Disciplines." *Across the Disciplines: A Journal of Language, Learning, and Academic Writing* 8 (2). https://doi.org/10.37514/ATD-J.2011.8.2.07.

Driscoll, Dana Lynn. 2013. "Connected Pedagogy and Transfer of Learning: An Examination of Graduate Instruction Belief vs. Practices in First-Year Writing." *Journal of Teaching Writing* 28 (1): 54–83.

Driscoll, Dana Lynn, Gwen Gorzelsky, Jennifer Wells, Carol Hayes, Ed Jones, and Steve Salchak. 2017. "Down the Rabbit Hole: Challenges and Methodological Recommendations in Researching Writing-Related Student Dispositions." *Composition Forum* 35. http://compositionforum.com/issue/35/rabbit-hole.php.

Driscoll, Dana Lynn, and Roger Powell. 2016. "States, Traits, and Dispositions: The Impact of Emotion on Writing Development and Writing Transfer across College Courses and Beyond." *Composition Forum* 34. https://compositionforum.com/issue/34/states-traits.php.

Driscoll, Dana Lynn, and Jennifer Wells. 2012. "Beyond Knowledge and Skills: Writing Transfer and the Role of Student Dispositions." *Composition Forum* 26. https://compositionforum.com/issue/26/beyond-knowledge-skills.php.

Friere, Paulo. 2000. *Pedagogy of the Oppressed: 50th Anniversary Edition*. New York: Bloomsbury Academic.

Gere, Anne Ruggles. 2001. "Kitchen Tables and Rented Rooms: The Extracurriculum of Composition." In *Literacy: A Critical Sourcebook*, edited by Ellen Cushman, Eugene R. Kintgen, Barry M. Kroll, and Mike Rose, 275–289. Boston: Bedford/St. Martin's.

Gorzelsky, Gwen, Dana Lynn Driscoll, Joe Paszek, Ed Jones, and Carol Hayes. 2017. "Cultivating Constructive Metacognition: A New Taxonomy for Writing Studies." In *Critical Transitions: Writing and the Question of Transfer*, edited by Chris M. Anson and Jessie L. Moore, 215–246. Fort Collins, CO: WAC Clearinghouse.

Gorzelsky, Gwen, Carol Hayes, Ed Jones, and Dana Lynn Driscoll. 2017. "Cueing and Adapting First-Year Writing Knowledge: Support for Transfer into Disciplinary Writing." In *Understanding Writing Transfer: Implications for Transformative Student Learning in Higher Education*, edited by Jessie L. Moore and Randall Bass, 113–121. Sterling, VA: Stylus.

Haskell, Robert E. 2001. *Transfer of Learning: Cognition, Instruction, and Reasoning*. San Diego: Academic Press.

Hayes, Carol, Ed Jones, Gwen Gorzelsky, and Dana L. Driscoll. 2018. "Adapting Writing about Writing: Curricular Implications of Cross-Institutional Data from the Writing Transfer Project." *WPA: Writing Program Administration* 41 (2): 65–88.

hooks, bell. 1994. *Teaching to Transgress: Education as the Practice of Freedom*. New York: Routledge.

James, Mark Andres. 2008. "The Influence of Perceptions of Task Similarity/Difference on Learning Transfer in Second Language Writing." *Written Communication* 25 (1): 76–103.

Keller, Daniel. 2014. *Chasing Literacy: Reading and Writing in an Age of Acceleration*. Logan: Utah State University Press.

Mina, Lilian W. 2017. "Social Media in the FYC Class: The New Digital Divide." In *Social Writing/Social Media: Publics, Presentations, and Pedagogies*, edited by Douglas M. Walls and Stephanie Vie, 263–282. Fort Collins, CO: WAC Clearinghouse.

Nelms, Gerald, and Ronda Leathers Dively. 2007. "Perceived Roadblocks to Transferring Knowledge from First-Year Composition to Writing Intensive Major Courses: A Pilot Study." *WPA: Writing Program Administration* 31 (1–2): 214–240.

Nowacek, Rebecca S. 2011. *Agents of Integration: Understanding Transfer as a Rhetorical Act*. Carbondale: Southern Illinois University Press.

Perkins, David N., and Gavriel Salomon. 2012. "Knowledge to Go: A Motivational and Dispositional View of Transfer." *Educational Psychologist* 47 (3): 248–258.

Reiff, Mary Jo, and Anis Bawarshi. 2011. "Tracing Discursive Resources: How Students Use Prior Genre Knowledge to Negotiate New Writing Contexts in First-Year Composition." *Written Communication* 28 (3): 312–337.

Roozen, Kevin. 2012. "Comedy Stages, Poets Projects, Sports Columns, and Kinesiology 341: Illuminating the Importance of Basic Writers' Self-Sponsored Literacies." *Journal of Basic Writing* 31: 99–132.

Russell, David. 1995. "Activity Theory and Its Implications for Writing Instruction." In *Reconceiving Writing, Rethinking Writing Instruction*, edited by Joseph Petraglia, 51–77. Mahway, NJ: Lawrence Erlbaum Associates.

Salomon, Gavriel, and David N. Perkins. 1989. "Rocky Roads to Transfer: Rethinking Mechanism of a Neglected Phenomenon." *Educational Psychologist* 24 (2): 113–142.

Shepherd, Ryan P. 2015. "FB in FYC: Facebook Use among First-Year Composition Students." *Computers and Composition* 35: 86–107.

Shepherd, Ryan P. 2018a. "Digital Writing, Multimodality, and Learning Transfer: Creating Connections between Composition and Online Composing." *Computers and Composition* 48: 103–114.

Shepherd, Ryan P. 2018b. "The Literacy of Facebook: SNS Literacy Practices and Learning Transfer in FYC." *Journal of Multimodal Rhetorics* 2 (2): 70–86.

Shepherd, Ryan P. 2020. "What Reddit Has to Teach Us about Discourse Communities." *Kairos* 24 (2). https://kairos.technorhetoric.net/24.2/praxis/shepherd/index.html.

Shor, Ira. 1992. *Empowering Education: Critical Teaching for Social Change*. Chicago: University of Chicago Press.

Smit, David W. 2004. *The End of Composition Studies*. Carbondale: Southern Illinois University Press.

Wardle, Elizabeth. 2009. "'Mutt Genres' and the Goal of FYC: Can We Help Students Write the Genres of the University?" *College Composition and Communication* 60 (4): 765–789.

Yancey, Kathleen Blake, Matthew Davis, Liane Robertson, Kara Taczak, and Erin Workman. 2019. "The Teaching for Transfer Curriculum: The Role of Concurrent and Inside- and Outside-School Contexts in Supporting Students' Writing Development." *College Composition and Communication* 71 (2): 268–295.

Yancey, Kathleen Blake, Liane Robertson, and Kara Taczak. 2014. *Writing across Contexts: Transfer, Composition, and Sites of Writing*. Logan: Utah State University Press.

PART III

Multimodality and Transfer across the Writerly Life

7
DRAWING WORLDS TOGETHER
Tracing Semiotic Practices along Histories of Literate Activity

Kevin Roozen

Throughout her adolescent years, Laura Shilling (a pseudonym) routinely turned to her engagement with art, especially the freehand pencil and ink drawings she fashioned on the pages of the sketchbook that was her constant companion. No matter where she was—at home, at school, in the car—if she had a spare moment, Laura could be found picking up a pencil or pen and turning to a fresh page of her sketchbook. Explaining the many functions her drawing served for her, Laura stated during one of our early interviews: "I would draw when I had nothing to do or when I had a lot on my mind. It was, like, very relaxing. Like, drawing would be, like, my place to go. [It] would be kind of like my safe haven."

Laura's detailed sketch of the lion face shown in figure 7.1, for example, had its beginnings during some downtime she had between high school classes. Looking for a way to make the time pass and let her mind wander away from her academic work, Laura stated, "I just pulled up an image [of a lion face] that I liked on my phone, looked at it a couple of times, sat down, grabbed a pen, and just started drawing." Laboring over the sketch at odd moments, it took Laura several days to finish it, but when she was done, she was immensely proud of how it had turned out.

Laura's artistic talents did not go unnoticed by her friends. After catching some over-the-shoulder glimpses of Laura's drawings in her sketchbook or viewing some of the ones she posted on social media, many of Laura's friends routinely sought her out for drawings they could use to decorate their school lockers or their bedrooms, and others asked her to sketch out designs for tattoos they were considering. As Laura stated, "My friends saw that I could draw, because I would post my art and stuff [on social media], and then from there, they'd be, like, 'hey, could you draw me a tattoo?' Lions I drew so much in high school. But, like, a lot of people had requested lions for tattoos, so I had to get comfortable with it."

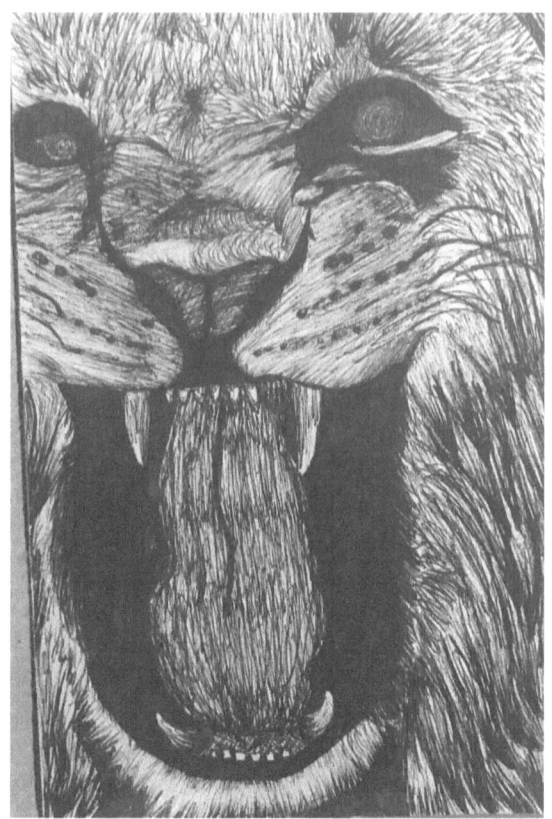

Figure 7.1. Ink drawing of a lion face Laura crafted in her sketchbook during her high school years

Laura's engagement with drawing served as a crucial means of relaxation and escape. And yet, as I have come to realize through researching her literate activities with her, drawing as a representational practice would trace a lengthy, unpredictable, yet highly consequential path through the richly literate landscape she would navigate throughout her life. In this chapter, I draw from a longitudinal study with Laura of her literate activities that collected a wide variety of her texts—supplemented by a series of observations of and text-based interviews about her textual practices over three years—and that also reached back to her earlier literate life, to explore how her drawing would come to texture her trajectory of engagement with science and medicine. Ultimately, I argue for taking up "literate activity" as a way to extend multimodal transfer research in ways that attend more fully to the richly embodied histories of semiotic tools and practices people continually act with and act from in composing literate lives across an ever expanding landscape of experiences.

LINKING MULTIMODALITY TO WRITING TRANSFER

In *The End of Composition Studies*, David W. Smit (2004, 132) asserted that beyond the basic knowledge that learners find ways of linking together seemingly diverse experiences with writing, there may be little more that research might reveal regarding how those linkages are made and the long-term impact they have on writing development. The years immediately following Smit's publication saw a wealth of writing studies scholarship address the question of "writing transfer," how students re-deploy writing-related knowledge and abilities to meet the textual demands of what seem like the novel contexts of college coursework (Beaufort 2007; Bergmann and Zepernick 2007; Reiff and Bawarshi 2011). Recognizing that dominant conceptions tended to emphasize the straightforward transmission or application of writing-related knowledge, Michael-John DePalma and Jeffery M. Ringer (2011) developed a theoretical perspective they referred to as "adaptive transfer" as a means of reconceptualizing understandings of transfer to illuminate how writing knowledge is transformed along students' histories. Challenging static models by addressing the dynamic, idiosyncratic, cross-contextual, rhetorical, multilingual, and transformative dimensions of how students carry forward writing knowledge, "adaptive transfer" served as a means of emphasizing "not only how students carry forward or reuse prior writing knowledge to fit new contexts, but also how they reshape or reform such prior knowledge" (135).

Considering a growing body of scholarship that examines students' multimodal composing practices (Alexander and Rhodes 2014; Buck 2012; Palmieri 2012; Selfe 2009), DePalma (2015) argued that notions of adaptive transfer also needed to extend beyond addressing multiple languages to include the dynamic reshaping of writing knowledge across multiple media and modalities. Among a number of productive lines of cultural historical activity theory that could be useful, DePalma reached specifically to Paul Prior and Jody Shipka's (2003) examinations of the rich histories of "repurposing," which they define as "the re-use and transformation of some text/semiotic object" (192, 238) that comes to be drawn into and shapes writers' activities as a particularly rich model for reconceptualizing the "interactions between activity systems, semiotic resources, and media" (DePalma 2015, 617)—particularly writers' "literate activities across media" (618). In suggesting Prior and Shipka (2003), DePalma echoed a similar move made by Kathleen Blake Yancey (2004) more than a decade earlier in her CCCC chair address where she also pointed to Prior and Shipka's (2003) research as a productive approach to expand not only the wealth and variety of semiotic repurposings that come to be woven into writer's literate activities but also the lengthy, continually emerging, and unpredictable histories along which those reuses come to take shape.

Coupling attention to multiple media and modalities with transfer offered writing transfer scholarship purchase on the wealth and variety of semiotic work at play in students' academic writing. In examining advanced undergraduate students, DePalma's (2015) multimodal perspective illuminated the print-based writing-related knowledge students adapted to create digital stories for class and pointed suggestively to students' refashioning of other literacies (e.g., religious worship, composing music) for use in their academic work. In their examination of advanced undergraduate and graduate students in digital writing classes, DePalma and Kara Poe Alexander (2015) gave attention to transfer across media that illuminated students' practices of weaving together multiple media to meet the rhetorical demand of digital composing. More recently, Ryan P. Shepherd's (2018) attention to multimodal transfer illuminated first-year composition students' histories with the semiotic tools associated with various social media platforms—such as Instagram, Snapchat, Pinterest, and YouTube—and gestured toward their more extensive histories with other semiotics.

Scholarship has increasingly called for studies that can account as fully as possible for the continually emerging circulations of bodies, texts, technologies, and material spaces that make writing possible (Ringer and Morey 2021; Rule 2019; Anson, foreword, this volume; Knutson, chapter 5, this volume). In this chapter, I echo and extend Yancey's (2004) and DePalma's (2015) invitations to take up Prior and Shipka's (2003) attention to the rich semiotic histories mediating writers' activities as a productive lens for conceptualizing and mapping the chains of semiotic practices that trace across people's lives and lifeworlds. In particular, I elaborate "literate activity" (Prior 1998; Prior and Shipka 2003) as generative ground for expanding contemporary approaches for multimodal transfer scholarship to address the richly and historically multi-semiotic character of embodied textual practice.

ATTENDING TO LITERATE ACTIVITY

To gain some purchase on Laura's history of engagement with drawing, I turn to "literate activity" as a way of understanding the multiple and complex semiotic-material histories that shape people's experiences of what we typically refer to as "writing." Drawing together sociocultural perspectives that posit human activity as mediated by people acting with semiotic tools along dialogic histories of action (Bakhtin 1986; Holland et al. 1998; Voloshinov 1973; Vygotsky 1987; Wertsch 1991, 1998) and rhizomatic material ontologies (Barad 2007; Latour 2005), Prior (1998, 2015) forwards "literate activity" as a construct that productively challenged the notion of "writing" as a discretely bound act of transcribing a text-privileging written language as the dominant semiotic mode. Defining literate activity as not "located in acts of reading and writing, but *as* cultural forms of life saturated with textuality that [are] strongly motivated and mediated by texts" (138, original emphasis), Prior (1998; see also Durst 2019; Prior 2006, 2015; Prior and Shipka 2003; Prior and Smith 2020; Ware 2022) sought to address writing as a fully embodied activity emerging from and extending along the dialogic histories of textuality that come to texture people's lives.

As a framework, literate activity stresses three particularly important ideas. First, literate activity makes visible people's concrete engagements with a rich variety of semiotic resources. In describing literate activity as "cultural forms of life saturated with textuality," Prior (1998, 70) signals the notion that writing is implicated in and emerges from historically unfolding threads of activity layered with confluences of multiple semiotic tools and modalities, including "talk, text, bodily stance and gesture, graphics, mathematics, and other symbolic activity woven together in threads of interactional history." Literate activity, then, invites attention to the ways people's textual engagements implicate what Prior and Steve Thorne (2014, 46) would come to describe as the "multiple semiotics" of fully embodied people acting with semiotic artifacts in the world, including "reading, talk, embodied action and gesture, visual design, observation and manipulation of material and virtual objects, inner semiotics of thinking, feeling, and attention." The diverse arrays of semiotic tools made visible by attending to literate activity would lead Prior and a series of coauthors and colleagues toward constructs that include "semiotic performance" and "semiotic remediation" (Prior and Hengst 2010; Prior et al. 2006), "semiotic agility" (Prior 2010), and "semiotic becoming" (Prior 2018; Prior and Olinger 2019; see also Ware 2022) as a way of addressing how writing comes to be implicated across acts of semiosis and how deftly people's embodied entanglements with semiotic resources as "artifacts-in-activity" (Prior 2006, 58) weave together and across multiple semiotic modes.[1]

Second, a literate activity perspective illuminates the length, breadth, and complexity of the semiotic histories that shape writing. "Writing," Prior (2006, 64) suggests, "emerges out of far-flung historical networks, and the trajectories of a particular text trace delicate paths through overgrown sociohistoric landscapes"; thus, it invites writing researchers "to trace and understand an increasingly complex semiotic phenomena dispersed across widening spatiotemporal networks of activity and mediated by a growing array of tools." In their oft-cited definition of literate activity as "the dispersed and fluid chains . . . that come to be tied together in trajectories of literate action," Prior and Shipka (2003, 181) assert that such historical chains not only reach across people's engagements with various "places, times, people, and artifacts" but also extend along "trajectories of activity that are often ambiguous and fuzzy; that may be tied, untied, and retied; and that stretch across official cultural boundaries" (208). Rather than locating people's embodied histories with semiotic tools as corralled within discrete, autonomous moments, acts, or contexts as containers, literate activity locates them dispersed along far-flung histories of meaning-making experiences that reach back to the embodied lifeworlds of near and distant pasts and are propelled toward lifeworlds of near and distant potential futures.[2] In this sense, literate activity does not just address people's uses of a wide array of semiotics but also offers a dialogic semiotics that addresses the profound "acrossness" histories of entanglements as they are continually reworked through time and space (Prior and Smith 2020; Ware 2022).

Third, literate activity invites attention to development, to the ways the complex histories of acting with semiotic resources are not just avenues of travel across time, space, and modalities but rather function as the very pathways along which people, artifacts, practices, and social worlds are continually in the making.[3] In this sense, literate activity not only addresses "a process whereby texts are produced, exchanged, and used, but [is] also part of a continuous sociohistoric process in which persons, artifacts, practices, institutions, and communities are being formed and reformed" (Prior 1998, 139). To describe the important role semiotically equipped histories of embodied activity through the world play in the ongoing production of people, artifacts, practices for acting with them, and the social worlds they populate, Prior (2018) would draw on Karen Barad's (2007) notion of "intra-action" to describe these pathways as "trajectories of semiotic becoming" (also Smith and Prior 2020). These are emergent pathways laid down as embodied activity draws confluences of semiotic tools into focal engagements in which all elements are brought together, elaborated, and then propelled toward later moments of intra-action further along the stream of ongoing life—a process through which semiotic elements slowly, incrementally come to be textured with a continuous potentiality for reuse. Because such trajectories emerge from the interweaving of multiple semiotic material histories textured with varying degrees of agency, synergy, turbulence, and consequence (Ware 2022), they are continually emergent and thus do not track neatly through predictable routes and stages or toward pre-established teleological endpoints. For Smith and Prior (2020, 1), these continually and unpredictably emergent trajectories that interweave multiple histories "across activity systems, across practices, across identities, across semiotic modes, and across the moments that add up to (re)make both the person and social life" function as the pathways "for becoming throughout all domains of the lifeworld and throughout the lifespan" (Prior and Smith 2020, 9).

Literate activity, then, offers a productive way of conceptualizing the pathways writing traces through the flow of lived experience, especially "how thoroughly and necessarily life involves the historically unfolding blend (and it is always a blend) of multiple semiotic resources including oral language, embodied action and gesture, perception of environments, written texts, films, music, and touch" (Prior 2014, 160). A focus on literate activity highlights the confluences of semiotic practices people act with across engagements that range from fleeting to sustained. It likewise makes visible the ways those semiotic histories reach across dominant mappings of timescales and social worlds and points to the function of these trajectories in propelling the continual becoming of people, the semiotic artifacts they act with, their practices for acting with them, and the social worlds they impact.

In the sections that follow, I take up literate activity to first examine Laura's engagement with drawing. Next, I explore how Laura's drawing as a representational practice comes to be woven into her interest in studying medicine across her semiotic performances for a high school art class.

"YOU KNOW, YOU CAN DO THAT. YOU HAVE TALENT"

Laura, the youngest of three daughters, grew up in a small town in the northern midwestern United States. Throughout her childhood, her two main interests involved sports and art, both of which were central features of her family life. While she credits her father, who coached her softball team, with fostering her fondness for sports, she acknowledges that her oldest sister—almost six years older than Laura—sparked her interest in art. Her oldest sister, Laura indicated, was really into art, especially drawing and painting, and had majored in art and design at the large public university she attended. Laura reported looking throughout her childhood at all of the pieces of her sister's artwork her mother had hung all over their house. In addition to a painting of her other sister, Laura recalled that she was especially drawn to one of her oldest sister's self-portraits showcased on a wall in the family's living room that featured "just her face, and she had drawn it out of lyrics of one of her favorite songs. So it's all words. The entire portrait is words."

Recalling seeing her sister working on her art pieces and talking with her about them during her weekend visits from college, Laura stated "and I was, like, 'that's cool.' And my mom was, like, 'you know, you could do that. You have talent.' And I was, like [sarcastically], 'sure. Sure I do.'" Encouraged by her mother's entreaties for her to "just pick up a pencil and start," eventually Laura stated that "I started to draw a little bit, and then I really got into it once people were telling me, like, 'oh, you're good.' So I was, like, 'I guess I'll keep doing it.'" She enrolled in community art classes during middle school, and by the time she was around fourteen she noticed that art had become her "thing" and that she started to gain some recognition as an artist. Recalling one of the pieces she did during middle school, Laura stated, "I remember that I did this painting of a Laffy Taffy logo. And . . . the principal liked it so much that he kept it in his office. That's when I was kind of, like, 'oh, people see me if I do art. And I liked the attention, in a good way. So then I was, like, 'well, let me keep doing it.'"

Eventually, Laura gravitated toward drawing, particularly with a fine-pointed ink pen. "I did a lot with painting," Laura stated, "but I realized that I really like pen because I can control it. I feel like I have more control over it. And I feel like you get more out of it. More depth and more detail." She added that while it might not look like it, drawing with pen "is a lot more personal than it seems to be." As we browsed through the pages of her sketchbooks, Laura indicated that her drawings have always tended to be what she called "very nature-focused." Initially, they featured outdoor scenes, particularly of mountains and other kinds of terrain she wanted to see and experience one day or of geographic features of her favorite places around her hometown. Slowly, she gravitated toward drawing animals, typically focusing on their heads and faces (figure 7.2). As her friends began to request designs for tattoos, she also devoted more time and space in her sketchbook to coming up with small designs they might like to use and that she herself might want to get one day.

As we browsed through her drawings, Laura frequently commented on the affective dimension of her artwork. "It's very emotional," she stated while we were looking through the fifty pages of sketches in her most recent sketchbook. "Everything [I draw] has to do with emotional

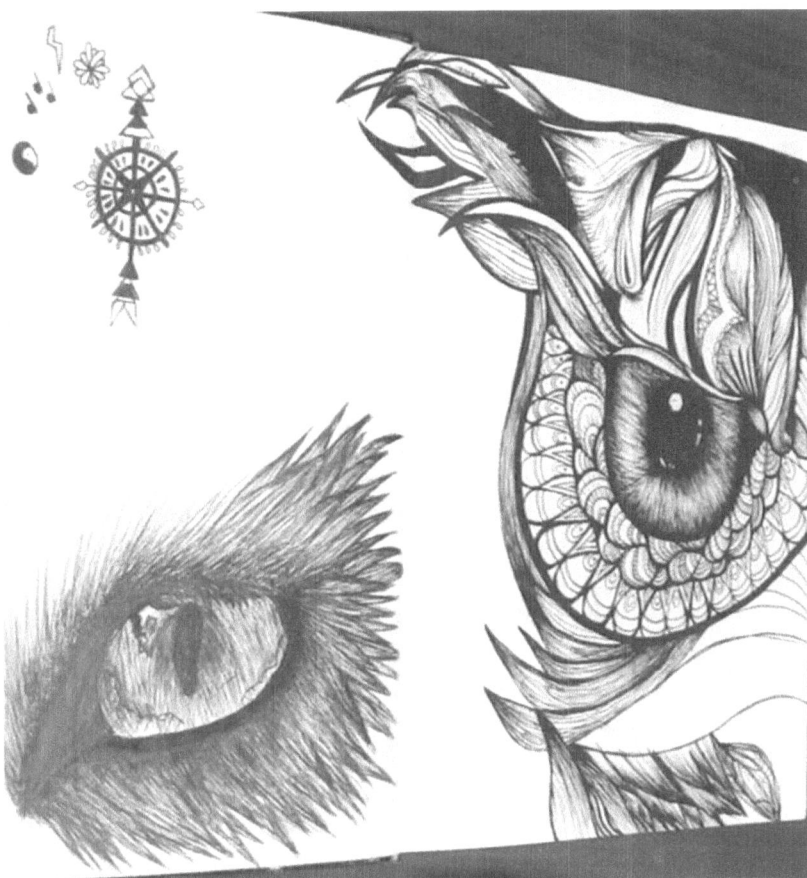

Figure 7.2. Two facing pages from a sketchbook Laura kept during her high school years. At top left are some tattoo designs she had been experimenting with. The two large sketches are versions of eyes Laura was considering for drawings of a series of different animals she had been working on. At bottom left is an eye of a lion. At right is an eye for an owl.

ties [I have] to it . . . All these animal [drawings] are about, these have to do with the emotion I connect with that animal. Like, when you think of lions, what do you think of? You think of being on top, being strong. When I think of an owl, I think of being confident and smart."

Laura's inclination toward drawing figured prominently in her relationships with her family and friends. It also shaped the pace and path of her engagement with medicine at key moments and in crucial ways throughout her ongoing life. I turn now to partially tracing the history of this semiotic practice as it comes to be entangled with Laura's encounters with medicine across her high school coursework.

"LET'S START THINKING ABOUT WHAT YOU WANT TO DO"

Anticipating her final year of high school, Laura recalled that although she knew college was in her future, she did not have a sense of what she wanted to focus on. While many of her friends had known all throughout high school what they would major in as undergraduates, Laura indicated that "that was not me. I wasn't, like, 'okay, I'm going to go to college for *this*.' I didn't really know what I wanted to study in college. So I was, like, 'let's start thinking about what you want to do.'" Throughout high school, she had enrolled in whatever courses had interested her, regardless of how coherently they pointed toward any particular field. She recalled briefly considered pursuing a major in art, as her oldest sister had recently completed a BA in art and design and had taken a design position in a marketing department at a large corporation. She stated, though, that she did not give art any serious consideration, in part because she did not want to be seen as simply following in her oldest sister's footsteps and also because she did not see herself as talented enough to make a living with her drawing.

According to Laura, one possibility she had entertained every now and again involved studying medicine and health. She had navigated a number of illnesses as a child, including an irregular heartbeat, and one of her younger relatives had been diagnosed with a genetically inherited condition. These experiences had prompted an interest in human science courses. Despite her curiosity regarding some medicine-related field and perhaps even medical school or nursing school, she was somewhat reluctant to focus her efforts in that direction. While she had enjoyed her human science courses, she confessed that she had not always performed well in them. "What's weird," she stated, "is that I liked science, but it wouldn't show in my grades . . . I don't remember doing that great . . . So I was kind of like 'and college is going to be *so much* harder [than high school].'"

One of the courses Laura was slated to take during her final year of high school was a two-semester IB (International Baccalaureate) studio art class with a teacher who encouraged her students to select a particular theme to explore across the various projects they would be working on throughout the year. As a way of determining if medicine might be a viable major for her, Laura decided she would focus her work on what she referred to as "medical-based stuff."

One of the major projects during the first semester of the class introduced students to three-dimensional modeling with clay. Laura's work began with creating a series of detailed life-size models of major bodily organs (e.g., the heart, the brain) (figure 7.3) and appendages (e.g.,

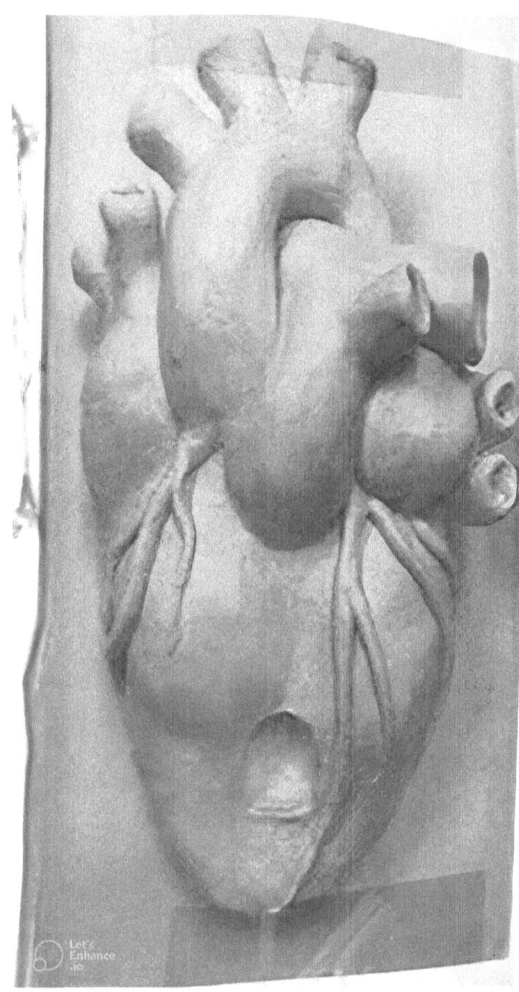

Figure 7.3. Black-and-white photograph of a clay model of a life-size heart Laura created in her studio art class. Laura kept this photograph taped to a page of her sketchbook.

hands, feet), eventually leading to her creating a life-size model of a heart fully enclosed in a ribcage (figure 7.4).

Laura recalled that her initial forays with "medical-based stuff" throughout her first semester of studio art had been productive, so much so that for the second semester of her senior year, while still taking the studio art class, she decided to enroll in IB Medical Terminology, a class focused on introducing students to the common root words, prefixes, and suffixes used in medical discourse. On the first day of Medical Terminology, Laura's teacher invited the students to take home some of the old biology and anatomy textbooks the school had previously used so that students could use them as resources. Laura helped herself to an

Figure 7.4. Facing pages of Laura's sketchbook as she and I interact with some of the contents through talk and gesture. On the left page are black-and-white photographs of the life-size clay model of a rib cage surrounding a broken heart that Laura created for her studio art class. On the right is a quick doodle of a heart pierced by an arrow.

armload of the books, and she recalled using them regularly to supplement the main course materials.

According to Laura, those old textbooks also offered a ready source of inspiration for her studio art projects that semester. Rather than finding and viewing images and information solely on her phone or her computer, she often found herself browsing the pages of the biology and anatomy texts, looking at the images and skimming the prose. One of the major studio art projects during the spring semester invited students to elaborate on the theme of "loss" using a multiple-panel drawing or painting. Inspired by some of the detailed images of the human heart she had encountered in the biology text she had taken home, Laura decided to represent "heartbreak" using anatomically detailed drawings of the human heart and other bits of medical discourse to depict the

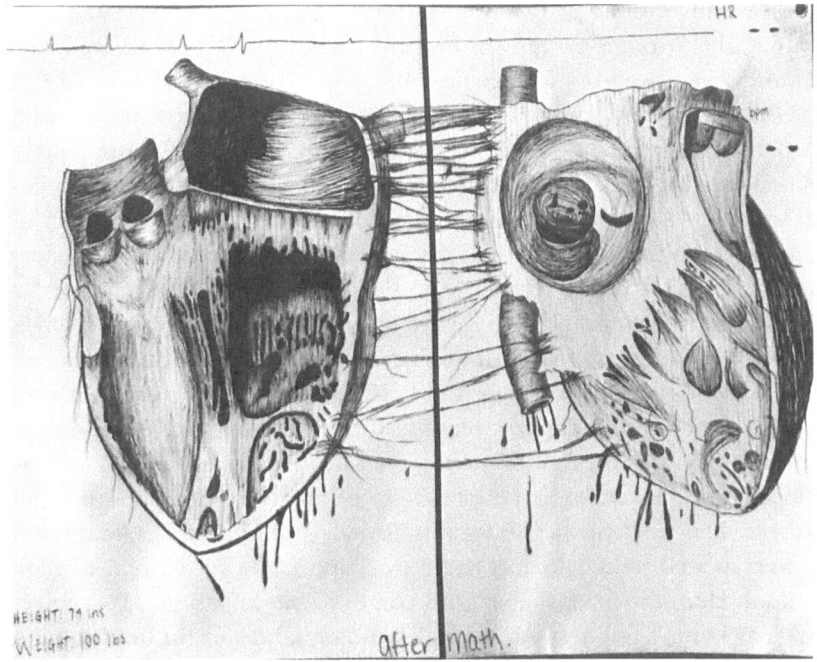

Figure 7.5. Image of the bottom portion of Laura's "heartbreak" project created during the second semester of studio art

physiological changes the human heart goes through as two people fall in love, become content, and then break up.

The final version of her project took the form of four 8.5- × 11.0-inch panels pinned to a large, dark poster-size background. Laura used the two panels at the top to represent "love" and being "content," providing for each a detailed drawing she did of the human heart in that state as well as numerical figures for heart rhythm accompanied by the line (oscillating wave) offered on an EKG reading for heart beats per minute and for the person's height and weight.

Laura used the two panels at the bottom of the poster to depict the physiological changes a person encounters as the relationship ends (figure 7.5), by offering anatomically detailed drawings of a human heart that has been cleaved in half. As with her representations of the other stages, this one also provides numerical figures for heart rhythm accompanied by the line offered on an EKG reading (*top*), for heart beats per minute (*toward top right, almost eclipsed by the heart*), and for the person's height and weight (*bottom left*). She includes the words "after math" across the panels (*bottom center*).

Illustrative of how "the trajectories of a particular text trace delicate paths through overgrown historical landscapes" (Prior 2006, 64), Laura's extensive work for her heartbreak piece emerges along a stream of literate activity woven from far-flung histories of experiences with a dense array of the "multiple semiotics" Prior and Thorne (2014) describe. This work offers a history of dynamic entangling that includes at least, but is certainly not limited to: Laura's childhood experience of illness, including her irregular heartbeat; her embodied experiences with art, which reach across encounters with multiple generations of her family members and include the piece of her sister's artwork (which entangled word and image) hanging on the wall of the family home; Laura's own artwork (creating the Laffy Taffy painting, doing her own drawings and tattoo designs, sending images of them on her phone to social media postings) and encounters with community and school art classes; and her embodied experiences of breaking up with significant others. This work further illustrates how all of those threads, and many others as well, entangle and come to shape Laura's final year of high school. Here the work shapes, and comes to be shaped by, experiences such as Laura's felt desire to identify a potential major for her future as an undergraduate; her focus on "medical-related stuff" for the studio art class, which includes making clay models and drawings of body parts during the first semester and later, during the second term, creating the "heartbreak" piece; and her decision to enroll in Medical Terminology, where she encountered a host of semiotic representations of medical discourse—including talk, visual images, and written language across the pages of textbooks, phones, and laptops. The semiotic activity of Laura's heartbreak piece, in other words, draws all of this together.

It is along this pathway of entangled semiotic material histories—a path that reaches "across activity systems, across practices, across identities, across semiotic modes, and across the moments that add up to (re)make both the person and social life" (Prior and Smith 2020, 1)—that Laura's drawing as a meaning-making practice has come to be a means of participating in the academic study and practice of art to and of exploring medicine as a potential academic major. The social world of her studio art class has come to be a space where Laura could explore medicine as a potential undergraduate major and possible career. This pathway had implications for Laura's identity as well. By the end of her senior year of high school, Laura had decided to pursue a focus on medicine for her undergraduate work when she started college in the fall, with the possibility of attending medical school or nursing school. By the end of her first year of college, her goal was to earn a spot in her university's nursing program.

ENTANGLING ART AND MEDICINE ACROSS COLLEGE YEARS

Laura's entangling of art and medicine did not just lead a brief, fleeting half-life and then disappear. The interweaving of these semiotic material histories, which was certainly not without multiple tensions and challenges, would continue to be drawn into and along a trajectory of becoming that would have consequence throughout her life. Below, I offer brief vignettes of just two points during her college years where Laura's drawings rewove her trajectories of art, medicine, and life.

One afternoon while visiting her parents' house during the summer after her first year of college, Laura began to browse through some of the old textbooks her high school Medical Terminology teacher had given her, which were stored in her bedroom closet. Scanning the pages, she became intrigued with a series of images offering front and back perspectives of the human leg muscles. She had not done any drawing for a while, so she decided to create her own versions of the images in her sketchbook (figure 7.6). As Laura stated, "I was really, I was kind of bored, and I was, like, 'well, let me try and draw this [the image of the leg muscles], but more realistic.' And so I did a detailed version of it, and it was like very unproportional but I was, like, 'whatever, just let me try to get, like, the scale to it.'" Using the image in the old textbook as a kind of guide, Laura worked in brief but intense spurts over the next two weeks, devoting about sixteen hours to generate sketches of both front and back perspectives.

This drawing, among others she did that summer (including, incidentally, a series of detailed drawings of human hearts she referred to as her "heart sketches"), would impact Laura's life and learning in a number of ways as she struggled through the coursework for her nursing program over her next two years of college. And it would come to figure prominently in her decision to explore the field of medical illustration, a decision that would eventually prompt her to forgo participation in the nursing program so she could enroll in her university's newly founded interdisciplinary studies major and assemble a curriculum that allowed her to take coursework with a dual emphasis in biomedicine and art.

Laura's entangling of her semiotic material histories with art and medicine would also figure prominently throughout her final year of college as she worked to identity potential career directions.

This drawing (figure 7.7) of a skeleton that Laura did for her Drawing I class—one of the first art classes she took during the beginning of her final year of college—would also come to shape Laura's life. One of several skeleton drawings Laura worked on throughout the course, it would eventually function as one of the pieces Laura submitted as part of her application materials for a competitive internship with the art therapy program at one of the city's large hospitals. It is one of three she selected to send because she "felt like they showcased my drawing abilities, especially with organic form."

Based in part on the drawings she submitted, Laura was selected for the internship, a position in the hospital's oncology unit making art with patients as they received chemotherapy treatments. Her working with oncology patients on their art prompted Laura to recognize a need for someone who could, as she described it excitedly to me, "make art *for* them, so they can understand their diagnosis." Through making art with patients, Laura hit on the idea of serving as a type of oncology patient advocate who would "teach patients about their diagnosis through visuals and art . . . like, to help them with understanding what their body is going to go through. And use layman's terms rather than the Latin and confusing terms that doctor's use" by creating a personalized guidebook for each patient under her care. The guidebooks she envisioned would "provide patients with a lot of information . . . about symptoms, for each step of their treatment, like radiation, chemo, surgery, post-op, just all of that stuff, and then certain medications, what the symptoms would be, why they are going to happen, certain things like that. And I would also include images, um, I would want to, for

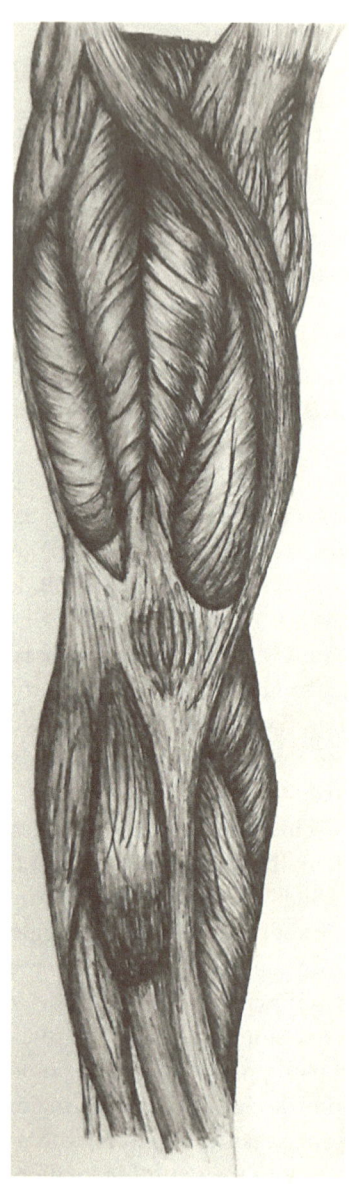

Figure 7.6. Laura's sketch offering a front perspective of the human leg muscles, based on an image she encountered in one the old textbooks she received from her high school Medical Terminology teacher.

Drawing Worlds Together 161

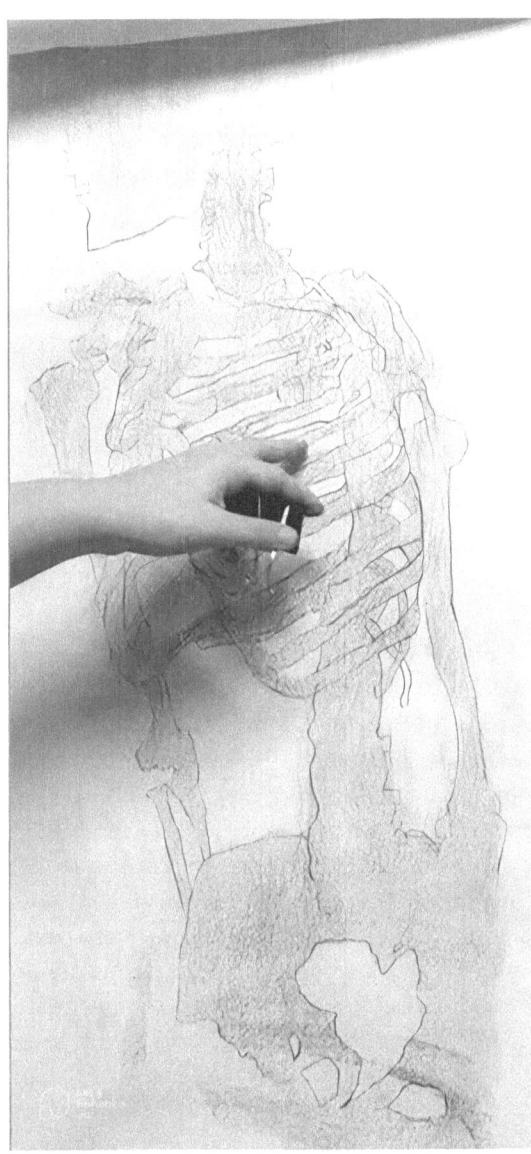

Figure 7.7. Laura interacts through talk and gesture with an early, in-process version of one of the skeleton sketches from her Drawing I class she would later choose to include with her internship application.

surgery, create, like, a video of what's going to go on. And then also add visuals of, like, why certain things happen. Things I would draw. So if I were to talk to a patient about something and they did not understand it, I would draw it for them."

Throughout her final semester of college, Laura worked hard to try to chart a career path that would allow her to extend her history of weaving together art and medicine. Still interested in pursuing a career in medical illustration, Laura drafted statements of intent and selected a handful of her drawings for the portfolio she needed to apply to two graduate medical illustration programs that had captured her interest. She also explored patient advocate positions, seeking to identify or possibly create for herself a job in which she could fashion the kinds of patient guidebooks she had imaged. Despite taking an overload of classes, Laura met with everyone she knew who worked in healthcare, from nurses to patient advocates to her mother's physician, to get their input about career possibilities. As she stated, "I am trying to go to all these different healthcare specialists to get their input on how I can do what I want to do." When she could not meet with them in person, Laura contacted healthcare professionals by phone to explore how she might go about creating the kind of patient advocate position she envisioned for herself. By the time she graduated at the end of the term, she had decided that her best move would be to "apply for jobs as a patient advocate. That's a start."

REACHING TOWARD FULLER ENGAGEMENT WITH HISTORIES OF SEMIOTIC PRACTICE

Chris M. Anson (2016, 542–543) argues that writing transfer research is well positioned to usher teachers across the university toward "understanding much deeper and more challenging ideas about interrelationships between students' existing knowledge or experience and the nature, constraints, and activity systems of the writing they are asked . . . to produce." The "deeper and more challenging ideas" Anson envisions would need to emerge, at least in part, from detailed accounts of writing as part of literate activity and learning as a facet of semiotic becoming that attend to the rich diversity of semiotic practices people act with and how those practices come to have consequence for people's lives. It's crucial, then, that writing research provide accounts of writing and becoming that address the richly equipped semiotic material histories that tangle together to make up the continually unfolding confluence of lived, embodied experience. If, as Prior (2018, introduction) writes, becoming emerges from "spaces that are never pure or settled, where discourses and knowledge are necessarily heterogeneous, and where multiple semiotic resources are so deeply entangled that distinct modes simply don't make sense," then we'll need to acknowledge and value that rich diversity. It matters, then, and matters a great deal, how capaciously we understand the semiotic practices that are relevant to making meanings and living and how capaciously we configure the lengthy, heterogeneously situated histories through and along which people's actings with a wealth of semiotic resources unfold and come to matter.

For multimodal transfer researchers, coupling multimodal composing with adaptive transfer has brought a great deal into view. As the blurry, blended, continually unfolding, and imminently unpredictable trajectories of semiotic materialities come into view, it is vitally important to understand and trace those pathways without occluding, confusing, and severing the very histories writing research seeks to comprehend. Literate activity offers productive theoretical and methodological grounds for doing so. What directions, then, might this very partial tracing of the delicate paths literate activity draws throughout Laura's socio-historic lifeworld open for researchers working at the intersections of multimodal composing and transfer?

First, attention to literate activity illuminates the wealth and variety of semiotic tools people act with and that come to be entangled throughout literate action. By attending to rich semiotic textualities rather than the narrow semiotics typically associated with "writing" and "reading," literate activity is attuned to the ways diverse, blended semiotics animate a broad array of meaning-making activities across continually unfolding flows of life. To focus exclusively on any particular semiotic resource or even a privileged few brings some moments of such flows into finer focus but obscures others; the result is that the flow can come to appear as a series of discrete, autonomous, isolated pools in need of being bridged. Focusing on Laura's tactile engagement with the clay models of hearts would certainly illuminate her engagement with that medium in her high school studio art class but would occlude her other engagements with hearts (her experience of her heart condition, her drawings of hearts, the images of hearts she encountered on the pages of print sources such as textbooks, and so on). A tight focus on the visual dimensions of Laura's artwork, whether on paper pads or digital screens, would foreground her drawings but obscure how they are interwoven with written prose in her heartbreak piece; her embodied engagements with the oncology patients she has been seeing, talking with, and co-experiencing strong emotions with during her internship; and her use of images in the patient guidebooks she envisions. Attending to literate activity can help multimodal transfer research more fully account for the wealth and diversity of semiotic tools that shape writing and can help keep the complexity of material semiotic histories alive in analyses and accounts of writing and becoming.

Second, attention to literate activity illuminates how concrete acting with semiotic resources—the lived experience of semiotic practice—shapes action. Rather than merely offering a way of attending to an expanded list of inert, disembodied semiotic resources, attending to literate activity invites viewing those resources as artifacts-in-activity, as semiotic tools acting with people to do work in the world. Laura's engagements with her drawings, for example, involve not just creating them on the pages of her sketchbook but also the embodied activity of acting with them by showing them to other people—which involves Laura and others in enlivening the drawings with talk, gesture, and gaze; engaging with affective intensities associated with them; taking photos of them and posting them to social media; combining them with written prose and other images, and so on. In addition to providing multimodal transfer researchers with a way to attend to what people do with the semiotic tools they encounter, attention to literate activity also invites attention to the impact such practices have on action. It invites, in other words, attention to what entanglements of semiotic tools do and how they do it, to ways tools do less and more than what people might consciously intend, and to ways they draw together seemingly disparate worlds and activities. Attention to literate activity, then, can help multimodal transfer researchers work toward accounts of what people do with semiotic tools, what tools do with people, and the enduring impact and consequence they have (Kell 2015). It likewise encourages researchers to examine the synergies and tensions (Ware 2022) that animate entanglings of people acting with tools and to be alert to how such assemblages are not located in individuals and contexts but rather are dispersed along chains of semiotic practice.

Third, attention to literate activity illuminates the expansive histories people acting with semiotic artifacts trace through the world, the synergies and tensions that animate those histories, the fleeting and enduring timescales they extend across, and how "unpredictable encounters" (Tsing 2015, 20) transform flows in myriad ways. Focusing on the flows of semiotic materialities only as they circulate within the assumed temporal, spatial, and social borders of routine, culturally given territories brings some moments of the flow into finer focus, but it also severs the flow, truncating the historical materiality of their becoming. Laura's drawing as a representational practice as she grew up with her sister and mother, for example, traces a history that is not confined to her family life. It weaves through her semiotic repurposing of her drawing as a practice during encounters with community art classes, with high school and college coursework, with a hospital internship, and into the potential futures she imagines for herself in terms of a career. As a semiotic practice, Laura's drawing emerges as a lifetime in the making across acts, modalities, people, and artifacts. Focusing only on the histories within privileged official spaces can make it appear that those are the only moments in which becoming occurs, or at least that they are the moments that matter the most. Attention to literate activity, then, can help multimodal transfer researchers understand the expansive histories along which becoming occurs and the ways those histories continually reach across, and thereby weave together, seemingly separate domains of life.

The kinds of "ethnographically oriented and longitudinal studies" Anson (foreword, this volume) calls for that trace those histories across settings and throughout sites are essential for making visible the ways people and semiotic resources are reworked across a historically linked series of actions. Attention to the far-flung histories of literate activity also encourages multimodal transfer research to continue to extend the productive directions that have already emerged from its studies, particularly challenges to the "alphabetic-centric bias" and the strong focus on schooling that Yancey (afterword, this volume) identifies as continuing to dominate notions of what writing is and where it is learned and perhaps particularly toward exploring the wealth and variety of inscriptions and inscriptional practices (Roozen 2020, 2021) that entangle throughout what a growing number of scholars have come to call "the everyday" (Barton and Hamilton 1998; Cintron 1997; Sinor 2002; Yancey 2020; Yancey et al. 2020) and the consequences they hold as they come to be entwined in literate development.

"Becoming," Prior (2018, conclusions) writes, "is entangled complexly, materially, historically." Accounts of the delicate paths through the overgrown socio-historic landscapes textualities trace as they come to be—fine-grained accounts that acknowledge and value multiple semiotics and that address fuzzy, blurry, lengthy histories—are indeed complex and messy, and necessarily so. However complex and messy they might be, I would argue that it is vital to build accounts of the diversity of semiotics continually being assembled into textual moments, changed in those dynamic intra-actions, propelled out along the pathway of literate life, then pulled again into later moments of action—only to be further changed and then cast out yet again and again and again. Without perspectives that can account for the rich diversity of semiotic tools people act with and their historical repurposing along the confluent flow of ongoing life, we will miss so much of what writing is and what it entails, of what it does and how it does it, of the heterogeneous activities it implicates. Without following trajectories of people and tools across the twisting, braiding, entangling worlds they trace over time, we will miss so much of the lived experience of assembling a life across landscapes saturated with textuality. And without those hard-won insights, we will struggle to come to terms with how we might more equitably and responsively support the historical becoming of people and tools, of practices of being and knowing, and of our emerging and continually emergent social worlds.

NOTES

1. Taking up *semiotic* as the grounding for literate activity addresses a number of issues associated with the term *multimodal*, including researchers' strong tendency to conflate multimodality with digitality (Fraiberg 2017; Shipka 2011), to focus on objects rather than practices, and to focus attention on various modalities themselves as separate channels and thus to elide people's embodied entanglings of them across moments of action.
2. As it reaches across seemingly disparate social worlds, literate activity also entangles those worlds. Prior draws on Goffman's (1974, 1981) notion of lamination—the way multiple, heterogeneous social frames and footings are dynamically and agentively woven into moments of action; how multiple activities coexist, are immanent, in any situation— to conceptualize the way literate acts come to be textured by an accumulated and ever accumulating heterogeneity and heterochronicity of social action. In this sense, a literate activity perspective makes visible how each moment of literate activity, according to Prior (1998, 277), "implicates multiple activities, weaves together histories, and exists within the . . . networks of lifeworlds where boundaries of time and space are highly permeable." In other words, literate activity "melds together supposedly separate domains of life" (Prior and Shipka 2003, 205).
3. For Prior (2006, 55), the term *act with* highlights an explicit recognition that action is accomplished by people acting with semiotic tools as an irreducible entanglement. In examining people's literate activities, "act with" also serves as a way of explicitly signaling people's lived, embodied, material engagement with such tools as "artifacts-in-activity" (58) in ways that can be easily obscured by terms such as *writing* and *reading*.

REFERENCES

Alexander, Jonathan, and Jacqueline Rhodes. 2014. *On Multimodality: New Media in Composition Studies.* Champaign, IL: National Council of Teachers of English.

Anson, Chris M. 2016. "The Pop Warner Chronicles: A Case Study in Contextual Adaptation and the Transfer of Writing Ability." *College Composition and Communication* 67 (4): 518–549.

Bakhtin, Mikhail. 1986. *Speech Genres and Other Late Essays.* Translated by Vern W. McGee. Edited by Caryl Emerson and Michael Holquist. Austin: University of Texas Press.

Barad, Karen. 2007. *Meeting the Universe Halfway: Quantum Physics and the Entanglement of Matter and Meaning.* Durham, NC: Duke University Press.

Barton, David, and Mary Hamilton. 1998. *Local Literacies: Reading and Writing in One Community.* London: Routledge.

Beaufort, Anne. 2007. *College Writing and Beyond: A New Framework for University Writing Instruction.* Logan: Utah State University Press.

Bergmann, Linda, and Janet Zepernick. 2007. "Disciplinarity and Transference: Students' Perceptions of Learning to Write." *WPA: A Journal of Writing Program Administration* 31 (1): 124–149.

Buck, Amber. 2012. "Examining Digital Literacy Practices on Social Network Sites." *Research in the Teaching of English* 47 (1): 9–38.

Cintron, Ralph. 1997. *Angels' Town: Chero Ways, Gang Life, and Rhetorics of the Everyday.* Boston: Beacon.

DePalma, Michael-John. 2015. "Tracing Transfer across Media: Investigating Writers' Perceptions of Cross-Contextual and Rhetorical Reshaping in Processes of Remediation." *College Composition and Communication* 66 (4): 615–642.

DePalma, Michael-John, and Kara Poe Alexander. 2015. "A Bag Full of Snakes: Negotiating the Challenges of Multimodal Composition." *Computers and Composition* 37: 182–200.

DePalma, Michael-John, and Jeffrey M. Ringer. 2011. "Toward a Theory of Adaptive Transfer: Expanding Disciplinary Discussions of 'Transfer' in Second-Language Writing and Composition Studies." *Journal of Second Language Writing* 20: 134–147.

Durst, Sarah. 2019. "Disciplinarity and Literate Activity in Civil and Environmental Engineering: A Lifeworld Perspective." *Written Communication* 36 (4): 471–502.

Fraiberg, Steve. 2017. "Pretty Bullets: Tracing Transmedia/Translingual Literacies of an Israeli Soldier across Regimes of Practice." *College Composition and Communication* 69 (1): 87–117.

Goffman, Erving. 1974. *Frame Analysis: An Essay on the Organization of Experience.* Cambridge, MA: Harvard University Press.

Goffman, Erving. 1981. *Forms of Talk.* Philadelphia: University of Pennsylvania Press.

Holland, Dorothy, William Lachicotte, Debra Skinner, and Carole Cain. 1998. *Identity and Agency in Cultural Worlds.* Cambridge, MA: Harvard University Press.

Kell, Catherine. 2015. "Making People Happen: Materiality and Movement in Meaning-Making Trajectories." *Social Semiotics* 25 (4): 423–435.

Latour, Bruno. 2005. *Reassembling the Social: An Introduction to Actor-Network Theory.* Oxford: Oxford University Press.

Palmieri, Jason. 2012. *Remixing Composition: A History of Multimodal Writing Pedagogy.* Carbondale: Southern Illinois University Press.

Prior, Paul. 1998. *Writing/Disciplinarity: A Sociohistoric Account of Literate Activity in the Academy.* Mahwah, NJ: Lawrence Erlbaum Associates.

Prior, Paul. 2006. "A Sociocultural Theory of Writing." In *Handbook of Writing Research,* edited by Charles A. MacArthur, 54–66. New York: Guilford.

Prior, Paul. 2008. "Flat CHAT? Reassembling Literate Activity." Paper presented at Writing Research across Borders. Santa Barbara, CA, February 22–24.

Prior, Paul. 2010. "Remaking IO: Semiotic Remediation in the Design Process." In *Exploring Semiotic Remediation as Discourse Practice,* edited by Paul Prior and Julie Hengst, 206–234. London: Palgrave/Macmillan.

Prior, Paul. 2014. "Semiotics." In *The Routledge Companion to English Studies,* edited by Constant Leung and Brian Street, 160–173. London: Routledge.

Prior, Paul. 2015. "Writing, Literate Activity, Semiotic Remediation: A Sociocultural Approach." In *Writing(s) at the Crossroads: The Process/Product Interface,* edited by Georgeta Cislaru, 183–202. Philadelphia: John Benjamins.

Prior, Paul. 2018. "How Do Moments Add Up to Lives: Trajectories of Semiotic Becoming vs. Tales of School Learning in Four Modes." In *Making Future Matters,* edited by Rick Wysocki and Mary P. Sheridan. Logan: Computers and Composition Digital Press and Utah State University Press. http://ccdigitalpress.org/makingfuturematters.

Prior, Paul, and Julie Hengst. 2010. "Introduction: Exploring Semiotic Remediation." In *Exploring Semiotic Remediation as Discourse Practice,* edited by Paul Prior and Julie Hengst, 1–23. New York: Palgrave/Macmillan.

Prior, Paul, Julie Hengst, Kevin Roozen, and Jody Shipka. 2006. "'I'll Be the Sun': From Reported Speech to Semiotic Remediation Practices." *Text and Talk* 26 (6): 733–766.

Prior, Paul, and Andrea R. Olinger. 2019. "Academic Literacies as Laminated Assemblages and Embodied Semiotic Becoming." In *Re-Theorizing Literacy Practices: Complex Social and Cultural Contexts*, edited by David Bloome, Maria Luna Castanheira, Contant Leung, and Jennifer Rowsell, 126–140. New York: Routledge.

Prior, Paul, and Jody Shipka. 2003. "Chronotopic Lamination: Tracing the Contours of Literate Activity." In *Writing Selves, Writing Societies: Research from Activity Perspectives*, edited by Charles Bazerman and David R. Russell, 180–238. Fort Collins, CO: WAC Clearinghouse.

Prior, Paul, and Anna Smith. 2020. "Editorial: Writing Across: Tracing Transliteracies as Becoming across Time, Space, and Settings." *Learning, Culture, and Social Interaction* 24: 1–9.

Prior, Paul, and Steve Thorne. 2014. "Research Paradigms: Product, Process, and Social Activity." In *Handbook of Writing and Text Production*, edited by E.-M. Jakobs and Daniel Perrin, 31–54. Boston: Mourton de Gruyter.

Reiff, Mary Jo, and Anis Bawarshi. 2011. "Tracing Discursive Resources: How Students Use Prior Genre Knowledge to Negotiate New Writing Contexts in First-Year Composition." *Written Communication* 28 (3): 312–337.

Ringer, Jeff, and Sean Morey. 2021. "Posthumanizing Writing Transfer." *College English* 83 (4): 289–311.

Roozen, Kevin. 2020. "Coming to Act with Tables: Tracing the Laminated Trajectories of an Engineer-in-the-Making." *Learning, Culture, and Social Interaction* 24: 1–12.

Roozen, Kevin. 2021. "Acting with Inscriptions: Expanding Perspectives of Writing, Learning, and Becoming." *Journal of the Assembly for Expanded Perspectives of Learning* 26: 23–48.

Rule, Hannah J. 2019. *Situating Writing Processes: Perspectives on Writing*. Fort Collins, CO: WAC Clearinghouse.

Selfe, Cynthia. 2009. "The Movement of Air, the Breath of Meaning: Aurality and Multimodal Composing." *College Composition and Communication* 60 (4): 616–663.

Shepherd, Ryan P. 2018. "Digital Writing, Multimodality, and Learning Transfer: Crafting Connections between Composition and Online Composing." *Computers and Composition* 48: 103–134.

Shipka, Jody. 2011. *Toward a Composition Made Whole*. Pittsburgh, PA: University of Pittsburgh Press.

Sinor, Jennifer. 2002. *The Extraordinary Work of Ordinary Writing: Annie Ray's Diary*. Iowa City: University of Iowa Press.

Smit, David W. 2004. *The End of Composition Studies*. Carbondale: Southern Illinois University Press.

Smith, Anna, and Paul Prior. 2020. "A Flat CHAT Perspective on Transliteracies Development." *Learning, Culture, and Social Interaction* 24: 1–11.

Stornaiuolo, Amy, Anna Smith, and Nathan Phillips. 2017. "Developing a Transliteracies Framework for a Connected World." *Journal of Literacy Research* 49: 68–91.

Tsing, Anna. 2015. *The Mushroom at the End of the World*. Princeton, NJ: Princeton University Press.

Voloshinov, Valentin. 1973. *Marxism and the Philosophy of Language*. Translated by Ladislav Matejka and Irwin Titunik. Cambridge, MA: Harvard University Press.

Vygotsky, Lev. 1987. *Problems of General Psychology: The Collected Works of L. S. Vygotsky, Volume 1*. Translated by Norris Minick. New York: Plenum.

Ware, Ryan. 2022. "'God's Absence during Trauma Took Its Toll': Dialogic Tracing of Literate Activity and Lifespan Trajectories of Semiotic (Un)Becoming." *Written Communication* 39 (1): 129–165.

Wertsch, James V. 1991. *Voices of the Mind: A Sociocultural Approach to Mediated Action*. Cambridge, MA: Harvard University Press.

Wertsch, James V. 1998. *Mind as Action*. Oxford: Oxford University Press.

Yancey, Kathleen Blake. 2004. "Made Not Only in Words: Composition in a New Key." *College Composition and Communication* 56 (2): 297–328.

Yancey, Kathleen Blake. 2020. "Everyday Writing: An Introduction." *South Atlantic Review* 85 (2): 1–6.

Yancey, Kathleen Blake, Joe Cirio, Jeff Naftzinger, and Erin Workman. 2020. "Notebooks, Annotations, and Tweets: Defining Everyday Writing through a Common Lens." *South Atlantic Review* 85 (2): 141–168.

8
RHETORIC IN ITS FULLNESS
Metalanguage and Multimodal Transfer

Logan Bearden

Inquiries into writing knowledge transfer have explored the role of key terms in helping (student) writers theorize their composing practices across contexts (e.g., Yancey, Robertson, and Taczak 2014). Scholarship in this area suggests that composers can develop a "transfer mind-set" with/through *key terms*, because "key terms provide a conceptual foundation for writing knowledge developed in the course, guiding the assigned readings, class activities, and major assignments, and serving as a focal point for students' reflective work" (Yancey et al. 2018, 43). This mind-set assists composers in performing more effectively in the various contexts they might encounter by helping them better understand their composing choices using those key terms. Similarly, research in writing program administration details the importance of the language used in outcomes statements to articulate and communicate curricular values (Yancey 2005). According to Anis Bawarshi and Mary Jo Reiff (2010, 94, emphasis added), outcomes can function as a metagenre for programs, impacting programmatic culture by providing a "shared *vocabulary* for assigning, producing, reflecting on, and assessing student writing."[1] In describing the curricular content of our programs, we craft a (meta)language that we deliver to students, one that can influence their ability to adopt (or not) a transfer mind-set. In other words, language, especially as it pertains to course and programmatic design, is key in transfer.

Multimodality complicates our understanding of this relationship by expanding the resources available to students in processes of transfer. Specifically, multimodal theory's more accurate reflection of the way humans make and share meaning makes it imperative that those of us working in writing studies cultivate new language for describing *composing* process(es) and the transfer of *composing* knowledge (instead of alphabetic writing alone). The New London Group's pedagogy of multiliteracies, developed in the 1990s and early 2000s, began this work, emphasizing the importance of a "tool kit for working on semiotic activities," a way of "talking about language, images, texts, and meaning-making interactions . . . [in order] to identify and explain differences between texts" (Cope and Kalantzis 2000, 24). That toolkit included terms such as *design, mode, grammar, ensembles of meaning,* and *aptness,* to name a few—terms that are capacious enough to help students and instructors theorize how to create and consume new and varied forms of texts beyond alphabetic writing. This new metalanguage, these scholars argued, would help realize the goal of the pedagogy—"creating a kind of person, an active designer of meaning, with a sensibility *open to differences, change and innovation*" (Cope and Kalantzis 2009, 175, emphasis added). More recently, scholars in writing studies have taken up this work. Kara Poe Alexander, Michael-John DePalma, and Jeffrey M. Ringer's (2016, 34, emphasis added) concept of adaptive remediation, for example, assumes that a "rhetorical choice that works well in one context or medium (e.g., a print-based essay) might not work as well in another (e.g., a digital story or other multimodal text) . . . [It] also assumes that composers can be trained to think about their motives or rhetorical purposes in ways that allow them to . . . reshape prior knowledge *across media.*" In a course that emphasizes adaptive remediation, students study rhetorical concepts to understand rhetorical moves, which, in turn, allows them to make more effective rhetorical choices regardless of the medium in which they work.

Thus, over time, we have begun to develop a framework for fostering multimodal transfer: a curriculum that delivers to students rhetorical key terms and concepts that will help them compose multimodally across contexts and purposes. However, as of yet, we have not been able to implement this framework in a significant number of composition programs (Bearden 2019, 2022; Khadka and Lee 2019), in part because we have not sufficiently attended to the way the language of our programmatic documents fosters or inhibits multimodal transfer. This tension poses an urgent question I take up in this chapter: how might we craft programmatic language that can be used to facilitate multimodal transfer in first-year composition (FYC) and beyond? To answer this question, I organize this chapter into four sections. First, I synthesize interrelated but distinct areas of scholarship to understand what multimodal transfer requires of a curriculum. Then, to temper the optimism of published scholarship with the realities of the day-to-day work of composition programs, I share examples from a study in which I analyzed ten composition programs that have demonstrated an ongoing and intentional commitment to incorporating multimodality into their curricula, especially in their programmatic documents. Comparing published research to how programs have taken up and adapted that scholarship uncovers a practical but theoretically informed metalanguage and framework that teachers and administrators might apply to their own composition programs to create an environment that will foster multimodal transfer. Third, to demonstrate what it might look like for those individuals to do so, I consider how I might apply this knowledge in my own program, the First-Year Writing Program (FYWP) at Eastern Michigan University (EMU). Finally, to reveal how we might foster multimodal transfer in FYC and beyond, I scale that metalanguage up from the First-Year Writing Program to our professional writing major. I argue that we can use this knowledge to work toward a more sophisticated composition curriculum, one that extends beyond the first year of university education and helps prepare students to compose multimodally across the contexts they will encounter in the future.

MULTIMODAL TRANSFER AND CURRICULA

Transfer and multimodality are symbiotic concepts: transfer has *always* been at the core of multimodal theory and multimodal composition curricula. The pedagogy of multiliteracies, which first described how and why multimodality should be integrated into the classroom, emerged as a response to a "multiplicity of communications channels" and "the increasing salience of cultural and linguistic diversity" of the mid-1990s, which led to the need for a pedagogy that "focuses on modes of representation much broader than [textual-alphabetic] language alone" (Cope and Kalantzis 2000, 5). Expanding the content of the curriculum and the kinds of texts students are able to create reinvigorates the role of rhetoric in composition, because composing multimodally requires rhetorical knowledge as much as technical skill (Sheppard 2009); using multiple modes of communication increases student knowledge of rhetorical situation; (Ferruci and DeRosa 2019); and in deepening their understanding of the meaning-making potentialities of various modes, media, and technologies, students increase their rhetorical dexterity and meta-awareness (Graban, Charlton, and Charlton 2013; VanKooten 2016). This combination of rhetorical knowledge and multimodal experience allows students to cross (more) contexts (more) effectively.

Cross-contextual meaning making is what the New London Group termed *transformed practice*, which Carol Westby (2010, 68) defines as a practice in which "students are redesigning by taking meaning out of one context and adapting it in such a way that it works well somewhere else." This is the culmination of a pedagogy of multiliteracies, a meaning-making process that "involves students' transfer, reformulation, and redesign of *existing texts and meaning-making practice from one context to another*" (Angay-Crowder, Choi, and Yi 2013, 38, emphasis added). Nicola Yelland and coauthors (2008, 202) put it another way; writing that "transformed practice relates to the transfer in meaning-making practice that puts knowledge to work in new contexts or cultural sites." Transformed practice is an act of transfer—taking text and meaning made for one location and rhetorically repurposing it for another. Too, because the pedagogy of multiliteracies emphasizes multimodal texts, transformed practice is necessarily multimodal—a rhetorically informed process of theorizing the potentialities of different communicative resources (e.g., modes, media, genres) and selecting the most appropriate to translate meaning across contexts. Rhetoric and metalanguage are essential parts of this process. According to Anne Cloonan (2011, 24), "Without a metalanguage, or grammar, for describing multimodal texts, understandings remain tacit rather than explicitly articulated or brought to consciousness . . . Without language to name structures and features and frameworks to organise thinking about the modes in texts, developing understanding will be limited." Terms such as *genre, mode, purpose, audience,* and *context* (just to name a few of those centered within the pedagogy of multiliteracies) help students develop an understanding of literacy and of composition that they can use to conceptualize the rhetorical moves necessary to cross contexts and cultures because with this metalanguage, students are able think through what constitutes rhetorical effectiveness in any context.

Thus, this scholarship suggests that there are two curricular components necessary to foster multimodal transfer:

- **Multimodal transfer requires a rhetorical metalanguage.** Key terms and a metalanguage rooted in rhetorical terms allow students to theorize and enact multimodal rhetorical performances.
- **Multimodal transfer requires that students understand, orchestrate, and deploy the semiotic potentials of various communicative resources.** Multimodal transfer invokes rhetoric in its fullness—a *techne*, a theory of practice considering the full available means of communication that will allow (student) composers to take meaning made in one context and transform it for another.

To put it plainly, metalanguage cultivates meta-awareness, and meta-awareness allows students to achieve as multimodal transfer. This framework, however, has not been adopted in most composition programs.[2]

To offer a solution to this problem, the remainder of this chapter will explore the lessons we might learn from ten programs that have endeavored to make multimodal composition and multimodal transfer meaningful parts of their first-year composition curricula. These programs suggest that there are certain programmatic outcomes and assignments that can foster an environment that moves students in the direction of multimodal transfer, a necessary lesson for those interested in updating their classrooms and programs to align more closely with contemporary calls to center multimodality within the content of composition. This is important not only in FYC but throughout the university experience, because FYC cannot be the sole location in which students learn and practice composition. A vertical composition curriculum—that is, an intentionally designed sequence of courses that integrates what students learn at the introductory level into the intermediate and advanced levels—can provide us with a better opportunity to foster multimodal transfer by requiring that students encounter key terms and concepts reiteratively and recursively, deepening their familiarity with those concepts and strengthening their rhetorical practices over time. Thus, the data I share in this chapter are gleaned from FYC programs, but I use those data to work toward a framework that can be extrapolated to other FYC contexts *and* scaled up vertically.

MODEL PROGRAMS

Programmatic documents can be a valuable resource for (or an impediment to) fostering multimodal transfer. As I mentioned at the beginning of this chapter, the language we invoke in our outcomes and the values underlying that language can create, constrain, and influence the environments in which students work and learn. Outcomes, according to Chris Gallagher (2012, 44), "give teachers and students targets to shoot for. They provide focus, stability, clarity, and transparency. Further, they are helpful for accountability purposes: they allow us to measure and document students' performances vis-à-vis expressed goals." As a part of the textual ecologies that define programs, outcomes can inflect assignment sheets, impact pedagogical practices, motivate professional development opportunities, and inform assessment practices. Correspondingly, they can be an invaluable resource in our efforts to update the work of composition programs. To be clear, *outcomes alone cannot ensure that students achieve multimodal transfer*. Not all programs utilize outcomes assessment; not all programs require that all instructors use the same outcomes; not all instructors are motivated by outcomes in the same way; and not all students experience outcomes and curricula in the same ways. However, we can utilize these documents *and others* in the creation of an overall environment that fosters multimodal transfer (see Naftzinger, chapter 10, this volume, for a more detailed discussion of the role of infrastructure in the creation/development of programmatic community and culture).

To demonstrate this capacity, I turn to ten programs that have made multimodal composition a meaningful part of their curricula. These data come from a larger, mixed methods research project, the results of which I share in my book, *Making Progress* (Bearden 2022). In that project, I studied the phenomenon of multimodal curricular transformation, an ongoing and intentional effort to make multimodal composition a meaningful part of a composition program's curriculum through the interplay of programmatic practices and documents. To study multimodal curricular transformation, I:

- Collected and analyzed outcomes statements from eighty+ different composition programs for a panoramic understanding of the curricular values at various institutions, discovering that there are certain outcomes and values that foster multimodal composition and others that prevent its inclusion
- Conducted interviews with the model program directors, which uncovered that the process of entering into multimodal curricular transformation is collaborative and utilizes the feminist pragmatic rhetorical strategy of perceiving resistance to multimodal composition as a productive moment of opportunity for discussing (perhaps competing) pedagogical values
- Reviewed multimodal assignments from those ten programs, discovering that a majority of the programs *ask students to perform multimodal transfer (not just multimodal composition)* through an act of remediation in which students take a previously composed assignment (most typically a research paper) and transform that assignment for a different audience, purpose, context, or combination of the three.

For the purposes of this chapter, I will focus on the outcomes statements guiding these model programs *and* assignments that animated those outcomes by requiring multimodal transfer. Table 8.1 provides a brief bit of demographic context for the programs.

This demographic information suggests that multimodal curricular transformation is not limited to one specific institutional type; thus, these programs can provide rich material for us to examine and apply in our efforts to help students work toward multimodal transfer. Specifically, these programs create curricular environments that foster multimodal transfer by emphasizing the importance of a rhetorical

Table 8.1. Program information

Program Name	Institutional Type	Student Population	Curricular Description
Program 1	Public college	~18,000	Theme-based focus on academic literacies in first course and public, digital literacies in second course
Program 2	Public college	~16,000	Theme-based, focusing on the role of inquiry in writing
Program 3	Public, land-grant research university	~24,000	Introduction to rhetoric and writing, emphasis on argumentation
Program 4	Public, regional research (R2) university	~20,000	Introduction to rhetoric and writing
Program 5	Public research (R2) university	~24,000	Introduction to rhetoric and writing
Program 6	Private Jesuit university	~8,500	Theme-based, focusing on academic literacies and inquiry
Program 7	Private, Ivy League research (R1) university	~22,000	Theme-based, writing-in-the-disciplines approach
Program 8	Public research (R1) university (Hispanic-serving institution)	~25,000	Introduction to rhetoric and writing
Program 9	Public liberal arts university	~11,000	Theme-based approach, emphasis on rhetoric
Program 10	Public research (R1) university	~30,000	Introduction to rhetoric and writing

knowledge and rhetorical key terms, allowing students the opportunity to compose multimodally, and requiring multimodal transfer in the form of a remediation project.

These programs suggest that rhetorical key terms are necessary to craft programmatic language used to facilitate multimodal transfer in FYC and beyond. These terms function as a metalanguage students can utilize to adapt their rhetorical practices and performances across contexts and purposes, which is part of multimodal transfer. A rhetorical vocabulary helps strengthen student meta-awareness because, according to Crystal VanKooten (2016), a rhetorical knowledge gives students the "ability to move consistently between enacting compositional choices and articulating how and why those choices might be effective or ineffective in a rhetorical context." All ten of the model programs included outcomes that pertain to rhetoric/rhetorical knowledge, and several of them emphasized the importance of rhetorical key terms. Table 8.2 provides a summary.

Table 8.2. Rhetorical outcomes

Program	Rhetorical Outcome(s)
Program 1	Pay careful attention to rhetorical concepts such as "style, tropes, genre, audience, and purpose" to apply in their own composing
Program 2	"Recognize and practice" key rhetorical terms according to the rhetorical situation
Program 3*	"Learn and use key rhetorical concepts [such as purpose, audience, and context] through analyzing and composing a variety of texts"
Program 4	Gain practice "identifying rhetorical qualities in composing situations"
Program 5	Demonstrate the ability to "write effectively for different contexts"
Program 6	Compose "rhetorically effective" texts
Program 7	Learn the "fundamentals of rhetoric," such as genre, audience, and purpose, to name a few examples.
Program 8	Address multiple rhetorical situations in addition to reading a "range of texts" to apply those texts to multiple contexts
Program 9	"Understand and apply" rhetorical concepts such as audience, rhetorical situation, and rhetorical appeals
Program 10	Address multiple audiences and rhetorical situations

* *Program 3 uses the most recent version of the* Outcomes Statement *released by the Council of Writing Program Administrators (2019).*

I wish to highlight two main points about these rhetorical outcomes. First, six programs (Programs 1, 2, 3, 4, 7, and 9) stipulate in their outcomes that students will gain proficiency with specific rhetorical key terms. When taken up by students, these terms function as a kind of Burkean terministic screen (or, as Maynard illustrates in chapter 9, this volume, a metacognitive framework), allowing students to notice rhetorical qualities in composing situations *and* to effectively apply those concepts in their own work. This delivers to students the metalanguage necessary to theorize transfer, which, I demonstrate in the coming paragraphs, can foster an environment that makes multimodal transfer possible. Specifically, Program 1's outcomes argue that students need a rhetorical vocabulary to understand and employ the "conventions appropriate" for various contexts. Through this knowledge, students are able to "adapt writing and composing conventions (including your style, content, organization, document design) . . . to your rhetorical context." Similarly, in Program 4, students develop and utilize their vocabulary to understand the rhetorical qualities of composing situations. This, in turn, the outcomes suggest, will allow them to *enact* rhetoric in the construction of "persuasive" or effective texts. Program 7 summarizes the relationship between metalanguage and rhetorical proficiency by suggesting that in learning the "fundamentals of rhetoric" (genre, audience, and purpose, to name a few examples), students will be able to "transfer easily" the knowledge they cultivate in the program "to the many new writing situations" they will face in the future.

In other words, rhetorical concepts heighten rhetorical meta-awareness, which heightens rhetorical skill. All of this increases the likelihood that students will be able to enact multimodal transfer, a complex rhetorical task, if or when it is asked of them.

Second, while only six of these programs list specific rhetorical key terms that students will be expected to learn, all ten emphasize flexibility in that they do not prescribe alphabetic writing as the means through which students must realize their rhetorical goals. For example, these programs ask students to:

- "Address a range of audiences."
- "Address multiple rhetorical situations."
- Compose "rhetorically effective" texts.

Such outcomes focus more on cultivating meta-awareness than on prescribing that students work with/in writing, which realizes an emerging goal of those who are implementing assignments that enact multimodal composition in their classrooms and programs. In the words of VanKooten and Angela Berkley (2016, 161), this approach to FYC seeks to "equip students with a versatile array of processes and habits . . . that will help them tackle whatever sort of writing obstacles await them outside our classroom walls." Emphasizing rhetoric over writing makes space for outcomes that value multimodal composition and assignments that require multimodal transfer, two features necessary for an environment that fosters multimodal transfer.

These model programs also included outcomes related to multimodal composition, which build from the rhetorical metalanguage and flexibility emphasized in the rhetorical outcomes. Table 8.3 summarizes those outcomes.

These outcomes build from the metalanguage cultivated by the rhetorical outcomes and use that language to describe multimodal composing as a way of effectively enacting rhetoric. In so doing, these outcomes help students work toward adaptive remediation, "a set of strategies composers can draw on in order to adapt or reshape composing knowledge across media" (Alexander, DePalma, and Ringer 2016, 34), which is part of multimodal transfer. For example, several of these outcomes use the concept of "rhetorical situations" to define the work students will complete. In those programs, students can utilize the concept of

Table 8.3. Multimodal outcomes

Program	Multimodal Outcomes
Program 1	Use multiple media to compose for "multiple rhetorical situations"
Program 2	Use multimodal technologies to "address a range of audiences"
Program 3	"Learn common formats and/or design features of different kinds of texts" *and* "adapt composing processes for a variety of technologies and modalities"
Program 4	"Compose using digital technologies, gaining an awareness of the possibilities and constraints of electronic environments"
Program 5	Develop an awareness of the limitations and affordances of technologies, both digital and non-digital
Program 6	Compose texts for different audiences in "different modes of presentation"
Program 7	Use digital media to write for "non-academic audiences"
Program 8	Develop "composing processes" according to the audience and assignment
Program 9	Understand that "images, sounds, animations—in addition to words" are necessary parts of communication
Program 10	Employ "appropriate composing modalities" to address a variety of rhetorical situations

rhetorical situation and its constituent parts to think through what defines effective rhetorical performances. However, in those situations, students are expected to use the "composing modalities," "media," and "multimodal technologies" most appropriate and effective depending on that situation. The metalanguage here provides a way of re-seeing the rhetorical task, one that highlights that not all rhetorical choices work in all rhetorical contexts; these outcomes position multimodal composition as a way to make the most effective rhetorical choices.

To that end, these outcomes do not prescribe the materials with/in which students work. Students are not required to demonstrate proficiency in any specific kind of technology or media. Rather, they are expected to perform rhetoric—understanding the limitations and affordances of different media, addressing a variety of rhetorical situations, and adapting their composing processes accordingly. Thus, these outcomes value rhetoric in its fullness. They emphasize the differing needs and expectations of various audiences and encourage students to make their own choices when it comes to the assembly and delivery of texts. This creates an environment that centers rhetoric, values multimodal composition, and accounts for the limitations and affordances of various communicative resources. Within this environment, I contend, multimodal transfer is possible. However, it must be asked of students.

REMEDIATION INVITES MULTIMODAL TRANSFER

While these outcomes can create an environment in which multimodal transfer is possible, that environment must be activated by an assignment that requires multimodal transfer. These programs do so using what I will call a Remediation Project. In my investigations into multimodal curricular transformation, I discovered that this is the most common assignment programs invoke to enact a multimodal composition curriculum: nine of these ten programs required a version of the Remediation Project. While the assignment has gone by many names in various forms of scholarship (e.g., radical revision, remix, composition in three genres, multi-genre campaign),[3] the basic elements remain the same: students take a previously composed assignment—typically an argument or insight presented in a research paper—and translate/transform/adapt that argument for a different audience, purpose, context, medium, or some combination. This kind of assignment, transfer research has demonstrated, can be "a turning point for many students in understanding the key terms for the course . . . [and can] help students enact key terms" (Yancey, Robertson, and Taczak 2014, 142). In other words, allowing students to focus on the rhetorical reshaping of their work, rather than producing new inquiry or arguments, helps them understand how and why it is necessary to adapt their work to the audience, context, and task at hand. In so doing, they gain a more nuanced understanding of multimodality and rhetoric, knowledge they can utilize to achieve (multimodal) transfer. Table 8.4 briefly summarizes the assignments.

While the descriptions of these assignments are fairly simple, this is the complex work of multimodal transfer. In these projects, students take existing content and focus on reshaping that content depending on audience needs, modal/media affordances, and similar factors. Program 5's remediation project requires that students adapt a "previous piece of writing" using "digital media and perhaps multimodality" to address a new audience, emphasizing apt choices in terms of modes, media, and genres. In Program 8, students compose a video that "advocates for action on a social issue" using research conducted for a previous assignment: an annotated bibliography related to the social issue addressed in the video. Here, students transform content for a new purpose, using a combination of previously composed work and multimodal transfer to perform advocacy. Similarly, the "transformed research project" required in Program 4 focuses on the "affordances . . . of available media" with "specific attention to adapting classroom research for a public audience using an appropriate medium and genre."

Table 8.4. Multimodal assignments

Program	Assignment Title	Brief Description
Program 1	Research remediation/remix	Presenting a "remixed" research paper "through multiple modes"
Program 2	Digital portfolio	Digital portfolio presenting student work
Program 3	Visual argument	Visual representation of previously conducted research
Program 4	Multimodal interactive presentation	Remediated version of a research paper topic presented at an event
Program 5	Remediation	Remediating previous writing for a new audience
Program 6	Podcast	Audio version of previously composed research project
Program 7	Digital editorial	Research presented in the form of an editorial for an online magazine
Program 8	Advocacy video	Researched advocacy video adapted from literature review
Program 9	Research remediation	Multimodal version of a research paper
Program 10	Research remediation	Multimodal version of a research paper

These kinds of assignments require multimodal transfer, the rhetorical reshaping of material for new audiences and purposes with careful attention to the limitations and affordances of the various communicative resources available. These programs suggest that we can (begin to) create environments that foster multimodal transfer using outcomes and assignments. Composition programs are made up of texts and practices. Outcomes, as programmatic documents, help compose the environment of a program—influencing assignment descriptions, assessment practices, professional development needs, and similar factors. While not completely constitutive of a curriculum, they are and can be influential. The outcomes I have shared thus far create an environment that emphasizes rhetorical metalanguage and informed choices in multiple forms of communication. The assignments here activate and align those emphases—students need rhetoric (and a rhetorical vocabulary) to employ the full potential of various semiotic resources *and* doing so strengthens their rhetorical knowledge. In the remainder of this chapter, I explore how we might implement this model in our programs *and* scale that model up vertically to make space for and invite multimodal transfer beyond the first year.

REVISED, VERTICAL OUTCOMES

These programs, then, offer compelling models demonstrating how composition programs can embrace rhetoric in its fullness and invite students to recompose and repurpose prior work, thereby inviting multimodal transfer. They invite us to return to our own programs, outcomes, and assignments—reconsidering the environments they create or constrain, especially as they pertain to multimodal transfer. In doing so, we can craft a comprehensive composition curriculum that is in alignment with contemporary scholarship and informed by what composition programs are already doing. To demonstrate how we might apply these models in our own contexts, I will utilize Program 4's outcomes and assignments. Program 4, the First-Year Writing Program at Eastern Michigan University, is the program in which I work. We are guided by five core principles: rhetoric, process, conventions, multimodality, and reflection. These core principles translate to outcomes, some of which I shared earlier in this chapter. Here, though, I ask: can we craft better outcomes (and better assignments) that will foster multimodal transfer?

Following the lead of scholarship *and* the model programs I shared in the previous section, we know that rhetoric is the cornerstone of a curriculum that fosters multimodal transfer because of the metalanguage and meta-awareness rhetoric cultivates. If our program did not include rhetoric in its guiding documents and curricular descriptions, the first step in fostering multimodal transfer would be to add it. Luckily, however, rhetoric is already one of Program 4's guiding principles. Our program includes two complementary outcomes related to rhetoric, which read:

- You will have practiced using language consciously and *identifying rhetorical qualities* in composing situations.
- You will have *enacted rhetoric* by consciously constructing persuasive texts.

These outcomes do good work: they use the term *rhetoric* and make the case that a rhetorical knowledge will allow students to produce persuasive and effective texts. But I believe we can improve them following the model of other exemplary programs and contemporary scholarship. For example, these outcomes might be revised to *name* the specific rhetorical qualities and concepts to which students might be introduced, as in Program 9 (e.g., exigence, *kairos*, ethos) or Programs 1 and 7 (genre, audience, purpose). Outcomes that name specific rhetorical concepts like these can infuse the culture of the program with a rhetoric-based metalanguage with which students can theorize the potentialities of various composing technologies, genres, and media. This metalanguage assists students in (beginning to) cultivate a transfer mind-set *and* functions as a foundation that can be expanded upon in future courses. Such outcomes might read:

- You will have practiced identifying rhetorical concepts and key terms (such as genre, audience, purpose) at work in various composing situations.
- You will have used your knowledge of rhetorical concepts and key terms to enact rhetoric in multiple contexts.

To be clear, outcomes cannot ensure that all students have the same learning experiences or that all outcomes will be applied evenly throughout the program, but we *can* use them as a (meta)genre to make space for new ways of programmatic being. By naming rhetorical concepts in our outcomes, we create the possibility of increasing, expanding, and nuancing the metalanguage delivered to students.

In addition, emphasizing rhetoric instead of alphabetic writing skills expands narrow definitions of what counts as writing or composition (see Alexander, Cassady, and DePalma, chapter 4, this volume) and makes space for multimodal composition within the curriculum. These programs provide a framework for multimodal outcomes as well: ask students to engage with multiple kinds of semiotic materials to achieve their rhetorical ends. Such outcomes are vital, I contend, in creating an environment that fosters multimodal transfer, because multimodality highlights the symbiotic relationship between rhetorical knowledge (including key terms) and material affordances, which is the foundation of multimodal transfer. As mentioned previously, another one of Program 4's guiding principles is multimodality. The outcomes related to this principle are:

- **Multimodal transformation**: You will have adapted your writing to distinct rhetorical contexts, drawing attention to the way composition transforms across contexts and forms.
- **Multimodal design**: You will have composed using digital technologies, gaining awareness of the possibilities and constraints of electronic environments.

These outcomes point the attention of students, instructors, and external audiences to the ways composition necessarily changes across contexts and to the necessity of using of the possibilities and constraints of different media. However, our second outcome prescribes the digital, which inherently limits the kinds of texts students can make and circulate (see Shipka 2013, for example).

The model programs I have presented in this chapter, however, offer different outcomes that attend to the capaciousness of multimodality and highlight flexibility, transformation, and adaptation without (necessarily) requiring a computer. Program 6 allows students the opportunity to compose "for different audiences in different modes of presentation" without predetermining what those modes might be. Similarly, Program 2 simply requires that students use multimodal technologies to "address a range of audiences." Both programs emphasize material-rhetorical flexibility depending on audience needs. Program 3, which uses the Council of Writing Program Administrators outcomes, phrases its outcomes in the following way. Students will:

- "Learn common formats and/or design features of different kinds of texts" and
- "Adapt composing processes for a variety of technologies and modalities."

Collectively, these models depict multimodal composition as something that must be rhetorically adapted to situation, audience, purpose, and mode/genre/media potentiality—all of which prepares students to do the work of multimodal transfer. Following these models, outcomes that foster multimodal composition and create an environment that can lead to multimodal transfer might read:

- You will adapt/transform texts you have composed to multiple rhetorical contexts, paying attention to the possibilities and constraints of different forms and contexts.
- You will use your knowledge of rhetorical concepts (e.g., audience, purpose, *kairos*, appeals) to perform multimodal composition effectively in multiple contexts.

These updated outcomes emphasize adaptability and flexibility *through* a rhetorical metalanguage. This kind of informed flexibility is at the heart of (multimodal) transfer, because students must possess a flexible set of composing strategies to transform texts for new audiences and purposes. To me, this suggests that outcomes like these are those for which EMU's FYWP should strive to help create an environment that fosters that kind of (meta)awareness.

As mentioned earlier, outcomes are animated by assignments, and these updated outcomes would simultaneously more accurately reflect one of our program's current assignments and challenge us further. Currently, our program invites students to demonstrate multimodal transfer at our semiannual showcase of student writing. The project for this event requires that students present their research in a way that will be accessible and engaging to those who attend—mostly students and instructors from other sections of FYW, university administrators, and students seeking learning experience credit for general education purposes. Students present their research through a variety of texts (e.g., flyers, posters, interactive games, videos), and they are assessed on their ability to transform that research for their given audience. While this is multimodal transfer, we could ask our students to embrace transformed practice more fully in the circulation of their texts, which could increase their attention to audience, medium, and genre—thereby strengthening their multimodal transfer skills. The New London Group's concept of transformed practice asks students to take meaning made for one context and transform that meaning for another. Our showcase does that, but the audience is still an academic audience associated with the university. It might be differently challenging to require that students communicate those arguments to folks *beyond* the academy as in Program 8, where students compose advocacy videos for real-world audiences. For example, in our program, students have conducted and communicated research about the gentrification of Ann Arbor, Michigan. Rather than presenting at the showcase, those students might communicate their arguments to Ann Arbor residents. In so doing, they would be invited to consider more deeply the specific needs and abilities of their audience, increasing their attention to the concept of rhetorical situation. Too, a more concrete, real-world audience could influence the kinds of texts students create to share their research. An informational video could be more effective than a flyer or a pamphlet. Increasing the stakes in this way would offer students the opportunity to enact their rhetorical metalanguage, demonstrate their multimodal meta-awareness, and achieve multimodal transfer. These kinds of assignments, the model programs suggest, are those we might compose to cultivate an environment that fosters multimodal transfer.

We can also take these lessons and scale them up, crafting a *vertical* composition curriculum that can foster multimodal transfer at the introductory, intermediate, and advanced levels. According to the introduction to the Council of Writing Program Administrators' (2019, emphasis added) *WPA Outcomes Statement for First-Year Composition (3.0)*, "As students move beyond first-year composition, their writing abilities do not merely improve. Rather, their abilities will *diversify* along disciplinary, professional, and civic lines as these writers move into new settings where *expected outcomes expand, multiply, and diverge*." Similarly, research in transfer suggests that the TFT curriculum can indeed be successfully scaled up into writing across the curriculum/writing in the disciplines contexts if the core features of the curriculum remain: a focus on an evolving set of key terms to understand composing *and* requiring students to compose across contexts to cultivate a comparative understanding of those different contexts (Yancey et al. 2018, 60–61).

Following these claims and the lead of the model programs, we can craft a vertical composition curriculum that attends to rhetorical metalanguage, multimodal proficiency, and comparative practice. To illustrate what this might look like in practice, at EMU we are developing a vertical composition curriculum that implements our FYWP's outcomes up through our major in professional writing.

We are currently working on an intermediate-level composition course that would help bridge the gap between FYC, which most students take in their first year, and the writing students are asked to do in their majors, which most students do not encounter until their third or fourth years at the institution. This course would build on the knowledge and metalanguage students develop in FYC but (begin to) help them specialize their (multimodal) rhetorical expertise and experience *along disciplinary boundaries*. The course is titled WRTG 225: Writing in the Disciplines, and it explores composition within four "families" of academic inquiry: the natural sciences, the fine arts, the social sciences, and the humanities.[4] In this course, students "expand, multiply, and diversify" their (rhetorical, multimodal) metalanguage by examining the ways composing conforms to discipline-specific features. Building on those I explored in previous sections, outcomes for this class related to rhetoric might read:

- You will identify, understand, and operate within the rhetorical contexts of various disciplines using your knowledge of rhetorical concepts (e.g., audience, purpose, genre, exigence).
- You will identify, understand, and accommodate the needs (in terms of, e.g., evidence, appeals) of audiences in various disciplines.

By focusing on a metalanguage related to rhetorical knowledge in this way, students reiteratively and recursively encounter this vocabulary in multiple courses, increasing the likelihood that they will perform rhetoric effectively using their metalanguage across contexts. We could craft outcomes that cultivate material-rhetorical flexibility in composing tools, technologies, and materials *across disciplinary lines* as well. At the intermediate level, these might read:

- You will use your rhetorical knowledge (of, e.g., audience, purpose, genre) to respond to discipline-specific composing situations (e.g., reports) using appropriate and effective text formats (e.g., designs, layouts).
- You will transform your work (e.g., research, writing) for distinct multimodal-rhetorical contexts, paying attention to the limitations and affordances of different modes, media, and genres.

These outcomes ask students to draw upon *and* nuance their rhetorical metalanguage to realize their multimodal-rhetorical goals. To achieve these outcomes, students might follow the Teaching for Transfer curriculum model, conducting research on and composing about discipline-specific ways of composing. The students could then communicate their research to incoming first-year students as "how-to" guides for composing in various majors. This act of multimodal transfer, of focusing on the rhetorical reshaping of content for a specific audience with specific needs, instantiates those outcomes, demonstrating the utility of the framework I have synthesized in this chapter. We can do this at the advanced and graduate levels too, using outcomes and assignments to help students learn and enact key rhetorical terms, develop multimodal proficiency, and achieve multimodal transfer by circulating the work composed for school with audiences beyond.

This chapter addressed the question: how might we craft a curricular environment that can foster multimodal transfer in the first year and beyond? I looked to current trends in research related to the transfer of composing knowledge *and* how actual programs are fostering multimodal transfer. Reading across the evidence in this way revealed that we can utilize programmatic documents, such as outcomes and assignments, to foster multimodal curricular transformation. The programs I discussed in this chapter utilized their outcomes statements to argue for the importance of a rhetorical metalanguage and specific rhetorical terms. This metalanguage increases meta-awareness by allowing students to name and theorize their composing processes and choices. In addition, in focusing on rhetoric over alphabetic writing, these programs make space for multimodal composition as a rhetorical choice students can make to enact successful rhetorical performances. In other words, those programmatic outcomes create environments that value rhetoric in its multimodal fullness. Those environments are activated and animated by assignments that require students to demonstrate multimodal transfer, most commonly as a remediation project in which students translate previously composed work for a new context. These are the basics of a curriculum that fosters multimodal transfer: utilize programmatic documents to emphasize rhetoric and rhetorical key terms, make space for multimodal composition as a valuable part of the composition curriculum, and require that students utilize their multimodal-rhetorical skills to adapt their work to distinct contexts. I also suggested that we can utilize this framework to scale that environment up, creating an intentional, vertical composition curriculum that fosters multimodal transfer by having students encounter a rhetorical metalanguage and demonstrate multimodal transfer reiteratively and recursively. I utilized EMU's FYWP as an example of how we might do this, demonstrating how foundational outcomes can provide a throughline we can utilize to work toward a more sophisticated, vertical composition curriculum—one that prepares students not just to write in and for the academy but to rhetorically reshape meaning across the contexts they'll encounter in their lifeworlds.

NOTES

1. Janet Giltrow's (2002, 195) use of the term *metagenre* refers to "atmospheres of wordings and activities, demonstrated precedents or expectations—atmospheres surrounding genres." Michael Carter (2007, 393) elaborates on this definition by claiming that metagenres direct "our attention to broader patterns of language as social action." In this way, outcomes function metagenerically by impacting the pedagogical and curricular environments that constitute (composition) programs.
2. While multimodality is a popular trend in the research of the discipline, it has not been integrated consistently in composition curricula. Santosh Khadka and J. C. Lee (2019, 4), for example, argue that "multimodality . . . is largely ignored in most writing classes."
3. I provide a fuller treatment of various versions of the remediation project, the multimodal work it asks of students, how various programs have implemented it, and its strengths and weaknesses in Bearden (2022, chapter 4).
4. Michael Carter (2007) describes the rationale behind a course such as this more fully. The central claim he makes is that this comparative approach can demystify discipline-specific writing expectations, which increases student meta-awareness *and* helps faculty articulate their needs and expectations more clearly.

REFERENCES

Alexander, Kara Poe, Michael-John DePalma, and Jeffrey M. Ringer. 2016. "Adaptive Remediation and the Facilitation of Transfer in Multiliteracy Center Contexts." *Computers and Composition* 41 (September): 32–45.

Angay-Crowder, Tbua, Jayoung Choi, and Youngjoo Yi. 2013. "Putting Multiliteracies into Practice: Digital Storytelling for Multilingual Adolescents in a Summer Program." *TESL Canada Journal* 30 (2): 36–45.

Bawarshi, Anis, and Mary Jo Reiff. 2010. *Genre: An Introduction to History, Theory, Research, and Pedagogy*. Anderson, SC: Parlor.

Bearden, Logan. 2019. "Favorable Outcomes: How Outcomes Can Make Space for Multimodal Curricula." *WPA: Writing Program Administration* 43 (1): 139–160.

Bearden, Logan. 2022. *Making Progress: Programmatic and Administrative Approaches for Multimodal Curricular Transformation*. Logan: Utah State University Press.

Carter, Michael. 2007. "Ways of Knowing, Doing, and Writing in the Disciplines." *College Composition and Communication* 58 (3): 385–418.

Cloonan, Anne. 2011. "Creating Multimodal Metalanguage with Teachers." *English Teaching: Practice and Critique* 10 (4): 23–40.

Cope, Bill, and Mary Kalantzis. 2000. *Multiliteracies: Literacy Learning and the Design of Social Futures*. London: Routledge.

Cope, Bill, and Mary Kalantzis. 2009. "Multiliteracies: New Literacies, New Learning." *Pedagogies: An International Journal* 4 (3): 164–195.
Council of Writing Program Administrators. 2019. *WPA Outcomes Statement for First-Year Composition (3.0).* WPA Council. July. https://wpacouncil.org/aws/CWPA/pt/sd/news_article/243055/_PARENT/layout_details/false.
Ferruci, Stephen, and Susan DeRosa. 2019. "Multimodality, Transfer, and Rhetorical Awareness: Analyzing the Choices of Undergraduate Writers." In *Bridging the Multimodal Gap: From Theory to Practice*, edited by Santosh Khadka and J. C. Lee, 201–224. Logan: Utah State University Press.
Gallagher, Chris. 2012. "The Trouble with Outcomes: Pragmatic Inquiry and Educational Aims." *College English* 75 (1): 42–60.
Giltrow, Janet. 2002. "Meta-genre." In *The Rhetoric and Ideology of Genre: Strategies for Stability and Change*, edited by Richard Coe, Lorelei Lingard, and Tatiana Teslenko, 187–205. Creskill, NJ: Hampton.
Graban, Tarez Samra, Colin Charlton, and Jannika Charlton. 2013. "Multivalent Composition and the Reinvention of Expertise." In *Multimodal Literacies and Emerging Genres in Student Compositions*, edited by Tracy Bowen and Carl Whithaus, 248–281. Pittsburgh, PA: University of Pittsburgh Press.
Khadka, Santosh, and J. C. Lee, eds. 2019. *Bridging the Multimodal Gap: From Theory to Practice.* Logan: Utah State University Press.
Kress, Gunther. 2010. *Multimodality: A Social Semiotic Approach to Contemporary Communication.* London: Routledge.
Sheppard, Jennifer. 2009. "The Rhetorical Work of Multimedia Production Practices: It's More than Just Technical Skill." *Computers and Composition* 26 (2): 122–131.
Shipka, Jody. 2013. "Including, but Not Limited to, the Digital: Composing Multimodal Texts." In *Multimodal Literacies and Emerging Genres in Student Compositions*, edited by Tracy Bowen and Carl Whithaus, 73–89. Pittsburgh, PA: University of Pittsburgh Press.
VanKooten, Crystal. 2016. "Identifying Components of Meta-awareness about Composition: Toward a Theory and Methodology for Writing Studies." *Composition Forum* 33. https://compositionforum.com/issue/33/meta-awareness.php.
VanKooten, Crystal, and Angela Berkley. 2016. "Messy Problem-Exploring through Video in First-Year Writing: Assessing What Counts." *Computers and Composition* 40: 151–163.
Westby, Carol. 2010. "Multiliteracies: The Changing World of Communication." *Topics in Language Disorders* 30 (1): 64–71.
Yancey, Kathleen Blake. 2005. "Outcomes, Standards, and All That Jazz." In *The Outcomes Book: Debate and Consensus after the WPA Outcomes Statement*, edited by Susanmarie Harrington, Keith Rhodes, Ruth Fischer, and Rita Malencyzk, 18–23. Logan: Utah State University Press.
Yancey, Kathleen Blake, Matthew Davis, Liane Robertson, Kara Taczak, and Erin Workman. 2018. "Writing across College: Key Terms and Multiple Contexts as Factors Promoting Students' Transfer of Writing Knowledge and Practice." *WAC Journal* 29: 42–63.
Yancey, Kathleen, Liane Robertson, and Kara Taczak. 2014. *Writing across Contexts: Transfer, Composition, and Sites of Writing.* Logan: Utah State University Press.
Yelland, Nicola, Bill Cope, and Mary Kalantzis. 2008. "Learning by Design: Creating Pedagogical Frameworks for Knowledge-Building in the Twenty-First Century." *Asia-Pacific Journal of Teaching Education* 36 (3): 197–213.

9
A CURRICULUM DELIVERED, A CURRICULUM REMEMBERED
Multimodal Transfer in Writing and Rhetoric Major Alumni

Travis Maynard

Kathleen Blake Yancey (2018, 16) argues that writing studies is in the midst of a "disciplinary turn," an ongoing shift from a "field" to a full-fledged discipline. Yancey cites four contemporary trends as primary catalysts for this disciplinary turn: a resurgence in empirical research, particularly in writing transfer; efforts to consolidate the knowledge of the field, including Linda Adler-Kassner and Elizabeth Wardle's (2015, 2020) two volumes on threshold concepts; the continued growth of undergraduate major programs in writing and rhetoric; and the institutional presence of the field codified by those programs. As the current volume and many other books and articles attest, writing transfer continues to be a pressing exigence for researchers, identifying ways students adapt their writing knowledge in new contexts and informing the development of pedagogies to facilitate transfer. By conducting research into writing transfer, we have begun to demonstrate the effectiveness of undergraduate writing programs in preparing students for future writing; to put it simply, transfer research provides evidence that our writing pedagogies *work*.

However, despite this widespread interest in writing transfer, few scholars (Hall, Romo, and Wardle 2018; Scott and Wardle 2015) have studied how undergraduate writing majors can better prepare students for transfer into multimodal environments and non-academic contexts. If we grant Yancey's claim that transfer research and undergraduate major programs contribute to our disciplinary development, transfer research within those programs can augment these disciplinary contributions: by researching the efficacy of programs to facilitate multimodal transfer, we can become more deliberate in designing and revising programs that prepare students for future non-academic rhetorical writing. Subsequently, by documenting the successes of undergraduate major

https://doi.org/10.7330/9781646425341.c009

programs in facilitating transfer, we can foster their continued development and further solidify our disciplinary presence within the contexts of higher education.

To better address these disciplinary contributions, this chapter presents the findings of a qualitative study identifying successful and failed multimodal transfer of alumni of Florida State University's editing, writing, and media (EWM) concentration. The experiences of alumni represent a rich site of inquiry given the three potential sites for transfer they offer: first, from their prior literacy experiences to a writing and rhetoric curriculum; second, from a writing and rhetoric curriculum to concurrent academic and co-curricular activities; and third, from a writing and rhetoric curriculum to post-graduation writing endeavors. While previous alumni studies (Blythe, Lauer, and Curran 2014; Cosgrove 2010; Weisser and Grobman 2012) have established alumni writing as thoroughly multimodal, they haven't addressed the dynamics of influence operating in the three sometimes overlapping contexts of prior literacies, study and practice in the major, and post-graduation writing lives. The study presented here identifies the ways alumni do or do not transfer writing knowledge across these contexts and, based on those findings, argues for strategies guiding the design of major programs that can better prepare students to transfer rhetorical knowledge into non-academic writing contexts after graduation.

The history and curriculum of the EWM program have been fully documented by Kristie Fleckenstein, Kathleen Blake Yancey, Matthew Davis, and Katherine T. Bridgman (2013) and Davis, Fleckenstein, and Yancey (2015). Briefly, the EWM program is one of three undergraduate concentrations in the English Department at Florida State University, alongside programs in creative writing and literature, media, and culture. The concentration was approved by a faculty vote in 2009, with the initial class graduating in the spring of 2010. Following this first graduating class, enrollment in the program exceeded departmental expectations of 200 students in two years; within the first nine months, 330 students had declared an EWM major (Davis, Brock, and McElroy 2012). Given the program's success in enrolling students, EWM alumni represent a rich source of data, thus guiding my research design of an IRB-approved study conducted during the 2017–2018 academic year. The study relied on a Qualtrics survey emailed to the then 1,184 graduates of the program—garnering 174 complete responses (14.7%)—and six one-hour interviews conducted via Google Hangout. While the study's survey and interviews produced macro- and micro-level accounts of EWM alumni's writing lives, I will focus primarily on the micro-level interview data, as they provide the most direct insight into areas in which transfer does and does not occur during and after the EWM program.

I begin by reviewing alumni studies of undergraduate writing majors, pertinent transfer literature, and the study's methodology and methods. I then discuss three themes in the interviews: missed opportunities for transfer, the successful transfer of alums' writing/rhetoric knowledge into collegiate contexts and post-graduation writing, and the rhetorical nature of alums' multimodal professional writing, spanning multiple media and genres and necessitating the metacognitive ability to move between them. Within each theme, I offer curricular strategies that can better lead to alums' multimodal transfer in their post-graduation writing lives. I close by suggesting directions for future alumni transfer research and the importance of that research for our emergent disciplinarity.

SYNTHESIZING ALUMNI STUDY AND TRANSFER RESEARCH

Writing transfer research has generated a preponderance of scholarship identifying and theorizing transfer and pedagogies that contribute to it. Comparatively, programmatic alumni studies have been neither as numerous nor as expansive—primarily identifying and describing alumni writing, with alums' perceptions of their education remaining a secondary focus. While these prior studies have done well to provide portraits of alumni writing, those portraits only depict so much; alums' perceptions of their education and writing are equally important, as they allow us to pull back the curtain and understand if and how undergraduate majors shape alumni writing practice. To simultaneously capture alumni writing and their perceptions of an undergraduate major, the full study from which this chapter is derived weaves together approaches from both prior alumni studies and transfer research. By emulating alumni studies of undergraduate majors, it contributes to the growing portrait of alumni writing and, by incorporating aspects of transfer research focusing on different time periods in student/alumni lives, identifies ways alumni transferred their writing and rhetoric knowledge during and after an undergraduate major. However, given the context of this chapter and volume, I will focus my attention solely on the examples of transfer that emerged in the data.

The alumni studies of Stuart Blythe, Claire Lauer, and Paul G. Curran (2014), Christian Weisser and Laurie Grobman (2012), and Cornelius Cosgrove (2010) have sought to characterize the writing lives of alumni and, collectively, have shown that writing major alumni lead multifaceted writing lives: writing professionally in an array of industries, completing civic and self-sponsored writing, and composing in a range of multimodal genres and technologies. In addition to these three programmatic studies, Bradley Hughes, Paula Gillespie, and Harvey Kail's (2010) work also examines alumni but differs in two ways. First, rather than looking at undergraduate writing majors, the study focuses on alums who served as writing center tutors; second, rather than documenting alumni writing, the study assesses alumni perceptions of how their training and experience as tutors shaped their subsequent writing and professional lives.

Like these prior alumni studies, the current inquiry documents alumni's professional trajectories following graduation and gathers information regarding the influence of the undergraduate major on their subsequent writing lives. However, rather than only examining the major's influence on alumni *after* graduation, I have broadened the scope to include alums' prior literacies and their academic/co-curricular writing while still enrolled in college. This broader scope allows for a more capacious sense of how students transfer writing knowledge both during and after their time in an undergraduate writing major, necessitating drawing on transfer research that examines these specific dynamics.

In addition to curricular-based research of transfer in first-year composition (Wardle and Downs 2011; Yancey, Robertson, and Taczak 2014), scholars have extended transfer research by examining dynamics of transfer across different time periods in students' lives, including the role of students' prior knowledge and literacy practices in academic settings as well as student/alumni transitions into non-academic contexts. In examining the influence of students' prior lives and literacies on their education, scholars have explored the influence of students' prior knowledge (Robertson, Taczak, and Yancey 2012) and emotional dispositions (Driscoll and Powell 2016; Driscoll and Wells 2012; Wardle 2012) on student writing in academic settings. Others have mapped the ways students transfer their prior literacies and co-curricular writing into academic settings (DePalma 2015; Roozen 2008; Rosinski 2016). Similarly, scholars have also examined the strategies students use to navigate the "transitions" from academic to non-academic writing contexts, highlighting how students transfer writing knowledge into their co-curricular, civic, and professional writing activities while still in college and beyond (Anson and Forsberg 1990; Beaufort 2007; Yancey et al. 2019).

By expanding alumni research to include transfer during and after the undergraduate major, we develop a deeper understanding of the ability of undergraduate majors to prepare students for their subsequent writing lives. The transfer of students' prior literacies into academic contexts can encourage student learning by helping them contextualize new rhetorical concepts within their preexisting literacies, making explicit tacit understandings of rhetoric in their self-sponsored writing. Given that this type of transfer can aid learning and, theoretically, better learning can lead to future transfer, it is important to track if and how alumni were able to draw upon their prior literacies in the undergraduate major. Furthermore, since a student's time in a major is significantly longer than it is in a single writing course, transfer is more likely to occur while they are still enrolled in a program; as such, it is important to determine if, when, and where concurrent transfer occurs. Incorporating these aspects of transfer research into an alumni study cataloging alumni writing ultimately contributes to a fuller sense of how a program does or does not prepare students for their post-graduation writing lives.

ADAPTING CURRICULAR FRAMEWORKS FOR ALUMNI STUDY

The extended chronological scope of this study necessitates a methodological framework accounting for student experiences over time. As such, this study adapts Kathleen Blake Yancey's curricular framework developed in *Reflection in the Writing Classroom* (1998) and *Teaching Literature as Reflective Practice* (2004) and adapted for programmatic study with Kara Taczak in their chapter in *Naming What We Know: Threshold Concepts of Writing Studies* (Taczak and Yancey 2015). Yancey's framework consists of three different curricula—the curriculum as delivered, lived, and experienced—and serves as a heuristic for understanding how students incorporate their prior experiences into an academic curriculum; however, researching how alumni transfer their academic experiences into their lives after graduation requires the addition of a fourth component to the framework, which I have called the remembered curriculum.

The delivered curriculum consists of the institutional materials that define a program of study—programmatic outcomes, course descriptions, syllabi, readings, assignment prompts, and others. Briefly, the EWM program's delivered curriculum "emphasizes the production, analysis, and interpretation . . . of texts [and] engages students in praxis . . . [to develop their] editorial expertise and writing skills" (English Department at Florida State University n.d.). After taking an entry-level Introduction to English Studies course, students complete three gateway courses in rhetoric, composition, and history of text technologies; three advanced courses in composition, rhetoric, visual

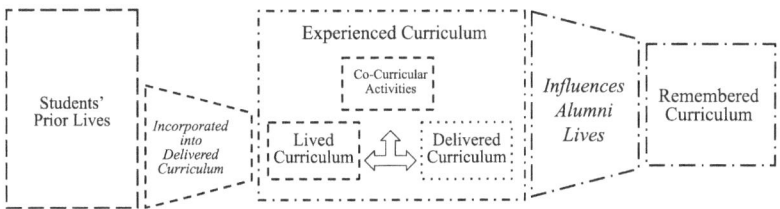

Figure 9.1. Yancey's curricular framework, expanded for alumni study

rhetoric, editing, and/or publishing, allowing students the autonomy to specialize in areas that align with their interests; four electives in the department; and a required internship in writing, editing, or both.

The lived curriculum encompasses the elements of a student's previous knowledge, experiences, and literacies—what Kevin Roozen describes as "literate activity" (chapter 7, this volume)—that they incorporate into the delivered curriculum of a program, which gives rise to the experienced curriculum. The experienced curriculum is conceived of as the sum total of a student's educational experiences, including what they learn, the projects they complete, the lived curricula they incorporate into a program, their co-curricular activities, and the relationships they form and learn from. Once a student graduates, the experienced curriculum draws to a close; ideally, students carry forward their experienced curriculum—or elements of it—so it shapes their subsequent writing practice. These elements constitute alumni's remembered curriculum.

The interrelationships among these curricula are dependent on the animating force of transfer in three areas. First, the lived curriculum emerges from elements of students' prior lives they transfer into academic and co-curricular contexts; second, within the experienced curriculum, students may transfer their academic learning into other disciplinary and co-curricular contexts (or vice versa); and third, the remembered curriculum is defined by elements of alums' educational experiences they transfer into their post-graduation writing lives. This study delineates these dynamics of transfer by identifying elements of alums' lived, experienced, and remembered curricula and traces the influence these elements exert on alumni's lives during and after the program.

Using this curricular framework, I designed a mixed methods study documenting alumni's writing lives and identifying these three areas of transfer. As with prior alumni studies, I relied on a survey to provide a macro-level portrait of five areas: demographics, reasons for enrolling in the major, academic and professional experiences following graduation, the spheres and genres in which alumni compose, and quantitative ratings of the program's impact on their current writing. The majority of the survey provides a portrait of alumni writing, but two areas—reasons for enrolling and quantitative ratings of the program—provide surface-level snapshots of alums' lived and remembered curricula. By determining reasons for enrolling in the major, we gain perspective on what, if any, elements of their lived curricula led them to the program to begin with; and the quantitative ratings allowed alums to holistically assess the degree to which their education influences their current writing, that is, their remembered curricula.

To complement the macro-level account of the survey data, the six interviews provide micro-level testimony honing in on alums' experienced and remembered curricula. The subjects were selected using a multi-tier principle of selection, representing relative diversity in their spheres of current writing, graduating class, and demographics. My subjects included:

- **Leslie**: white female, Class of 2016, logistics specialist at a national paper company
- **Marcia**: Latinx female, Class of 2012, senior recruiter for an international cruise line and an MBA student
- **Hannah**: African American female, Class of 2015, communications assistant in municipal government
- **Rose**: white female, Class of 2010, senior digital editor at a national wedding publication
- **Claire**: white female, Class of 2014, field marketing specialist for an international footwear brand and an MA student in parks and recreation
- **Eli**: white male, Class of 2011, senior strategist at an international social media consulting firm

Each interview opened with two mapping activities modeled after an informal study conducted at the University of Massachusetts–Amherst to develop their integrative experience requirement—one map documenting relationships among their current writing in the professional, public, and private spheres, and another map representing influences among their academic, co-curricular, and professional writing experiences during college. These maps prompted subjects to begin thinking about if and how these different areas of writing influence one another, preparing them for the semi-structured interview questions that followed.

I began with the remembered curriculum, asking about the relationships on their first map, their current writing activities and process, and rhetorical awareness of context, audience, and genre—inferring the expression of rhetorical thinking in those responses to be the influence of the undergraduate major. I then transitioned to the experienced curriculum, asking explicitly about the influence of the program on other courses, co-curriculars, internships, jobs—and vice versa. I closed by returning to the remembered curriculum and asking them to read across both of their maps, articulating what influence the undergraduate major had on their current writing lives. These interview questions had subjects articulate the dynamics of influence among the different spheres of their lives; as a result, they point to specific instances in which alums attempted, succeeded, or failed to transfer their knowledge into and beyond the EWM program, helping to identify areas in which undergraduate majors can potentially improve in the future.

MISSED OPPORTUNITIES FOR TRANSFER

Given the proliferation of digital multimodal composing, the lived curricula students and alumni can draw on in writing majors is potentially expansive—at least in concept. However, only Marcia and Hannah indicated that they had prior multimodal composing experience; like prior studies documenting negative or stifled transfer (Anson 2016; Davis, Brock, and McElroy 2012; Nowacek 2011), their interviews show that they had minimal opportunities to transfer those multimodal practices into the major.

Marcia came into the major with prior graphic design experience, stating "I had a background in graphic design, more so just from my school and a hobby"; however, she could only point to one instance in which her graphic design experience influenced her undergraduate education: the visual design of an ePortfolio. Hannah represents an even more pronounced case of missed opportunities for transfer, as her prior multimodal experiences were more expansive: she had completed web design and blogging and helped local artists develop their presence on social media prior to the program. But in spite of Hannah's multimodal literacies, she did not identify instances in which they influenced her coursework; in fact, she went so far as to say her coursework *displaced* her prior multimodal writing: "Before [college], I would blog, and I had a website and [would] just write . . . outside of class, but I stopped doing that because of the amount of writing that I was doing for class."

Marcia's and Hannah's minimal transfer of their previous multimodal composing indicates that the program did not offer opportunities or emphasize the potential for alumni to draw on their prior composing to shape their academic experiences. While Marcia transferred her graphic design experience into an ePortfolio assignment, neither she nor Hannah could further transfer their knowledge into multimodal programmatic contexts. In fact, transfer occurred just as frequently around or alongside the program, as both Marcia and Hannah applied their multimodal literacies in other, non-programmatic contexts: Marcia worked as a graphic designer in the university's publications office designing newsletters, and Hannah, without an outlet to complete her online writing, supplemented her multimodal composing by helping friends complete video projects. As both Anna V. Knuston and Ryan P. Shepherd argue (chapters 5 and 6, respectively, this volume), encouraging students to incorporate their home literacies into writing classrooms can help them forge connections between the delivered curriculum of a writing program and the "other curriculum" of their writing lives, thus making the possibilities for multimodal transfer more visible to students. To emphasize these possibilities for transfer, instructors might have students generate an inventory of their composing practices across all contexts and encourage (or require) them to complete an assignment in an already familiar medium or genre. Alongside such an inventory, Michael-John DePalma's (2015) adaptive transfer reflection prompts can also guide students to consciously articulate how they are integrating their previous multimodal experiences into course projects. At the programmatic level, faculty can encourage this type of reflection and transfer of students' prior literacies in mentoring or advising contexts.

CONCURRENT AND SUBSEQUENT TRANSFER

Despite alums' minimal transfer of their multimodal literacies into the program, the six interview subjects identified several instances of transfer out of the program, including both concurrent transfer (what Yancey and her coauthors [2019] refer to as "just-in-time" transfer) into classes, co-curriculars, and internships during college, and subsequent transfer into their professional writing following graduation. Considering alums' concurrent transfer, all six claimed their coursework in writing and rhetoric had impacted their college experiences in some form or fashion, including writing classes better preparing them for other alphabetic assignments. While less common than transferring alphabetic writing knowledge, concurrent multimodal transfer appears to be concentrated in alums' internships, where they used advanced composing technologies to complete client-based writing in professional contexts. For example, Leslie cites a course in which she learned the Adobe Creative Suite as directly influencing her multimodal composing in her internship at a summer camp:

> So, my advanced editing and writing class . . . we [learned] how to use InDesign and Photoshop . . . So when I went to my internship, I created their parent handbook. I was pretty much on my own, so I took my [rhetorical] concepts, and my ability to use InDesign, [and] I would not have created the parent handbook if I did not have that ability in InDesign. What I originally did was edit the camp staff manual, but then I added on the handbook to just be like "oh, this is something else that we need and is something I have the ability to do."

Two programmatic experiences influenced Leslie's completion of the parent handbook: learning the Adobe Creative Suite and developing the rhetorical thinking necessary to successfully design the handbook. The advanced course appears to be the primary catalyst for this instance of multimodal transfer, as it provided her with technical knowledge of InDesign, and she "would not have created the parent handbook if I did not have that ability." But as she explains the handbook further, we see that it wasn't just her technical knowledge that influenced the task; her rhetorical thinking played an equally important role by allowing her to identify the rhetorical need for a handbook. In recognizing that "oh, this is something else we need," Leslie displays her ability to identify a *kairos*, and in drawing on "my [rhetorical] concepts," she was able to include information appropriate for the genre and pertinent to the audience of campers' parents. This confluence of technical knowledge and rhetorical thinking facilitated Leslie's transfer out of the program and into the internship.

The interviews also show ways alums' writing knowledge influences their writing following graduation—specifically in professional writing contexts. Like their concurrent transfer above, the six subjects identified ways they have been able to apply alphabetic writing knowledge in new contexts, but they also spoke to how the program prepared them to complete multimodal professional writing tasks. For example, Eli transferred the rhetorical thinking he had gained in his coursework into an internship, and he was so successful that he was hired as a paid employee after graduation. Further, Claire cites an ePortfolio assignment that "really helped me see how I could specifically use this stuff," using the ePortfolio as a supplement to her job applications. Eli's transition from student-intern to alumni-employee and Claire's completion of the ePortfolio show how these two high-impact practices (Kuh 2008) can contribute to students' nascent identities as writing professionals, allowing them to begin to envision their writing in future contexts and thus establishing potential avenues for alums' transfer.

Even though Hannah's experiences were a notable example of missed opportunities for transfer, she spoke at length about how her rhetorical training has given her a "competitive edge" at her job. Specifically, Hannah spoke to the major's gateway writing course as contributing to that competitive edge. When asked about the course, I reminded her of the assignment sequence in which students complete projects for print, screen, and online environments; she proclaimed "okay, yeah, that is my job—like, all the way." Elaborating on the influence of the course on her job, she described having to circulate emergency messaging across multiple media during an approaching hurricane:

> One of the things my instructor instilled was different methods—how you write with a pen or a typewriter—it all just depends. We learned during the hurricane [that] how you write something to the news versus how you write something on your website is totally different. People are gonna be looking at information differently on the news; they're gonna pull out whatever stands out, versus on the website they're looking for detailed communication, and they want it placed a certain way. So, like, arrangement and things.

Despite initially citing the alphabetic examples of writing with a "pen" and "typewriter," Hannah's description of this task shows how her coursework directly influenced her multimodal professional writing, teaching her how writing must shift across contexts; as she says, "it all just depends." Delineating differences between the two contexts of "the news" and her city's website, Hannah pays specific attention to how audiences will interact with her writing. When reading or watching the news, audience members look for "whatever stands out," that is, urgent, pertinent information; website readers seek out "detailed communication" and expect it to be visually presented in a "certain way"—something Hannah describes as "arrangement," which could be taken to mean layout or an invocation of the rhetorical canon. In weaving together considerations of genre conventions, audience expectations, and "arrangement," Hannah shows that she can keep her rhetorical wits about her, even in the high-stakes context of an emergency.

These examples highlight multiple aspects of alumni experiences influencing their concurrent and subsequent multimodal transfer and offer insight for developing undergraduate majors that can better lead to these types of transfer. Leslie, Eli, and Hannah spoke to the importance of rhetorical thinking for their internships and jobs, a mind-set they learned through their coursework; for Leslie and Eli, their internships provided them with non-academic contexts in which they could apply that rhetorical thinking. These experiences suggest that programs should provide students with a foundation of rhetorical knowledge—what Logan Bearden calls a "rhetorical metalanguage" (chapter 8, this volume)—and offer a variety of non-academic writing contexts in which they can apply it, as non-academic writing was most conducive to alums' multimodal transfer. Programmatically, those non-academic contexts may take the form of internships or in-class assignments such as service-learning or client-based projects with "real" audiences (Rosinski 2016). Further, Claire's curation of an ePortfolio enabled her to envision how she could transfer her knowledge to other contexts, using it for job applications after graduation. Claire's ePortfolio illustrates the high impact of such an assignment—whether embedded in a course or as a program requirement—as it allows students to reflect on their growth as writers over time and envision how their current composing can aid and assist them in the future. Finally, Leslie's, Hannah's, and Eli's descriptions of their professional writing tasks establish the importance of being able to compose in a range of multimodal composing environments and specialized composing tools—a theme that becomes more prominent by further examining the group's multimodal writing.

GENRE, MEDIA, AND METACOGNITION

Beyond isolating instances of transfer, the interviews also identified the types of writing alumni complete in their post-graduation lives. Alumni spoke most frequently of their professional writing, defined by two key characteristics: first, it occurs in a range of media and genres; second, this range of tasks necessitates a strong sense of metacognitive rhetorical awareness, requiring alumni to remain consistently cognizant of the relationships among purpose, audience, and genre as they move across contexts. In considering the six interview subjects' writing lives, Marcia, Eli, Rose, and Hannah produce more multimodal professional writing, so this section focuses on these four subjects.

As seen in table 9.1, the four subjects complete varying types of multimodal writing spanning several genres, and the degree to which they complete multimodal writing is seemingly determined by their respective positions and the industries in which they work. As Marcia and Eli work in corporate professional environments, their professional writing is defined by more conventional workplace genres. Rose and Hannah, who, respectively, work in publishing and government communications,

Table 9.1. Alums' multimodal professional writing genres

Interview Subject	Professional Writing Genres

Marcia	• Résumé design
	• Multimedia presentations
	  – Slideshows
	  – Videos
	  – Data visualization

Eli	• Newsletters • Slideshows • Emails • Whitepapers
Rose	• Alphabetic articles (print and digital) • Search engine optimization web writing • Social media posts • Video copy
Hannah	• Press releases • Email blasts • Social media posts • Feature articles for newsletters • Video scripts • Document design • Web design

compose in a wider range of media and genres, as writing is a primary responsibility of their positions.

When addressing the range of her writing responsibilities, Rose observes that at least in the publishing industry, this repertoire of multimodal capabilities has become the industry standard for writing professionals: "I know so many people now coming out of college [asking] 'what's the one skill I should have?' And, you know, everyone wants writers and editors to be video producers and coders now . . . so it's like you can't just be a writer anymore." Given the range of genres collected in table 9.1, alongside Rose's claim that "you can't just be a writer anymore," these alums' professional writing appears to be thoroughly multimodal. This suggests that to enable post-graduation transfer, undergraduate major programs should design opportunities for students to become proficient in a range of multimodal tasks, which may include designing print materials, preparing multimedia presentations (including audio or video composing or both), and completing online writing tasks.

METACOGNITIVE RHETORICAL AWARENESS

In discussing their professional writing tasks, Marcia, Eli, Hannah, and Rose exhibited varying degrees of rhetorical awareness, highlighting how considerations of context, audience, media, genre, or some combination informed their composing. For Marcia and Eli, their rhetorical considerations were defined by straightforward considerations of context and audience, suggesting some degree of transfer. However, Rose's and Hannah's descriptions of their professional writing went beyond context and audience to include fully integrated understandings of the interrelationships among rhetorical factors and how they function across contexts. In actively comparing the nuances of different writing contexts and detailing the rhetorical decisions those nuances require, Rose and Hannah exhibited a strong metacognitive awareness of how their writing must change across contexts, suggesting a higher degree of transfer from the undergraduate major.

As discussed in the prior section, Hannah's comparison of writing for broadcast news and the city's website during a hurricane exemplifies how metacognitive considerations of audience, media, and genre shape her thinking when working to address the same rhetorical exigence. Similarly, Rose's work as a senior digital editor requires metacognitive consideration of the interplay among purpose, audience, media, and genre. Part of her responsibilities include a kind of rhetorical curation, selecting which articles to circulate in the magazine's various print and digital forums. The task requires her to remain cognizant of the expectations of audiences in each of those spaces, a process she describes in some detail:

> We definitely have a different set of needs from our audience for every platform. Our Facebook audience, they want content that entertains them; they want a break from wedding planning. But our newsletter audience really cares about planning . . . they want to be told what to do. With our Instagram audience, it's all about the imagery, so they want lots of inspiration. And if you pick up the magazine, that means you want to sit and daydream a little . . . you kind of want the whole experience. All of our platforms really do differ, so we have to keep that in mind when we're selecting articles for whichever platform.

Rose articulates a sophisticated understanding of the rhetorical factors guiding her editing process, strategizing how to place the magazine's content at the intersection of audience motivations, rhetorical purposes, and media/genre conventions. Audience motivations appear to be her guiding principle; stemming from each audience's needs, Rose and her colleagues choose content that will simultaneously meet those needs and fit within the conventions of each of those different platforms—ultimately delivering entertainment, information, inspiration, or the "whole experience."

These descriptions of alums' professional writing highlight key aspects of multimodal writing in the workplace and present opportunities for undergraduate majors to better prepare students for transfer into professional writing after graduation. The range of alums' professional writing genres and Rose's observation that "you can't just be a writer anymore" suggest that students are likely to encounter an array of media, genres, and technologies in their post-graduation writing lives. To prepare students to meet the demands of these contexts, it is important that programs design assignments and experiences that reflect alumni writing lives in several multimodal contexts: composing in different genres, becoming comfortable in multiple media environments, and engaging with a variety of composing technologies. Such a range of multimodal experiences can develop avenues for concurrent and future multimodal transfer and better prepare students for post-graduation writing contexts.

However, that experience in and of itself is not sufficient for transfer; to succeed in multi-genre composing, alumni must also enact some degree of rhetorical awareness—at the very least, taking purpose and audience into account, like Marcia and Eli, or, like Hannah and Rose, actively incorporating metacognitive considerations of medium and genre conventions into their composing processes. Rose's and Hannah's stronger metacognition may be attributed to the wider range of media and genres in which they write relative to Marcia and Eli; since they more frequently contend with how to best adapt their writing to different contexts, their responsibilities may require them to think rhetorically more often, further developing their metacognitive awareness. No matter the cause of this difference, both Hannah's experience of preparing emergency hurricane messaging for multiple outlets and Rose's thick description of her team's considerations of audience and medium illustrate the rhetorical sophistication required of professional writers to communicate across contexts. To help students develop this metacognitive awareness before they leave a major, programs must teach them how to recognize, learn, work within, and deviate from media and genre conventions as rhetorical contexts call for it. To do so, instructors can have students not only complete reflective writing during multimodal assignments to encourage transfer of students' previous knowledge but also complete reflections after multimodal projects to articulate how they applied rhetorical concepts they have learned and begin developing strategies for becoming acclimated to new genres, technologies, and media environments—practicing the "mindful abstraction" Ryan P. Shepherd (chapter 6, this volume) describes as necessary to high-road transfer.

CONCLUSION

While not exhaustive of the interviews, the excerpts presented here establish pathways of multimodal transfer from an undergraduate major to alums' college experiences and post-graduation writing. All six interview subjects cited the importance of coursework, internships, and ePortfolios in providing them with rhetorical knowledge and the multimodal contexts to begin applying it—particularly non-academic contexts like internships or the use of an ePortfolio in a job search. Similarly, these alums' professional writing shows the wide variety of their writing contexts and the metacognitive thinking required to transfer writing knowledge into those contexts. However, despite the prevalence of transfer *out* of the program, there was a pronounced lack of multimodal transfer *into* the program, with alumni minimally drawing on prior multimodal literacies to complete course assignments. Taken together, these three findings offer ideas for the design or revision of major programs to improve student experiences by providing opportunities to integrate prior multimodal composing, apply their writing knowledge in non-academic contexts, and prepare them for the types of writing tasks they will likely encounter after graduation. As described above, programs should incorporate assignments and experiences that reflect alumni writing tasks, having students compose in multiple media and genres and, when possible, writing in non-academic contexts. Across those experiences, students should consistently engage in metacognitive reflective writing—during and after the completion of a multimodal assignment and in the form of a reflective ePortfolio—so they can see the interrelationships among their prior literacies, current learning, and writing futures and draw on them accordingly.

By designing and revising undergraduate major programs with these principles and strategies in mind, we can better prepare our students to transfer writing knowledge and demonstrate their expertise following graduation, no matter the academic or professional paths they take. However, to further improve undergraduate major programs, we should continue to develop research projects that examine alumni writing and transfer as well as workplace writing writ large. Studies in these areas can better survey the writing landscape our alumni enter, allowing us to identify non-academic genres relevant to alumni and the kinds of thinking and writing processes they find necessary to succeed in their writing lives. Doing so can result in pedagogies that focus less on assignments that provide a one-to-one genre correlation to alumni writing and instead help students develop the metacognitive habits and writing processes alumni rely on to succeed, regardless of context, audience, or genre. Beyond the local benefits of alumni research to any one program, growing our body of knowledge about alumni writing and transfer can contribute to writing studies' emergent disciplinarity in two key ways. First, if transfer research can establish the success of undergraduate major programs in preparing students to write in the academic, professional, and public spheres, those findings can foster the continued creation and development of major programs in writing and rhetoric. Second, the growth of undergraduate major programs can not only reinforce our disciplinary presence within institutions of higher education but can also establish the importance of undergraduate education in writing and rhetoric to stakeholders in non-academic contexts so that graduates of writing and rhetoric majors become valued members of professional and civic organizations, sought out by employers and civic leaders alike.

REFERENCES

Adler-Kassner, Linda, and Elizabeth Wardle 2015. *Naming What We Know: Threshold Concepts of Writing Studies*. Logan: Utah State University Press.

Adler-Kassner, Linda, and Elizabeth Wardle 2020. *(Re)Considering What We Know: Learning Thresholds in Writing, Composition, Rhetoric, and Literacy*. Logan: Utah State University Press.

Anson, Chris. 2016. "The Pop Warner Chronicles: A Case Study in Contextual Adaptation and the Transfer of Writing Ability." *College Composition and Communication* 67 (4): 518–549.

Anson, Chris, and Lee Forsberg. 1990. "Moving beyond the Academic Community: Transitional Stages in Professional Writing." *Written Communication* 7 (2): 200–231.

Beaufort, Anne. 2007. *College Writing and Beyond: A New Framework for University Writing Instruction*. Logan: Utah State University Press.

Blythe, Stuart, Claire Lauer, and Paul G. Curran. 2014. "Professional and Technical Communication in a Web 2.0 World." *Technical Communication Quarterly* 23: 265–287.

Cosgrove, Cornelius. 2010. "What Our Graduates Write: Making Program Assessment Both Authentic and Persuasive." *College Composition and Communication* 62 (2): 311–335.

Davis, Matthew, Kevin Brock, and Stephen J. McElroy. 2012. "Expanding the Available Means of Composing: Three Sites of Inquiry." *Enculturation* 14. https://enculturation.net/files/availablemeans/index.html.

Davis, Matthew, Kristie Fleckenstein, and Kathleen Blake Yancey. 2015. "A Matter of Design: Context and Available Resources in the Development of a New English Major at Florida State University." In *Writing Majors: Eighteen Program Profiles*, edited by Greg Giberson, Jim Nugent, and Lori Ostergaard, 175–189. Logan: Utah State University Press.

DePalma, Michael-John. 2015. "Tracing Transfer across Media: Investigating Writers' Perceptions of Cross-Contextual and Rhetorical Reshaping in Processes of Remediation." *College Composition and Communication* 66 (4): 615–642.

Driscoll, Dana Lynn, and Roger Powell. 2016. "States, Traits, and Dispositions: The Impact of Emotion on Writing Development and Writing Transfer across College Courses and Beyond." *Composition Forum* 34. https://compositionforum.com/issue/34/states-traits.php.

Driscoll, Dana Lynn, and Jennifer Wells. 2012. "Beyond Knowledge and Skills: Writing Transfer and the Role of Student Dispositions." *Composition Forum* 26. https://compositionforum.com/issue/26/beyond-knowledge-skills.php.

English Department at Florida State University. n.d. "Editing, Writing, and Media." https://english.fsu.edu/programs/editing-writing-and-media.

Fleckenstein, Kristie, Kathleen Blake Yancey, Matthew Davis, and Katherine T. Bridgman. 2013. "Program Sustainability: Curricular Resilience in Florida State University's Editing, Writing, and Media Concentration." *South Atlantic Review* 78 (1–2): 10–33.

Hall, R. Mark, Mikael Romo, and Elizabeth Wardle. 2018. "Teaching and Learning Threshold Concepts in a Writing Major: Liminality, Dispositions, and Program Design." *Composition Forum* 38. https://compositionforum.com/issue/38/threshold.php.

Hughes, Bradley, Paula Gillespie, and Harvey Kail. 2010. "What They Take with Them: Findings from the Peer Writing Tutor Alumni Research Project." *Writing Center Journal* 20 (2): 12–46.

Kuh, George. 2008. *High-Impact Educational Practices*. Washington, DC: American Association of Colleges and Universities.

Nowacek, Rebecca. 2011. *Agents of Integration: Understanding Transfer as a Rhetorical Act*. Champaign, IL: National Council of Teachers of English.

Robertson, Liane, Kara Taczak, and Kathleen Blake Yancey. 2012. "Notes toward a Theory of Prior Knowledge and Its Role in College Composers' Transfer of Knowledge and Practice." *Composition Forum* 26. https://www.compositionforum.com/issue/26/prior-knowledge-transfer.php.

Roozen, Kevin. 2008. "Journalism, Poetry, Stand-Up Comedy, and Academic Literacy: Mapping the Interplay of Curricular and Extracurricular Literate Activities." *Journal of Basic Writing* 27 (1): 5–34.

Rosinski, Paula. 2016. "Students' Perceptions of the Transfer of Rhetorical Knowledge between Digital Self-Sponsored Writing and Academic Writing: The Importance of Authentic Contexts and Reflection." In *Critical Transitions: Writing and the Question of Transfer*, edited by Chris Anson and Jessie Moore, 247–271. Fort Collins, CO: WAC Clearinghouse.

Scott, J. Blake, and Elizabeth Wardle. 2015. "Using Threshold Concepts to Inform Writing and Rhetoric Undergraduate Majors: The UCF Experiment." In *Naming What We Know: Threshold Concepts of Writing Studies*, edited by Linda Adler-Kassner and Elizabeth Wardle, 122–139. Logan: Utah State University Press.

Taczak, Kara, and Kathleen Blake Yancey. 2015. "Threshold Concepts in Rhetoric and Composition Doctoral Education: The Delivered, Lived, and Experienced Curricula." In *Naming What We Know: Threshold Concepts of Writing Studies*, edited by Linda Adler-Kassner and Elizabeth Wardle, 140–154. Logan: Utah State University Press.

Wardle, Elizabeth. 2012. "Creative Repurposing for Expansive Learning: Considering 'Problem-Exploring' and 'Answer-Getting' Dispositions in Individuals and Fields." *Composition Forum* 26. https://www.compositionforum.com/issue/26/creative-repurposing.php.

Wardle, Elizabeth, and Doug Downs. 2011. *Writing about Writing: A College Reader*. Boston: Bedford/St. Martin's.

Weisser, Christian, and Laurie Grobman. 2012. "Undergraduate Writing Majors and the Rhetoric of Professionalism." *Composition Studies* 40 (1): 39–59.

Yancey, Kathleen Blake. 1998. *Reflection in the Writing Classroom*. Logan: Utah State University Press.

Yancey, Kathleen Blake. 2004. *Teaching Literature as Reflective Practice*. Champaign, IL: National Council of Teachers of English.

Yancey, Kathleen Blake. 2018. "Mapping the Turn to Disciplinarity: A Historical Analysis of Composition's Trajectory and Its Current Moment." In *Composition, Rhetoric, and*

Disciplinarity, edited by Rita Malenczyk, Susan Miller-Cochran, Elizabeth Wardle, and Kathleen Blake Yancey, 15–35. Logan: Utah State University Press.

Yancey, Kathleen Blake, Matthew Davis, Liane Robertson, Kara Taczak, and Erin Workman. 2019. "The Teaching for Transfer Curriculum: The Role of Concurrent Transfer and Inside- and Outside-School Contexts in Supporting Students' Writing Development." *College Composition and Communication* 71 (2): 268–295.

Yancey, Kathleen Blake, Liane Robertson, and Kara Taczak. 2014. *Writing across Contexts: Transfer, Composition, and Sites of Writing.* Logan: Utah State University Press.

10
IF YOU BUILD IT, WILL THEY USE IT
Composing Infrastructures, Communities of
Practice, and Instructor Dispositions

Jeff Naftzinger

It almost goes without saying that our field believes in the benefits—and even the necessity—of embracing multimodal composing and incorporating more than just words into our classrooms (see Kress 1999; Wysocki 2004; Yancey 2004, among others). Our discussions focus on the pedagogical value of multimodal composing and argue that we should be adjusting our outcomes, offering new courses, and assigning multimodal projects (see Bearden, chapter 8, this volume, for discussions of these curricular efforts). One of the ways we have encouraged and supported these efforts on our campuses is by building what Stuart Selber (2009, 12) calls the "composing infrastructure" or the "institutional resources" that support digital and multimodal composing. This can include "internet backbones, email servers, library databases, wireless networks, spam filters, and more" (12), as well as "spaces—physical, pedagogical, organizational—within which computer-based activities [at an institution] are deeply situated" (12).

Because the composing infrastructure at an institution can facilitate or limit multimodal composing in our classes, edited collections on composing infrastructure (e.g., Carpenter et al. 2015; DeVoss, McKee, and Selfe 2009; Purdy and DeVoss 2015) focus primarily on building and supporting the physical infrastructure itself and less on getting instructors to integrate it into their pedagogies. To paraphrase a cliché, the implication seems to be: if you build the infrastructure, instructors will use it. But not all instructors will be prepared to use the composing infrastructure that is available to them, due to their own experience—or *in*experience—with digital technologies in the classroom and the dispositions they've formed toward the infrastructure (see Borgman 2019; Duffelmeyer 2003; Journet 2007). So then the question becomes: if we build it, *will* they use it? As the study discussed in this chapter shows, not all instructors will be interested in using the infrastructure, so we might also ask: how can we motivate them to be interested in using it?

One way to approach these questions is by looking at instructors' dispositions toward digital pedagogies and their campuses' composing infrastructures and how those dispositions shape their motivations and choices. "Dispositions," Dana Lynn Driscoll and Jennifer Wells (2012) explain, "are not knowledge, skills, or abilities—they are qualities that determine how learners use and adapt their knowledge" in ways that can "allow or prevent successful development from taking place." As Neil Baird and Bradley Dilger (2017, 689) add, these dispositions "can be generative or disruptive, affecting writers' willingness to engage in writing transfer"; they can help explain why some students will transfer writing knowledge from one context to another while other students will not—or, in the context of this chapter, why some instructors will make use of the infrastructure and assign digital projects and others will not. Instructors might have transferrable knowledge and experiences around multimodal composing and teaching that can help them make use of their campuses' composing infrastructures, but— much like some of the tutors discussed by Kara Poe Alexander, Becca Cassady, and Michael-John DePalma (chapter 4, this volume) or the alumni discussed by Travis Maynard (chapter 9, this volume)—that transfer might not happen. Dispositions are one way to understand why it does and does not.

This chapter argues that instructors' dispositions influence their decisions and that the communities of practice (CoPs)—or the "groups of people who share a concern, a set of problems, or a passion about a topic, and who deepen their knowledge and expertise in this area by interacting on an ongoing basis" (Wenger, McDermott, and Snyder 2002, 4)—the instructors identify with can shape these dispositions in productive and unproductive ways. Instructors who identify with CoPs that provide models of digital composing and illustrate its value are more likely to have dispositions that encourage them to use the composing infrastructure and are more likely to assign digital projects to their students; instructors whose CoPs don't do so are less likely to assign these projects. To that end, if we really want to encourage instructors to use the composing infrastructures they have access to, then we should help them establish generative dispositions by ensuring that they see how CoPs they identify with—locally, in the fields they identify with, or both—can model digital composing and demonstrate its value.

In what follows, I focus on the dispositions and digital pedagogies of four graduate instructors (GIs) from two programs—literature (lit) and rhetoric and composition (rhet/comp)—in the English Department at Florida State University (FSU). FSU has a robust composing infrastructure that includes spaces (like multiliteracy centers and computer classrooms) and curricular efforts (like a writing major[1] and multimodal outcomes in first-year composition [FYC]) that should encourage digital composing. Despite similar access, the GIs from the Lit program did not assign any digital projects, while the GIs from the rhet/comp program frequently assigned them. The major difference was that the rhet/comp GIs identified with CoPs that modeled the use and value of digital assignments and thus formed generative dispositions toward including them in their classes while the Lit GIs did not. I draw on these findings to make two arguments for those who want to encourage and support multimodal composing: first, that CoPs function as integral sites for forming dispositions about digital teaching practices; second, that building and fostering CoPs *alongside* composing infrastructures can help instructors use them.

COMPOSING INFRASTRUCTURES, DISPOSITIONS, AND COPS: BEYOND BUILDING, TOWARD ENCOURAGING AND MODELING

These arguments—that dispositions and CoPs are important—might *seem* intuitive, but discussions of composing infrastructure often demonstrate what's gained with or lost without access to a robust composing infrastructure. They often overlook, however, what encourages the use of that infrastructure once it's built. If we only focus on new spaces, new tech, and new software and de-prioritize the instructors, their CoPs, and their dispositions, then we might not get them to actually use the infrastructures we build. The section that follows highlights how using the frame of dispositions can help us better understand why some instructors gravitate toward the infrastructure and others shy away from it, how the instructors' CoPs can shape those dispositions, and how this can be useful to think about alongside composing infrastructures.

An institution's composing infrastructure, as Dànielle Nicole DeVoss, Ellen Cushman, and Jeffrey T. Grabill (2005, 16) explain, can "make possible and limit, shape and constrain, influence and penetrate" multimodal composing. When instructors want to assign multimodal projects to their students, they argue, the infrastructure shapes the kinds of projects they can assign and the kinds of support they can offer students as they compose. While DeVoss, Cushman, and Grabill focus on what instructors are *able* to do with the infrastructure once it's built, Ryan (Rylish) M. Moeller, Cheryl E. Ball, and Kelli Cargile Cook (2009) demonstrate the ways faculty are *unable* to assign digital projects to their students and engage in their own research agendas due to the technological limitations in their department. In both cases, the authors argue that we should build composing infrastructures to encourage digital composing. The literature on infrastructure replicates this pattern and focuses mostly on the importance of building—both the technological spaces and the courses and groups that support that infrastructure once it's constructed (for examples, see edited collections like Carpenter et al. 2015; DeVoss, McKee, and Selfe 2009). These examples focus on instructors who have no hesitations about multimodal composing and using the infrastructure and are instead limited only by not having access to it. They overlook what Jessie Borgman (2019, 44) describes as "the fear instructors have about using multimodal assignments" in their classes, which can limit the ways they use the infrastructure they have access to.

For Borgman's (2019, 49) instructors, these fears were based around overwhelming logistics, unnecessary complications, student misunderstandings, and external judgment from students and peers. Likewise, Barb Blakey Duffelmeyer (2003, 299)—in outlining the concerns of GIs teaching in computer classrooms for the first time—adds fears around shifting models of teaching, of control, of authority, and of the field's values that confront them in these new technological spaces. Similar concerns are mentioned by Debra Journet (2007, 110), who describes hesitations around "learning to use multimodal technologies" and "understanding how multimodality connects to the primary goals of . . . writing classes." Discussions like these, around the barriers to making use of the infrastructure once it's there, are just as important as discussions about constructing it. Research on dispositions is a useful frame for understanding these barriers and how we might overcome them.

Just as dispositions "affect writers' willingness to engage in writing transfer" (Baird and Dilger 2017, 689), the three examples above demonstrate how they also affect instructors' willingness to incorporate digital composing into their classes and make use of their composing infrastructures. More specifically, these examples illustrate two of the dispositions identified by Driscoll and Wells (2012): (1) "Self-Efficacy," which "explains the relationship between students' beliefs about their capabilities and the likelihood they will take the steps needed to achieve their goals," and (2) "Expectancy-Value Theory of Motivation" (or Value), which argues that "if students don't value what they are learning or don't see how what they are learning will be useful to them in the future, they will not engage in mindful abstraction." Just as students with low self-efficacy will avoid engaging with difficult writing situations, instructors with low self-efficacy related to multimodal composing and teaching will avoid those situations. And just as students who do not see the value of writing or of what they're learning will be reluctant to transfer that knowledge, instructors who do not see the value of multimodal composing will be reluctant to transfer that knowledge—or reluctant to look for places it might transfer.

These instructor-focused examples can also help us see how dispositions toward multimodality can shift from disruptive to generative and how that shift in "individual dispositions . . . might be directly linked to dispositions of fields" (Wardle 2012) the instructors identify with. One place where instructors' individual dispositions encounter their, or *a*, field's disposition (as much as it can be unified) is in CoPs at their institutions and in more field-connected activities such as attending conferences and engaging in research. As members of CoPs "spend time together, they typically share information, insight, and advice. They help each other solve problems. They discuss their situations, their aspirations, and their needs. They ponder common issues, explore ideas, and act as sounding boards" (Wenger, McDermott, and Snyder 2002, 4–5). Looking specifically at CoPs in English departments, Richard J. Selfe (2007, 168) explains that members can "provide a space within which to share stories of what works and what does not, learn more about effective strategies for instruction, and expand their understanding of technology" and its uses in the classroom. When instructors are part of CoPs that have generative dispositions toward multimodal composing, they are more likely to develop similar dispositions. These shifts are illustrated in Duffelmeyer's (2003) and Journet's (2007) case studies at an institution and as part of a field, respectively.

Duffelmeyer (2003) demonstrates how a CoP at an institution can shift its members' dispositions around multimodal self-efficacy. Many of the GIs teaching in the computer classrooms for the first time weren't confident in their ability to teach in them; as a result, they found it difficult to transfer their understandings of writing and teaching into these new spaces. Once the GIs formed a CoP of computer-classroom instructors and shared experiences, models, and support, "they developed or discovered some usable ways to look at how the computer could augment their writing classes and began to incorporate computers in ways that were meaningful to them" (309). In other words, thanks to the models of teaching and the avenues of support that were offered by their CoP, the instructors were able to shift their dispositions (especially those related to self-efficacy), overcome the initial hesitations about teaching in the computer classrooms, and utilize the composing infrastructure.

Journet's (2007) discussion of her own dispositional shift—from disruptive to generative—through the CoP model utilized at the Digital Media and Composition Institute (DMAC) exemplifies the role a more field-connected CoP can play in these shifts. At DMAC, Journet had "an impressive collection of people to lead me through the technology, access to all kinds of hardware and software, and supportive colleagues who were, like me, also learning [multimodal composing]" (113). Despite an initial "professional reluctance" (107) toward multimodal composing, interacting with members of the field in the DMAC CoP helped to make her more comfortable with multimodal composing and shift her disposition. The generative dispositions she interacted with at DMAC helped her to shift her own disposition and to gain both more confidence with this kind of composing and a better understanding of how her previous writing and teaching knowledge can transfer into multimodal contexts.

The field's disposition toward the value of multimodal composing has also played a role in the shifts described by Duffelmeyer and Journet. These authors have dispositions that value multimodal composing at least in part because they are members of a field that has advocated for it and demonstrated its value. Duffelmeyer's desire to better understand the role CoPs can play in shifting GIs' dispositions is related to the value she sees in these kinds of classrooms and this kind of composing. Similarly, Journet's initial desire to learn more about multimodal composing at DMAC was related to the work she saw happening in the field and in the classrooms around her, which encouraged her to seek out that CoP. Their dispositions around the value of multimodal composing have driven them to illustrate this value to others. In working toward expanding the use of multimodal composing at their institutions, the instructors clearly see a value in it, which helps them transfer that knowledge to their teaching; at the same time, they are working to convey that value to members of their CoPs—both locally and in the field—and shift or reify their dispositions so these instructors can engage in similar kinds of transfer.

These examples start to illustrate how dispositions can help us understand why some instructors use the infrastructure and others do not. At the same time, they show us how CoPs, locally or in the fields instructors identify with, can play a role in shifting those dispositions. These examples, however, only show positive shifts: from disruptive to generative. CoPs can also reinforce dispositions that limit instructors' use of the composing infrastructure. The remainder of the chapter provides one picture of this happening at FSU to illustrate how CoPs can shift or reinforce dispositions around digital pedagogies and the campus's composing infrastructure. Despite access to the same infrastructure, only the instructors who identified with CoPs that value and model the use of the infrastructure and who fostered generative dispositions toward its use included digital assignments in their classes, while the others remained largely indifferent to it and excluded digital projects.

DISCOVERING INSTRUCTORS' DISPOSITIONS TOWARD THE INFRASTRUCTURE AT FLORIDA STATE UNIVERSITY

To illustrate the connections among infrastructure, CoPs, and dispositions, this chapter draws on discussions with GIs from two of the academic programs within the English Department at FSU: Lit and rhet/comp.[2] The four GIs selected for this study were Tobias and Robert from the Lit program and Lawrence and Kelly from the rhet/comp program. The first interview consisted of three sections of questions that asked about (1) the instructors' experiences with digital technologies/composing; (2) their use of digital technologies in the classroom; and (3) the factors that influenced the instructors' decisions about assigning or not assigning digital projects. After conducting the interviews, I looked for references to what influenced the instructors' use or nonuse of the department's composing infrastructure; the patterns that emerged were used to develop questions for a second interview that focused on those patterns. I then looked across both sets of interviews to determine what factors had the largest influence on the instructors' decisions. It is important to note that at FSU, GIs are given a lot of control over their course design; they have shared outcomes/goals for the course and a shared textbook, but individual instructors are able to include any amount or kind of assignments they would like as long as they fit with the goals and outcomes.[3]

The instructors for this study were deliberately selected to find GIs who had similar experiences at FSU but who also represented a wide range of educational experiences, backgrounds, and research interests. All four of the GIs discussed here were in PhD programs, had taken both a summer FYC pedagogy survey and a two-semester pedagogy seminar at FSU, taught in the same building, and had taught multiple sections and versions of the FYC course at FSU. They all also used digital technologies in their personal lives to browse the internet, post on social media, and watch movies and TV. Despite these similarities, the number of years the instructors had been teaching; the number and type of institutions they attended before coming to FSU; the classes they had taken, taught, and were teaching; and their previous experiences with digital technologies in class, among other aspects, varied:[4]

- **Tobias** researches American authors such as Jack Kerouac and Ernest Hemingway. He attended a private research university for his master's degree but did not teach there. In the three years he had been teaching at FSU, he taught multiple sections of two different courses in the FYC program and of six different courses in the Lit program. Professionally, Tobias uses digital technologies often, but it's mostly for word processing, reading, and researching.
- **Robert** researches avant-garde authors such as Samuel Beckett and William S. Burroughs. He attended a public research university for his master's degree but did not teach there. In the two years he had been teaching at FSU, he taught multiple sections of two different courses in the FYC program and of two in the Lit program. Professionally, Robert almost solely uses digital technologies for word processing and researching, although toward the end of the study he had started working with a digital archive.
- **Lawrence** researches multimodality and writing program administration. He earned his master's degree at FSU and stayed to earn his PhD. In the four years he had been teaching at FSU, he taught multiple sections of three different courses in the FYC program. Professionally, he primarily uses digital technologies for word processing, but he has started making ePortfolios for his coursework, running a Tumblr site, and using Twitter to communicate with his students.
- **Kelly** researches embodiment and transnationalism. She earned her master's degree at FSU and stayed to earn her PhD. In the six years she had been at FSU, she had taught multiple sections of three different courses in the FYC program, of one course in the Lit program, and of two in the writing major. Although Kelly's "primary composing tool" in her professional life is a word processor, she also uses Wix, iMovie, and Omeka (an online archive tool) on WordPress.

As the next sections illustrate, the infrastructure ultimately played very little role in the instructors' decisions; instead, their dispositions and their CoPs most strongly influenced those decisions. Despite regularly interacting with each other and having opportunities to join CoPs that cover overlapping professional interests and shared spaces, instructors at FSU tend to identify primarily with the CoP most closely associated with their program: those in the Lit program primarily identify with the Lit CoP, while those in the rhet/comp program primarily identify with the rhet/comp CoP. Due to their membership in two different programs in the department, these instructors were able to illustrate how the CoPs that formed in the department around the major academic programs influenced their dispositions.

INSTRUCTORS' DISPOSITIONS ARE AFFECTED BY COPS AND AFFECT THEIR USE OF INFRASTRUCTURE

As our interviews made clear, the instructors' dispositions toward digital composing, especially dispositions related to self-efficacy and value, were linked to the local and field-related CoPs they identified with. Both Tobias and Robert explained that they did not feel very comfortable with digital composing and did not have much experience with it in the classroom. Neither of them saw much of this type of composing happening in the CoPs they identified with, and neither assigned a digital project in their classes outside of the single required assignment in the FYC course. In contrast, Lawrence and Kelly felt comfortable with digital composing in the classroom, had a lot of experience with this kind of composing in the CoPs they identified with, and assigned digital projects in every one of their classes—often more than one in each class. To highlight the influences of the instructors' dispositions and the role CoPs play in shaping them, the results in this section are organized around three categories: (1) the infrastructure at FSU, (2) the local CoPs, and (3) the field as CoP.

Florida State University's Infrastructure: Built for Digital Composing

FSU built a composing infrastructure that supports and encourages digital/multimodal composing.[5] Perhaps the most visible element of the composing infrastructure at FSU is its two multiliteracy centers (see McElroy et al. 2015), which are staffed by graduate students who can help students and instructors discover what software and technologies are available to use, what they can be used for, and how to use them. Instructors can also request to teach in one of two computer classrooms, which are filled with desktop computers and composing software, and two laptop-ready classrooms, which are designed to easily incorporate students' own machines. These computer classrooms are supported by a graduate student who can provide resources and advice for using them effectively. These efforts are intended to alleviate concerns instructors might have about access to and their own self-efficacy with digital technologies. Ideally, this should encourage instructors to make use of the infrastructure and assign digital projects in their classes.

Ultimately, this did not appear to be the case. Even though all four instructors were aware of these spaces when they were designing projects for their classes, believed they were ultimately helpful to students and teachers, and had used them in some cases, the infrastructure did not end up making a difference in the types of assignments they included in their classes. Although both Lawrence and Kelly had previously taught in the computer and laptop classrooms, they did not reference those spaces. The only aspect of FSU's composing infrastructure that any of the instructors mentioned was the multiliteracy center, but access to this space was not enough to shift their decisions about what they assigned in either direction. Both Tobias and Robert acknowledged the space, but their dispositions still resulted in them not assigning digital projects in any of their classes. At the same time, neither Lawrence nor Kelly was swayed by the infrastructure itself. As Lawrence put it, "It would definitely be more difficult to [assign digital projects] if we didn't have the [multiliteracy center]," but he believes he would still find a way to do so if it wasn't there. In other words, the instructors' dispositions toward digital composing, *not* their access to infrastructure, were the basis for their decisions about assigning these projects. As the next two sections illustrate, these dispositions were shaped through interactions with CoPs locally and in the wider fields they identified with.

The Local CoPs: Divided among Programs with Diverging Dispositions
At FSU, local CoPs have formed around the courses and programs in the English Department. In the case of the FYC courses, for example, there are formally arranged communities, such as a required summer course for first-time instructors and a pedagogy workshop in the fall and spring semesters for all GIs in their first year at FSU (regardless of their previous teaching experience). As part of this FYC CoP, instructors are introduced to pedagogical theories (including multimodality) and are given syllabi templates, assignment ideas, and access to experienced GIs (from all three programs at FSU) who serve as mentors. In the case of non-FYC courses, the CoPs are often more informal and consist of current and former instructors who share materials, experiences, and advice with each other. Despite access to a range of CoPs in the department, most instructors primarily identify with CoPs associated with their specific program of study that are made up of professors and fellow GIs (i.e., Lit GIs prefer CoPs focused on Lit studies and made up of Lit GIs and professors). This primary identification remained true even when instructors were teaching courses outside their disciplinary specialization, such as FYC, and despite the presence of CoPs with wider foci, such as general multimodal pedagogy or assessment practices. These programmatic CoPs play a large role in shaping instructors' dispositions around digital composing, especially when it comes to feelings of value and self-efficacy.

As previously mentioned, neither Tobias nor Robert felt very comfortable with digital composing, and these dispositions—which informed their decisions to exclude digital projects in their classes—were reified by participating in a CoP that was indifferent to it. As they saw it, the fact that their Lit instructors and colleagues did not seem to place much, if any, value on these types of assignments encouraged them to feel similarly. Although there was no outright bias *against* digital composing in their CoP, Tobias's and Robert's responses make it clear that this perceived indifference resulted in similar dispositions.

Tobias explained that his "scholarly identity" and the way he has constructed his own pedagogy have largely been influenced by the courses he has taken and the professors who taught them. His pedagogy, he explained, is a "sort of weird hodgepodge of all the different professors [he has] had in the past," and the way he constructs his syllabi is a result of his experiences with those professors. His experiences, and thus his identity and syllabi, are almost entirely devoid of digital composing; because he has not been asked to compose digitally by instructors he identifies with, he was left feeling unsure whether using digital technologies even "fit within the model of [his] own pedagogical method." In other words, Tobias's disposition toward digital composing was modeled after his previous instructors' dispositions, which left him uninterested in digital composing.

Robert's disposition was also informed by not having a model on which to base his use of digital technologies, but he pointed to another place where the model didn't exist: among the GIs in his Lit CoP. Robert explained that his friends and colleagues in the Lit program were not really assigning digital projects in their classes and, like him, were assigning traditional papers. Since he was already somewhat disinclined to assign digital projects in his classes, his experience of seeing the same disposition shared within this CoP helped solidify that disposition. As Robert put it, the instructors were encouraged as part of their CoP to assign "pretty much whatever you're comfortable with." The assignments these instructors were most comfortable with were the ones they had been asked to do in courses they had taken, the ones they had done for their own research, and the ones they had seen their colleagues do—in other words, non-digital projects. Although both Tobias and Robert mentioned not having a model for digital pedagogies, both had taken the required FYC pedagogy courses that argued for the value of multimodal composing, provided examples of digital assignments, and asked them to compose digitally; in addition, both instructors had assigned a single digital project in their FYC courses. These examples, however, were not from members of the CoPs they identified with and did little to shift their dispositions.

This stands in stark contrast to the experiences of Lawrence and Kelly in the rhet/comp CoP. Both said they had often been asked to compose using digital technologies in their coursework, and they felt their instructors had successfully modeled how and why to use these technologies in a class. These models helped the instructors establish dispositions that encouraged them to include digital projects in their classes—even if doing so didn't totally align with their non-scholarly dispositions. In one interview, for example, Lawrence joked that "for someone who studies multimodality, [he doesn't] really write a lot of multimodal things" in his personal life, but he explained that the digital projects he's been assigned by his professors helped him see their use and value, which encouraged him to assign them to his own students.

Kelly also pointed to the role the professors in the local rhet/comp CoP played in shaping her disposition toward digital composing. After taking a course that explored topics related to digital writing and rhetoric, Kelly's disposition toward digital composing and the need to bring it into the classes she taught shifted. Before the class, Kelly explained, she "didn't really think of [herself] as a computer user": she had one, she used it to write, and she liked it, but it was not a big part of her life. After taking this course, led by a professor in her CoP, she started to really think about "how many different ways there [are] to use technology" and how she could bring those different ways of thinking into her classroom to help her students have similar experiences. Kelly even transferred this thinking into the one literature course she taught, which included multiple multimodal and digital assignments. For both Lawrence and Kelly, experiencing these models of digital composing among members of their CoP helped shift their dispositions toward seeing the value of digital composing for their own students.

As part of their local programmatic CoP, the rhet/comp GIs also shared assignments, experiences, and pedagogical strategies with each other, which strengthened their self-efficacy and encouraged them to try assigning more digital projects. When I asked Lawrence how he came up with the digital projects in his classes, he joked that he "stole all of them" from other rhet/comp GIs. Likewise, Kelly attributed her digital pedagogy in part to the fact that "everyone else [in the program] is doing" it, which makes her feel more comfortable assigning digital projects to her students. As Lawrence and Kelly create and assign new digital projects, they share them with the other members of their CoP, replicating this process for others. These varying experiences and their impact on dispositions and use of the composing infrastructure resemble Logan Bearden's (chapter 8, this volume) argument that even if we "create an environment in which multimodal transfer is possible," in this case through a composing infrastructure that supports multimodal outcomes, "that environment must [still] be activated by an assignment that requires multimodal transfer." These examples go a step further, however, and indicate that for instructors, these assignments must come from the CoPs they identify with.

Field as CoP: Reinforcing Dispositions around Value
In addition to the local CoPs at FSU, the instructors' dispositions were influenced by the wider CoP of the field they identified with. While the local CoPs tended to shape dispositions around both self-efficacy and value through models of assignments, the instructors indicated that the conversations around digital composing in their fields primarily shaped their dispositions regarding its value. The Lit GIs did not see the value of digital composing being demonstrated in their field, which reinforced their dispositions and left them uninterested in assigning digital projects. The rhet/comp GIs, in contrast, *were* shown its value, which reinforced their dispositions and helped them look for more opportunities to include it in their teaching.

Tobias's and Robert's dispositions concerning the value of digital composing are the result of them not seeing it represented in their fields' conversations—at least not ones they felt connected to. Tobias said he had not attended or seen any conferences or panels that explained how digital technologies might be used or be useful in the classroom. Robert said that if there were panels on these topics at conferences, he wasn't interested in attending them. As with their local CoP, the parts of the CoP they identified with weren't demonstrating the value of digital composing. However, both instructors mentioned a possible shift in their field that was starting to feel more influential in their decisions about digital pedagogies: the rise of the digital humanities (DH). But the value demonstrated by this part of their CoP affected their dispositions in different ways, and this helps illustrate the role identification plays in shifting dispositions.

Tobias said he felt a little pressure from the DH part of his CoP but that the decisions some scholars made to incorporate digital technologies into their work "feels very calculated and opportunistic . . . as opposed to the outgrowth of something real." He said that if he truly felt that his work or his classes needed to incorporate digital technologies as indicated by his field, then he would do so, but right now he still feels comfortable with traditional alphabetic works. Because he didn't identify with those in DH, that part of the CoP did not shift his disposition.

Robert's disposition was beginning to be shifted by DH because he was able to identify with it. During our second interview, he had just started working with an online archive connected to his research, and he mentioned that the value illustrated by this aspect of DH has made him consider including a digital archive assignment and possibly others in future courses.

Again, this stands in contrast to Lawrence's and Kelly's experiences. They explained that the CoP of rhet/comp as a field played a large role in influencing their decisions and clearly illustrated the value of digital composing. Lawrence said that seeing presentations at conferences like the Conference on College Composition and Communication as well as Computers and Writing made him "realize that [he is] on the right track and that he should keep pushing forward" with the kinds of projects he was assigning his students. Similarly, Kelly said these presentations helped her see that there is "a community of scholars that are working through similar pedagogical problems," which helps her solve her own issues and encourages her to keep assigning digital projects. Because the rhet/comp instructors identified with this CoP in their field, which illustrated the value of these assignments, their dispositions were similarly aligned and they looked for opportunities to include these assignments in their classes.

IF WE BUILD GENERATIVE DISPOSITIONS, THEY WILL USE THE INFRASTRUCTURE

In returning to the question about composing infrastructure in the title of this chapter, these four instructors show us that they will use the infrastructure *if* they have dispositions that orient them toward doing so. Importantly, these examples also show that we can play a role in shaping dispositions by leveraging the CoPs our instructors identify with. Admittedly, this chapter discusses a small sample of instructors, and, as such, the results here may not be immediately generalizable across institutions; however, the programmatic and field-connected divisions these instructors inhabit, the ways they identify with some CoPs and not with others, and the implications this can have on their use of the composing infrastructure and adoption of digital pedagogies *are* found at many of our institutions. In the end, these results can still provide a starting point for us to think about how we encourage digital pedagogies and the use of our composing infrastructures. Based on these instructors' responses, there are two major steps we can take to begin shifting dispositions: (1) better embody and demonstrate the value of digital composing in the ways we teach and train instructors, and (2) do more to bridge the gaps between CoPs so instructors identify with members who are modeling ways to use the infrastructure and assign digital projects.

For the first step, we can do more to make sure instructors see how to use the infrastructure, how to assign digital projects that make use of it, and how these projects result in valuable outcomes for both their students and their field. When instructors have dispositions that already motivate them toward digital composing, it's easy for them to find ways to use the infrastructure and assign digital projects to their students. When they don't have these generative dispositions, however, they might overlook or ignore efforts to help them to do so. If we do more to model the assignments and values of digital composing in our own classes and in our workshops and seminars on instructional design and digital pedagogies, then we can help instructors see how they can incorporate these kinds of assignments in their classes. Similarly, we can provide materials and models of digital assignments for instructors to borrow (or "steal," to use Lawrence's phrase) for their own classes, which they can then reshape as they become more comfortable. These were the first steps Lawrence and Kelly took as they began to implement digital projects in their own courses. To do this, we can find instructors in our departments or universities who are using the infrastructure and ask them to demonstrate their projects and provide their materials to others. As Lawrence and Kelly illustrate, this step can help instructors establish stronger self-efficacy with the infrastructure and help them look for ways to bring it into their own classes. If we show instructors different kinds of projects, activities, and engagements they can have with the infrastructure and discuss why we include them, what they help us learn, and how to actually do them, then they will be more likely to incorporate them on their own. Interestingly, though perhaps not surprisingly (since all instructors were, at one time, students themselves), this step closely resembles some of the suggestions offered by Travis Maynard (chapter 9, this volume) to encourage transfer from the classroom to alums' professional contexts.

But as Tobias and Robert illustrate, we must also engage in a second step: making sure instructors identify with the CoPs that support digital composing. The models we provide might not actually impact instructors' self-efficacy or value-related dispositions if they don't identify with those modeling them. As we seek to model assignments and shift dispositions, we can try to seek out digitally productive members or projects from the CoPs our instructors identify with and make sure they are represented too. For example, despite having access to the rhet/comp and FYC CoPs that supported digital composing (including a group that maintained a digital archive), Robert didn't feel the need to incorporate digital composing into his classes *until* he saw it being used in the archival efforts related to his own research. In departments that train GIs, this second step might involve working to shift the dispositions of the instructors who mentor GIs to help them demonstrate the value of digital pedagogies in their fields. Perhaps if Tobias had seen one of his own instructors using digital projects, he would be more inclined to see its value.

Above all, these findings show us that it is not enough simply to build composing infrastructures; we must also build dispositions alongside them. Instructors need to know how the infrastructure can be used and, just as important, *why* it should be used, and they need to see these hows and whys demonstrated by the CoPs they identify with. If we do this, we can begin to shift instructors' dispositions in ways that help them use the infrastructure and assign digital projects to their students.

NOTES

1. This program and its curriculum are discussed in more detail by Maynard (chapter 9, this volume).
2. The study this chapter draws from involved eight instructors who represented three different programs of study (rhet/comp, Lit, and creative writing), two categories of instructors (GIs and full time), and two faculty types (professor and lecturer). The patterns discussed in this chapter held across program and faculty types, and the two groups discussed here are the most illustrative of those patterns.
3. One exception is that in FYC courses, instructors must include at least one multimodal assignment.
4. Although there are certainly a number of other factors—such as gender, race, ethnicity, age, experience, and socioeconomic background—that could influence instructors' decisions about using digital technologies, they were not considered when selecting the participants. Instead, the criteria used to select instructors for this investigation seemed most salient for discovering how Florida State's composing infrastructure influenced their teaching decisions.
5. More on these efforts can be found in Davis, Brock, and McElroy (2012); McElroy et al. (2015).

REFERENCES

Baird, Neil, and Bradley Dilger. 2017. "How Students Perceive Transitions: Dispositions and Transfer in Internships." *College Composition and Communication* 68 (4): 684–712. www.jstor.org/stable/44783589.

Borgman, Jessie. 2019. "Dissipating Hesitation: Why Online Instructors Fear Multimodal Assignments and How to Overcome the Fear." In *Bridging the Multimodal Gap: From Theory to Practice*, edited by Santosh Khadka and J. C. Lee, 43–66. Logan: Utah State University Press. www.jstor.org/stable/j.ctvg5bsxf.6.

Carpenter, Russell, Richard Selfe, Shawn Apostel, and Kristi Apostel, eds. 2015. *Sustainable Learning Spaces: Design, Infrastructure, and Technology*. Logan: Computers and Composition Digital Press and Utah State University Press. https://ccdigitalpress.org/sustainable.

Davis, Matthew, Kevin Brock, and Stephen J. McElroy. 2012. "Expanding the Available Means of Composing: Three Sites of Inquiry." *Enculturation* 14. http://www.enculturation.net/files/availablemeans/index.html.

DeVoss, Dànielle Nicole, Ellen Cushman, and Jeffrey T. Grabill. 2005. "Infrastructure and Composing: The When of New-Media Writing." *College Composition and Communication* 57 (1): 14–44. www.jstor.org/stable/30037897.

DeVoss, Dànielle Nicole, Heidi A. McKee, and Richard (Dickie) Selfe, eds. 2009. *Technological Ecologies and Sustainability*. Logan: Computers and Composition Digital Press and Utah State University Press. https://ccdigitalpress.org/tes.

Driscoll, Dana Lynn, and Jennifer Wells. 2012. "Beyond Knowledge and Skills: Writing Transfer and the Role of Student Dispositions in and beyond the Writing Classroom." *Composition Forum* 26. https://compositionforum.com/issue/26/beyond-knowledge-skills.php.

Duffelmeyer, Barb Blakey. 2003. "Learning to Learn: New TA Preparation in Computer Pedagogy." *Computers and Composition* 20: 295–311. https://doi.org/10.1016/S8755-4615(03)00037-9.

Journet, Debra. 2007. "Inventing Myself in Multimodality." *Computers and Composition* 24: 109–120. https://doi.org/10.1016/j.compcom.2007.03.001.

Kress, Gunther. 1999. " 'English' at the Crossroads: Rethinking Curricula of Communication in the Context of the Turn to the Visual." In *Passions, Pedagogies, and Twenty-First-Century Technologies*, edited by Gail E. Hawisher and Cynthia L. Selfe, 67–88. Logan: Utah State University Press. https://digitalcommons.usu.edu/usupress_pubs/119/.

McElroy, Stephen J., Jennifer Wells, Andrew Burgess, Jeff Naftzinger, Rory Lee, Josh Mehler, Jason Custer, Aimee Jones, and Joe Cirio. 2015. "A Space Defined: Four Years in the Life of the FSU Digital Studios." In *Sustainable Learning Spaces: Design, Infrastructure, and Technology*, edited by Russell Carpenter, Richard Selfe, Shawn Apostel, and Kristi Apostel. Logan: Computers and Composition Digital Press and Utah State University Press. https://ccdigitalpress.org/book/sustainable/s1/fsu/index.html.

Moeller, Ryan (Rylish) M., Cheryl E. Ball, and Kelli Cargile Cook. 2009. "Political Economy and Sustaining the Unstable: New Faculty and Research in English Studies." In *Technological Ecologies and Sustainability*, edited by Dànielle Nicole DeVoss, Heidi A. McKee, and Richard (Dickie) Selfe, 1–15. Logan: Computers and Composition Digital Press and Utah State University Press. https://ccdigitalpress.org/book/tes/01_moeller_ball_cargile_cook.pdf.

Purdy, James P., and Dànielle Nicole DeVoss, eds. 2015. *Making Space: Writing Instruction, Infrastructure, and Multiliteracies*. Ann Arbor: University of Michigan Press and DRC Sweetland Press. https://www.digitalrhetoriccollaborative.org/making-space/.

Selber, Stuart. 2009. "Institutional Dimensions of Academic Computing." *College Composition and Communication* 66 (1): 10–34. www.jstor.org/stable/40593513.

Selfe, Richard J. 2007. "Sustaining Multimodal Composition." In *Multimodal Composition: Resources for Teachers*, edited by Cynthia L. Selfe, 167–179. Cresskill, NJ: Hampton.

Wardle, Elizabeth. 2012. "Creative Repurposing for Expansive Learning: Considering 'Problem-Exploring' and 'Answer-Getting' Dispositions in Individuals and Fields." *Composition Forum* 26. https://compositionforum.com/issue/26/creative-repurposing.php.

Wenger, Etienne, Richard McDermott, and William M. Snyder. 2002. *Cultivating Communities of Practice*. Boston: Harvard Business School Press.

Wysocki, Anne Frances. 2004. "Opening New Media to Writing: Openings and Justifications." In *Writing New Media: Theory and Applications for Expanding the Teaching of Composition*, edited by Anne Frances Wysocki, Johndan Johnson-Eilola, Cynthia L. Selfe, and Geoffrey Sirc, 1–42 Logan: Utah State University Press. www.jstor.org/stable/j.ctt46nzc9.5.

Yancey, Kathleen Blake. 2004. "Made Not Only in Words: Composition in a New Key." *College Composition and Communication* 56: 297–328. www.jstor.org/stable/4140651.

Figure 11.1. Advent calendar

Figure 11.2. Alpine calendar

Afterword

TRANSFER HAPPENS; TRANSFER DOESN'T HAPPEN

Maps, Tensions, Questions, and Ways Forward

Kathleen Blake Yancey

In November, while visiting my six-year-old grandson Calder, I gave him an Advent calendar (figure 11.1), just as I do every year. Sitting together, we found the window for each day, imagining what might be behind it, and in December, as Christmas approached, he opened each window, day by day. Two months later, in January, another exciting event was planned: his family was going on a weekend skiing trip. To mark the days leading up to the trip, he decided to make his own calendar, one modeled on an Advent calendar (figure 11.2), which he and his family christened the Alpine calendar.

Transfer happens, even—perhaps often—when we don't expect it.

***

Nicole, an editing, writing, and media (EWM) major at Florida State University, was, by her own account, a multimodal composer. She'd thought about multimodality explicitly in Writing and Editing in Print and Online (WEPO), a required junior-level EWM gateway course supporting students' composing for print, screen, and network. She'd composed several digital multimodal texts and, as a culminating project, an electronic portfolio. In her subsequent classes, however, while she encountered opportunities to compose texts that would benefit from intentional multimodal design, she declined them.[1] For instance, enrolled in a classics course, Nicole composed her final project on a set of ancient visual objects, but the text itself was print-centric—which is not, of course, to say that it was mono-modal. As Cheryl E. Ball and Colin Charlton (2015) point out, all texts are multimodal, and this one was too. Still: although Nicole's text addressed a set of visual objects, it described them only in words, not additionally, as complement or supplement or illustration, in reproductions or representations of them, in photos, drawings, screenshots, or cartoons.

Ironically, when she and I talked about the process of composing the text, Nicole described an approach infused with multimodality: she used a camera to take photos of the seals that were the focus of the project, and she used the internet to verify the accuracy of her photo-based descriptions. She didn't consider these actions part of her writing process, however: Nicole categorized them as tactics she'd employed to save time, to help make her writing more efficient.[2] Moreover, when Nicole explained why she didn't incorporate images into the text, she located the reason in her theory of writing. Writing, she said, operates along a divide between "academic paper(s)" and a digital or internet "kind of thing." Her theory of writing—and as Jeff Sommers (2011) and Staci Perryman-Clark (2013) demonstrate, all students, tacitly or otherwise, have theories of writing—was founded on a divide between academic texts and other texts, a divide functioning as a Burkean terministic screen preventing her from seeing similarity across contexts, technologies, and composings. In sum, Nicole didn't include images in the project because her theory of writing precluded such a possibility.

Transfer doesn't happen, even with the support of rich curricula and exigent assignments.

**

This collection wonderfully maps the universe of multimodality, transfer, and, most especially, the intersections between them. In creating this map, the editors and authors provide instances of transfer, of not-transfer, of cross-media transfer, of linguistic transfer-via-translation, and of potential transfer—in the process demonstrating how rich and complex this intersection, this landscape, is. To create this map tracing transfer, multimodality, or both, some authors enact traditional research methods (e.g., interviews), while other authors, like Crystal VanKooten (chapter 1), intentionally devise multimodal methods mirroring the multimodality at issue. Moreover, in creating this map, the editors and authors have collectively surfaced a helpful set of tensions informing transfer of/and multimodality, some of which I identify below.

Is it the case, for instance, that students somewhat naturally transfer, as Kevin Roozen (chapter 7) suggests in his account of Laura and Anna Knutson (chapter 5) in her account of Kate? As both Roozen and Knutson point out, the environment contextualizes all transfer, a point also locating Logan Bearden's (chapter 8) observations about the role a curricular environment, as expressed through outcomes and assignment design, plays in transfer. Cues for transfer provided through software templates, as Jailei Jiang (chapter 2) explains, act as another environmental factor. Environments are human too, contextualizing writing and its teaching, as exemplified in Jeff Naftzinger's (chapter 10) account of competing communities of practice. Even with supportive, well-designed environments, though, even when presented with invitations and scaffolding, some students, as Ryan P. Shepherd (chapter 6) reports, perceive impermeable demarcations between kinds of composing that others see as constituents of the same phenomenon.

Which leads me to ask: why is it that in some contexts, students can compose in fully multimodal ways, even without encouragement, and in others, they don't see the potential or value in doing so? Why is it that in some contexts, students enthusiastically repurpose prior practices and knowledge, while in others they do not? Such questions have, of course, direct implications for those of us interested in supporting writers' development. If transfer is nature-based, we can concern ourselves less with programmatic issues of the kind outlined by Bearden, Naftzinger, and Travis Maynard (chapter 9); if transfer is largely nurtured, then programmatic designs and faculty development are of the moment. Put another way, one result of framing such tensions is to raise a question based in a familiar metaphor with literal reference: is transfer nature or nurture? As Calder demonstrates, people transfer all the time. As Nicole demonstrates, people don't transfer all the time. Clearly, it's not nature or nurture. What if it is nature and nurture?

***

Another way of thinking about the issues this collection maps is to locate a set of key questions.

What, for example, is writing? At some level, this may be the key-est of the key questions: if all writers identified writing as fully multimodal, the exigence for this collection would be considerably reduced. And yet, early on in life, multimodally is exactly how writers compose: the emergent literacy of four-, five-, and six-year-olds is rich with creative combinations and arrangements of words and images. It's largely as writers progress through school that they regress in multimodal composing—at the direction of the school—giving up visuals and creative formatting for words that are contained in and regulated through an MLA format.[3] An alphabetic-centric emphasis, furthermore, continues into higher education. Take, for instance, one of the threshold concepts (TC) outlined in the first TC collection: "words get meaning from other words."

Well, yes, they do—and from other modes, even in print (perhaps especially in print), including in layout and more particularly—especially in everyday writing—though their interaction with visuals. Writing, in other words, is considerably more complex and capacious than students often understand, and we who teach students contribute, often inadvertently, to that dearth of understanding. Which leads me to this question: how do we change this?

What, for another example, is multimodality? Ball and Charlton (2015, 42) cite the New London Group (NLG) (1996) as an originary source for multimodality, itself located in "five modes through which meaning is made: Linguistic, Aural, Visual, Gestural, and Spatial. Any combination of modes makes a multimodal text, and all texts—every piece of communication that a human composes—use more than one mode. Thus, all writing is multimodal." There is a sense, then, that modes work together to "distribute equal emphasis on how meanings are created, delivered, and circulated through choices in design, material composition, tools and technologies, delivery systems, and interpretive senses" (Ball and Charlton 2015, 42). As writers, we draw on all the relevant modes. As Wilson and Portz (chapter 3) demonstrate, some transfer may involve one primary mode—in their example, the linguistic mode—although most of the examples here point to texts with different modes working together. In such cases, what each mode brings to a text is perhaps best described in its own language—a proposition I make based in part on Michael-John DePalma's (2015) account of Noreen, who draws on her prior knowledge, practice, and experience of music to remediate a print story. Calling on classical music for inspiration, Noreen designs the structure of her remediated text: "In classical music things tend to happen in pairs. You have a primary thing, and you have a secondary thing. You have an antecedent, and you have a consequent. And so, with the structuring of the essay, I was very aware of that parallel. I'd always have something that goes back, like a counter-part before and after" (624).

Elsewhere I've discussed Noreen's multimodal transfer more fully (Yancey 2017), but suffice it here to say that her new text is beholden to what Noreen adapts from music quite intentionally, with a sophisticated language facilitating this adaptation, a point to which I'll return. The point for the moment: Noreen's prior experience of, knowledge of, and language for music, all located in a single mode, are required for the fullness of this multimodal text to be realized. Which leads me to these questions: does each mode, then, have its own vocabulary; if so, what is it; and if so, how do we create a larger lexicon that taps individual modes while assembling them for multimodality more generally?

What is transfer? And what does it mean to transfer writing? As a quick definition, transfer is the repurposing of the prior for the new; as quick, transferring writing is repurposing the prior for new rhetorical situations and tasks—and in each case I'm using prior to refer to a constellation of related capacities, among them knowledge, practice, experience, beliefs, attitudes, and values. Moreover, while we in writing studies have historically focused on the role of school in supporting the transfer of writing, recent research (e.g., Yancey et al. 2019) is identifying the multiple sites where students write, develop the prior, and repurpose it—including school but not exclusive to it. With a small group of internationally based colleagues, I've also been investigating what students make of what they learn in such sites, what we've called spheres of writing (O'Sullivan et al. 2022), including the academic but many others besides: self-motivated, co-curricular, internship, workplace, and civic. Which leads me to these questions: given these multiple sites, how/do we support students in writing in each, in writing across each, and in synthesizing what they learn in those writings? How might our curricula change if we took up this task? How might student understandings of writing— that is, students' knowledge of and about writing—change?

***

Given this collection and these observations, what are some steps we might take toward a world in which nurture and nature were seen as partners for writers and where multimodal transfer was (more) commonplace? No doubt, there are many possible steps we might consider; here I highlight four I believe to be critical.

First, as suggested above, we need a common vocabulary to describe writing, multimodality, and transfer. Currently, there is no common lexicon. The language for transfer is various, including adaptive transfer, dynamic transfer, repurposing: can we come to terms? The language for multimodality, likewise. To address this, Bearden and Maynard each propose the language of rhetoric, but I wonder if the conventional terms of rhetoric need some revision, amplification, or definition. To take one example, is the concept of audience capacious enough to include circulation of a digital multimodal variety; would we replace audience with circulation; or do we use both? And if we choose to include both, how do we avoid creating a vocabulary that's both too large and too unwieldy?[4]

Second, we need to conceptualize writing as lifelong and lifewide. Thinking in terms of a vertical academic curriculum, which several authors here do and which is the tendency of the field, is necessary but not sufficient: writers compose before they get to us, while they are with us, and after they leave us—a point Travis Maynard (chapter 9) explains well. Charles Bazerman (2020), as well as Norbert Elliot and Alice Horning (2020), among others, have advocated for our understanding of writing as a lifelong endeavor, but as important—especially for writing transfer—writing is also lifewide, occurring in the many spheres in which we participate, often concurrently. These spheres, like earlier and later occasions, set the stage for writing transfer. We need a more robust map of all the sites of writing we participate in; they also need to be fully included in our shared conception of writing.

Third, we need to incorporate a writer's identity into this conception of writing, and we need to link that identity to communities of practice.[5] Simply nurturing a writer's identity won't necessarily lead to transfer and in fact might work against it. Some research (Reiff and Bawarshi 2011; Yancey et al. 2023; Yancey, Robertson, and Taczak 2014) indicates that writers who claim a stronger writing identity, especially when linked to a clear sense of their future that is typically located in a specific community of practice, are less likely to transfer precisely because already committed to a theory of writing, they are less willing to consider revising it. Investigating more thoroughly the relationship of a writer's identity, especially the strength of that identity, relative to transfer will be important.

Fourth, we need to invite students' theories of writing into the classroom and help students continue to develop them. Some evidence (e.g., Andrus, Mitchler, and Tinberg 2019) shows that students are surprised when asked to theorize writing but that when asked to do so, they can—and that when they do, they develop a language that helps them describe writing, a discovery students appreciate. A key component in such theorizing is intentional, regular reflection on composing, as Kara Poe Alexander, Becca Cassady, and Michael-John DePalma (chapter 4) suggest; as the points above also suggest, such reflection should be nurtured as a lifewide and lifelong practice.

In sum, the map of transfer and/of multimodal writing, badly needed and presented here, shows us much about where we currently are within this intersection—and about where we might go next.

NOTES

1. For a fuller account, please see Yancey (2017).
2. Many students value efficiency in writing and look for ways to make their own writing more efficient; see Yancey et al. (2023).
3. For a fuller account, please see Yancey (2020).
4. As I write this, a CFP calling for entries to an encyclopedia on transfer has just been published; it begins with such a vocabulary.

5. Following Jeff Naftzinger (chapter 10), I'm referring to communities of practice here, but we might also think in terms of discourse communities, which Anne Beaufort (2017) identifies as the most important of her five kinds of writing knowledge.

REFERENCES

Andrus, Sonja, Sharon Mitchler, and Howard Tinberg. 2019. "Teaching for Writing Transfer: A Practical Guide for Teachers." *Teaching English in the Two-Year College* 47 (1): 76–89.

Ball, Cheryl E., and Colin Charlton. 2015. "All Writing Is Multimodal." In *Naming What We Know: Threshold Concepts of Writing Studies*, edited by Linda Adler-Kassner and Elizabeth Wardle, 42–43. Logan: Utah State University Press.

Bazerman, Charles. 2020. "Lives of Writing." *Writing and Pedagogy* 10 (3): 327–331.

Beaufort, Anne. 2017. *College Writing and Beyond: A New Framework for University Writing Instruction*. Logan: Utah State University Press.

DePalma, Michael-John. 2015. "Tracing Transfer across Media: Investigating Writers' Perceptions of Cross-Contextual and Rhetorical Reshaping in Processes of Remediation." *College Composition and Communication* 67 (1): 615–642.

Elliot, Norbert, and Alice Horning, eds. 2020. *Talking Back: Senior Scholars and Their Colleagues Deliberate the Past, Present, and Future of Writing Studies*. Logan: Utah State University Press.

New London Group. 1996. "A Pedagogy of Multiliteracies: Designing Social Futures." *Harvard Educational Review* 66 (1): 60–93.

O'Sullivan, Ide, D. Alexis Hart, Ashley J. Holmes, Anna V. Knutson, Yogesh Sinha, and Kathleen Blake Yancey. 2022. "Multiple Forms of Representation: Using Maps to Triangulate Students' Tacit Writing Knowledge." *Composition Forum*. https://compositionforum.com/issue/49/multiple-forms.php.

Perryman-Clark, Staci. 2013. "African American Language, Rhetoric, and Students' Writing: New Directions for SRTOL." *College Composition and Communication* 64 (3): 469–495.

Reiff, Mary Jo, and Anis Bawarshi. 2011. "Tracing Discursive Resources: How Students Use Prior Genre Knowledge to Negotiate New Writing Contexts in First-Year Composition." *Written Communication* 28 (3): 312–337.

Sommers, Jeff. 2011. "Reflection Revisited: The Class Collage." *Journal of Basic Writing* 30 (1): 99–129.

Yancey, Kathleen Blake. 2017. "Mapping the Prior: A Beginning Typology and Its Impact on Writing." In *Contemporary Perspectives on Cognition and Writing*, edited by Duane Roen, Patricia Portanova, and Michael Rifenburg, 313–330. Logan: Utah State University Press.

Yancey, Kathleen Blake. 2020. "Expanding the Inquiry: What Everyday Writing with Drawing Helps Us Understand about Writing and Writing-Based Threshold Concepts." In *(Re)Considering What We Know: Learning Thresholds in Writing, Composition, Rhetoric, and Literacy*, edited by Linda Adler-Kassner and Elizabeth Wardle, 135–161. Logan: Utah State University Press.

Yancey, Kathleen Blake, Sonja Andrus, Matthew Davis, Sharon Mitchler, Liane Robertson, Kara Taczak, Howard Tinberg, and Tanner Wouldgo. 2023. "Readiness to Learn: Variations in How Students Engage with the Teaching for Transfer Curriculum." *College Composition and Communication* 75 (2): in press.

Yancey, Kathleen Blake, Matthew Davis, Liane Robertson, Kara Taczak, and Erin Workman. 2019. "The Teaching for Transfer Curriculum: The Role of Concurrent Transfer and Inside- and Outside-School Contexts in Supporting Students' Writing Development." *College Composition and Communication* 71 (2): 268–295.

Yancey, Kathleen Blake, Liane Robertson, and Kara Taczak. 2014. *Writing across Contexts: Transfer, Composition, and Sites of Writing*. Logan: Utah State University Press.

INDEX

Locators with an *f* indicate a figure, locators with a *t* indicate a table, and locators with an *n* indicate a footnote.

academic inquiry, 5, 15, 30, 63, 186, 191
accessibility, 52, 54, 57, 59, 74
activism: art and, 115; political, 49
adaptation, xvi, 14, 67, 183, 184, 230
Adler-Kassner, Linda, 190
affordances, 3, 56, 96, 98, 100, 180, 181; audio, 7; defining, 64*n*2; material, 8, 183; modal, 8; multimodal, 73, 116
agency, 4, 33, 151; enacting, 120; researcher, 81; semantic, 81
Alexander, Jonathan, 7, 13
Alexander, Kara Poe, 17, 50, 63, 110, 113, 148, 171, 210, 232; inventorying and, 114; on multimodal composition, 132; remediation and, 28–29; writing transfer and, 57
alumni studies, 191, 206; curricular frameworks for, 194–97; transfer research and, 192–94
Animaker, 53, 59
animation, 49, 53, 54, 58, 62; potentials for, 55*f*
Animoto, 34, 38
Anson, Chris M., xiii, 47, 48, 51, 63, 162, 165; writing transfer and, 15–16
argumentation, xiii, 7, 113
art, 111; activism and, 115; classes, 154; making, 160; medicine and, 159–62
art history, 105, 111
artifacts: -in-activity, 149; semiotic, 149, 151
assessment practices, 3, 97, 118, 174, 181, 218
assignments, 11, 87, 138, 174, 181, 187, 219; alphabetic, 198, 221; design of, 119–20; digital, 211, 215, 220; multimodal, 8, 132, 181*t*, 205, 212; writing, 105, 110, 118, 120, 132
audience, 129, 134, 137, 180, 182, 197, 203, 231; addressing, 178; expectations of, 200; real-world, 185
audio, 31–32, 41, 94, 202
aural, 2, 42, 230; visual and, 33

Baepler, Paul, 29
Baird, Neil, 210
Ball, Cheryl E., 211, 227, 230

Barad, Karen, 150
Barton, David, xii
Baruch, 93; multimodal texts and, 90–91; rhetorical effect and, 91
Bawarshi, Anis S., 119, 170
Baylor University, 86, 87, 95, 97
Bazerman, Charles, 232
Bearden, Logan, 220, 228, 229, 231; metalanguage and, 18, 201
Beaufort, Anne, 11
Beckett, Samuel, 216
becoming, 151, 159, 164, 165, 166; accounts of, 163; semiotic, 149, 150, 162
Berkley, Angela, 178
Blackboard, 100
Black Lives Matter, 107
blogging, 111–17, 197
Blythe, Stuart, 30, 31, 131, 192
Bolter, Jay David, 110, 115, 116
Borgman, Jessie, 212
boundaries, 81, 120; agency of, 78; contextual, 80; cultural, 150; mapping, 79; social, 77
Bowen, Lauren Marshall, 85
Brand, Alice G., xi
Brent, Doug, 10
Bridgman, Katherine T., 191
brochure, 49, 52, 54, 58, 60, 87, 97; designs, 59; potentials for, 55*f*
Brown, Tessa, 67
Burroughs, William S., 216

Canva, 49, 52, 53, 57, 59
captions, 33, 109, 110, 111, 125, 129, 132
Cardinal, Alison, 30, 33
Carter, Michael, 188*n*1, 188*n*4
Cassady, Becca, 17, 210, 232
Charlton, Colin, 227, 230
charts, 87, 89, 132, 136
Clark, Irene L., 13
Cloonan, Anne, 173
coding, 29, 30–31, 34, 40, 43, 54, 130
College Collage: Not Going Back, A (video), 39, 40
comic books, 130

236   INDEX

communication, 7, 10, 14, 67, 78, 119, 131, 185, 204; detailed, 200; government, 201; landscape, 4; modes of, 6, 13; multimodal, 8, 68; multiplicity of, 172; online, 120; supplemental, 76; technical, 12, 19n2
communities of practice (CoPs), 210, 211–15, 216, 224; gaps between, 223; instructors and, 217–22; leveraging, 222; local, 218–22; rhet/comp, 215, 220
composition, x–xi, xiii, 11, 27, 47, 90, 176, 180, 186, 194; conceptualization of, 6; digital forms of, 50–51; discipline-specific ways of, 187; learning and, 39; material, 230; multicultural, 7; multi-genre, 204; multimedia, 7; multimodal, 13, 97; print-based, 48, 50–51; processes, 3, 4, 5, 7, 13, 15, 170, 184, 187, 198, 227; research on, 31; textual, 108; transfer and, 28; video, 38, 39; visual, 108
Composition Forum, 31
composition programs, xi, 171, 188n1; rhetoric and, 181–82
CompPile bibliographies, 5
computers, 53, 62, 209, 217; computer classrooms, 211, 213–14, 217
Computers and Composition Digital Press, 31
Computers and Writing, 222
Conference on College Composition and Communication, 147, 222
connections, 37, 57, 62, 100, 104, 106, 117, 126, 128, 132, 134, 135–36, 215; articulating, 95, 96; building, 137, 138, 198; mapping, 12; perceptions of, 129
constellation: fading, 134–36; maintaining, 136–37
content, 4; editing, 60, 61; rhetorical reshaping of, 187
context, xiii, 13, 49, 86, 95, 191, 197, 202, 203; academic, 106, 113, 120; connections across, 136, 138, 204; differences between, 200; disciplinary/co-curricular, 195; formal learning, 127; knowledge from, 105; multimodal, 186, 204; non-academic, 12, 205, 206; online, 107–11; rhetorical, 117, 176, 179, 186, 204; self-sponsored, 106, 120; WC, 99–101; writing, xiv, 135, 137, 138, 201, 204
conventions, 91, 111, 182; genre, 109, 200, 203, 204; writing/composing, 177
conversation, 14–16, 18, 43, 48, 62, 80; mapping, 3–5
Cook, Kelli Cargile, 211
Cope, Bill, 6, 13

CoPs. *See* communities of practice
copyright/fair use, 29
Cosgrove, Cornelius, 192
Council of Writing Program Administrators, 184, 185
Covid-19 pandemic, 63, 102n1
culture, 13, 148, 173, 191; development of, 175; pragmatic, 170
Curran, Paul G., 192
curriculum, 18, 89, 119, 133, 134, 171, 192, 197, 209, 228; composition, 172, 174, 182, 185, 186, 187, 188; development of, 3, 8, 10, 17, 231; engaging with, 127; hidden, 127, 127f; lived, 195, 196; multimodal composition and, 174, 180; multimodal transfer and, 172–74, 175; other, 126–30, 127f, 198; remembered, 194, 195; rhetoric, 191; transformation of, 187; vertical, 12, 174, 185, 186, 187; writing, 11, 12, 127, 127f, 137, 138, 139, 185, 198
Cushman, Ellen, 211

data, 15, 37, 174, 191; analysis of, 31, 32, 33, 39, 40, 42, 43, 75; audio, 31; classroom, 38; interpretations of, 43; interview, 54, 192; multimodal presentation of, 43; multisensory representations of, 30; survey, 54, 196; video, 30–31, 32, 33, 34, 42, 43
data collection, 16, 32, 107; methods for, 28, 88–89; multimodality and, 138; transfer and, 138
Davis, Matthew, 95, 191
demographics, 52, 54, 70, 175, 195, 196
DePalma, Michael-John, 9, 10, 17, 28, 50, 63, 110, 113, 147, 148, 171, 198, 210, 230, 232; inventorying and, 114; multimodal composing and, 13, 132; writing transfer and, 57
design, 55, 56, 87, 90, 95, 97, 100, 171, 223; assignment, 119–20; choices, 60, 62; curriculum, 12; effective, 54, 60; handbook, 199; multimodal, 13, 52, 58, 94, 183; processes, 53–54, 59, 61; visual, 33, 60, 97, 114; weakness of, 60–61. *See also* graphic design; website design
Devet, Bonnie, 95
DeVoss, Dànielle Nicole, 211
digital communities, studying, 29
digital composing, 39, 197, 209, 210, 212, 217–22, 223, 224; bias against, 219; moving to, 50
digital humanities (DH), 221
Digital Media and Composition Institute (DMAC), 214

digital practices, 6, 13, 28, 30, 31, 42
digital projects, xv, 28, 35, 210, 212, 215, 217, 218, 219, 220, 222, 223, 224
digital writing studies, transfer in, 49–52
Dilger, Bradley, 210
disciplinarity, 192, 206; transfer and, 12
discourse, 162; academic, 68; community, 4, 72; ethnic, 80; medical, 156–57
dispositions, 111, 211–15, 218, 219; answer-getting, 119; generative, 215, 222–24; influence of, 210; instructor, 215–16; positive/negative, 135; shifting, 222
diversity, 130, 162, 163, 165, 196; cultural/linguistic, 67, 172
Donahue, Christiane, 67, 117
Downs, Doug, 10, 11
Drawing I class, 159; interaction during, 161*f*
Driscoll, Dana Lynn, 95, 210, 212
Dryer, Dylan B., 118
Duffelmyer, Barb Blakely, 212, 213, 214

Eastern Michigan University (EMU), 182, 184, 186, 188
editing: internship in, 195; video, 29
editing, writing, and media (EWM) (FSU), 191, 192, 194, 197, 227
education, 4, 8, 52, 133, 231; focus on, 192; higher, xvi, 120, 206; as public good, 104; tutor, 86, 95, 99, 102*n1*
Elliot, Norbert, 232
Elon University: Research Seminars, 11; Elon Statement on Writing Transfer, 51
emotions, ix, xi, 33, 42, 55, 112, 116, 152, 163
EMU. *See* Eastern Michigan University
Enculturation, 31
End of Composition Studies, The (Smit), 147
engagement, 7, 51, 59, 76, 127, 129, 146, 148, 150, 151, 153; fuller, 162–66; textual, 149
English classes, social media and, 107–11
English Department (FSU), 191, 211, 215, 218
English language, 71, 87, 125
environments: curricular, 187; digital, 6; electronic, 183; learning, 106, 120; multimodal, 110, 190, 201; multiple media, 204; natural/built, 116; well-designed, 228
ePortfolios, 120, 197, 199, 201, 205, 227
essays: academic, 111; alphabetic, 96, 113, 114; analytical, 14; argumentative, xiii; print-based, 50, 61; problem-solution, 52; student reflection, 62; traditional, 111

ethics, 29, 30, 79
ethos, 37, 52, 55–56, 112, 182; awareness of, 54
EWM. *See* editing, writing, and media
"Expectancy-Value Theory of Motivation," 212
experiences, x, xvi, 99, 146, 151, 193, 201, 203, 204, 205; academic, 87–89, 111, 183, 194, 196, 198; alumni, 200; composition, 32, 39, 94; embedded, 158; extracurricular, 126; graphic design, 97; incorporating, 100, 194; knowledge and, 96; literacy, 30, 191; multimodal, 86, 87–90, 91, 93, 95, 100, 172, 197, 198, 204; prior, 87–90, 90–96, 195; professional, 89–90, 196; social media, 95, 136; writing, 30, 101, 137, 138, 196
extracurriculum, xvi, 18, 126, 127, 127*f*

Facebook, 107, 109, 110, 114, 125, 128, 203
feedback, xi, xiii, 9, 69, 78, 87
feminism, 17, 106, 111
first-year composition (FYC) courses, 52, 63, 138, 174, 178, 186, 211, 215, 216, 219, 224*n3*; CoPs, 218, 223; multimodal transfer in, 171, 176
first-year composition (FYC) students, 48, 49, 51, 52
First-Year Writing Program (FYWP): Baylor, 97; EMU, 172, 182, 184, 186, 188
Fleckenstein, Kristie S., 32, 191
flexibility, 112, 113, 114, 178, 183, 184; material-rhetorical, 186
Florida State University (FSU), 191, 211, 221, 227; composing infrastructure at, 215–16, 217–18; CoPs at, 218
flyers, 87, 88, 185
Forsberg, Laurie, xii, xiii
frameworks, 10, 15, 172, 173; curricular, 194–97; metacognitive, 177; pedagogical, 14; theoretical, 14, 101; transfer, 50
Freire, Paulo, 127
FYC. *See* first-year composition
FYWP. *See* First-Year Writing Program

Gallagher, Chris, 174
Gee, James Paul, xiv
gender, 44, 49, 53, 224*n4*; studies, 106; term, 71
genre, xiii, 3, 4, 5, 92, 104–6, 107–11, 116–17, 129, 137, 173, 180, 182, 184, 185, 186, 192, 197, 198, 201–2, 203; academic, 106, 108, 109, 114, 115, 119; analysis of, 86–87; antecedent, 110, 112, 116; digital, 106; media and, 104, 112, 120; meta-, 183; multimodal, 73–74, 88, 89, 91, 104,

105, 110, 112, 114, 117, 202*t*; online, 107; professional writing, 202*t*, 204; rhetorical, 118, 119; text length and, 117–19; transfer and, 104
Gentil, Guillaume, 71
Gere, Anne Ruggles, 126
gestures, 41, 76, 78, 164, 230
GIFs, 108, 109, 136
Gillespie, Paula, 193
Giltrow, Janet, 188*n1*
GIs. *See* graduate instructors
goals, 10, 67, 93, 174, 212, 215; rhetorical, 60, 61, 62, 178, 187; writing/learning, 13
Goffman, Erving, 166*n2*
Gonzales, Laura, 30, 31, 66–67, 131
Goodman, Bridget A., 68
Google: Hangout, 191; Sites, 53
Grabill, Jeffrey T., 211
graduate instructors (GIs), 210–11, 212, 213, 214, 215, 218, 224; rhet/comp, 220, 221
Graduate Writing Center (GWC) (Baylor), 86, 97
grammar, xii, 7, 133, 134, 171, 173
graphic design, 53, 97, 197, 198
graphics, 78, 87, 88, 90
graphs, 29, 31, 89, 132, 136
Grobman, Laurie, 192
grounded theory, 33, 52, 54, 87, 107
group management, 60, 61
Grusin, Richard, 110, 115, 116
Guerra, Juan, 105
GWC. *See* Graduate Writing Center

Halbritter, Bump, 30, 43
"Hall of Fame" (song), 35
Hannah, 196, 198, 200, 202; metacognition of, 204; multimodal literacies of, 197; professional writing and, 201, 203
Haraway, Donna, 79
healthcare, 162, 121*n1*
heart: changes for, 157; model of, 155, 155*f*, 156; sketch of, 157*f*
Hemingway, Ernest, 216
Hill, Heather N., 95
hooks, bell, 127
Horning, Alice, 232
Hughes, Bradley, 193
human expression, 7, 51, 59
hyperlinks, 55–56, 114

identity: ethnic, 66, 68, 71, 72; expressing, 120; heritage, 70, 73; linguistic, 66, 71; literacy, 72, 74; multifaceted, 114; scholarly, 219; student, 44; writing, 232
images, 29, 116, 132, 136; alignment of, 40; visual, 7

information: demographic, 54; flow of, 61; processing, 131
infrastructure, xvi, 210, 223; composing, 209, 211–15, 217–18, 221, 222, 224; disposition toward, 215–16; programmatic, 3; role of, 175; using, 212, 214
Instagram, 73, 74, 87, 95, 108, 136, 148, 203
interaction, 32, 73, 105, 106, 147, 171, 185, 218, 230; audience, 30, 76; participant, 72
interdependence, methodology of, 32, 33, 81
internships, xii, 164, 195, 197, 205, 231
interpretation, 43, 69, 93, 194, 230
interviews, 31, 32, 33, 34, 37–38, 39, 40, 52, 54, 59–60, 97, 107, 145, 205; coded, xvi; follow-up, 87; future, 130; interviewees, 70, 128–35, 131*t*, 136–37; protocol for, 70–73; semi-structured, 54, 196; social media writing and, 130–34; 3D, 30; transcripts, 54
Introduction to English Studies course, 194
inventorying, 114
IRB, 49, 52, 87, 130, 191

Jamieson, Kathleen M., 110
Jenkins, Henry, 29
Jennie, 97; multimodal composition and, 95, 96
Jiang, Jialei, 16, 29
journalism, 106, 108, 112
Journet, Debra, 212, 214

Kail, Harvey, 193
kairos, 31, 37, 119, 182, 184, 199
Kalantzis, Mary, 6, 13
Kazakh language, 70, 71, 72, 73, 74, 75, 78, 80; as educational language, 79; reclamation programs for, 66
Kerouac, Jack, 216
key terms, 100, 170, 183; rhetorical, 176, 177, 178, 187
Khadka, Santosh, 188*n2*
"Kitchen Tables and Rented Rooms" (Gere), 101
Klyshbekova, Maira, 68
knowledge, 29, 35, 39, 89, 180, 206, 229, 230; academic, 105, 113, 120; alphabetic, 110; antecedent, 105; composing, 13, 17, 34, 170; declarative, ix, x; design, 95; discourse and, 162; disposition toward, 9; gains in, 88, 104; generative, 99; genre, 105, 107–11, 116–17; knowing how/knowing that, xvi; multimodal writing, 28, 86, 87, 89, 90, 93, 94, 98, 99, 101; multisemiotic, 74; reshaped,

10, 40; rhetorical, 92; social, 70, 74; technical, 4, 199; transfer of, 14, 34, 48, 50, 51, 68, 79, 104, 105, 109, 120, 178, 197, 198, 210, 278; transforming, 50, 77; video, 94; website, 94. *See also* writing knowledge
Knutson, Anna V., 17, 63, 139*n1*, 198, 228
Korean language, 71, 72
Kress, Gunther, 7, 51, 59

Laffy Taffy painting, 152, 158
landscapes, 75, 166, 205; communication, 4; curricular, xvi; historical, 158, 165; literate, 147; sociohistorical, 150
language, x, 3, 67, 68, 72, 78, 104, 230; alphabetic, 7; body, 33, 35; critical understanding of, 73; home, 68; maintenance/revision of, 80–81; multiple, 147; oral, xiv; programmatic, 176; written, xiv, 149
language policies, 68, 70, 74, 77; monolingualist, 76; trilingual, 71
languaging, 67, 68, 72, 75, 80; multimodal, 69; political-rhetorical, 79
Lauer, Claire, 192
Lee, J. C., 188*n2*
Lindquist, Julie, 30, 43
linguistics, 67, 70, 118, 230
literacy, 4, 7, 30, 66, 77, 104, 125, 147, 148, 229; academic, 67; across borders, 68; alphabetic, xv, 131; autobiography, writing, xiii; conceptualization of, 6; diverse range of, 75; domains of, 100; home, 105, 198; institutional, 67, 76; Kazakh, 73, 74; multimodal, xv, 131–32, 205; network of, 100; preexisting, 194; print-based, 50, 61; prior, 191, 193–94, 195; Russian, 76; translation and, 69, 70–73, 76; writing, 110
Literacy in Composition Studies, 31
literate activity, 146, 158, 162, 166*n1*, 166*n2*, 166*n3*, 195; attention for, 148–51, 163–64; extracurricular, 17; histories of, 165
literature, 191, 210–11; transfer, 67, 104, 135, 192
logos, 37, 52, 54, 55, 56
longitudinal studies, xvi, 17, 105, 128, 138, 146, 165
Lovato, Demi, 42

Making Progress (Bearden), 175
mannerisms, 27, 35, 43
material ontologies, rhizomatic, 149
materiality, 3, 149; semiotic, 158, 159, 162, 163, 164, 183

Maynard, Travis, 18, 177, 210, 223, 224*n1*, 229, 231, 232
McCarthy, Lucille, 11
Mckoy, Temptaous, 29, 30
McLeod, Susan, xi
meaning-making, 3, 6, 8, 78, 120, 150, 158, 163, 171, 173; cross-textual, 172; modes of, 230
media, 4, 47, 48, 49, 63, 172, 173, 179, 182, 186, 191, 201–2, 203, 204; digital, 50, 51, 180; genres and, 104, 112, 120; knowledge across, 116; leveraging, 112; multiple, xvi, 6, 55, 147, 148, 192, 200; potentiality, 184; role of, 107–8; transfer across, 28, 32, 34, 39, 42, 104
medicine: art and, 159–62; engagement with, 146, 153
medium of education (MoE), 71, 77
Medway, Peter, 119
memes, 49, 129
mental health, 42, 111, 116
meta-awareness, 38, 50, 53, 100, 101, 113, 172, 176; cultivating, 178; multimodal, 185; rhetorical, 178
metacognition, 13, 192, 201–2, 203, 204, 205
metalanguage, 18, 170, 172, 177–78, 179, 183, 185; meta-awareness and, 173; rhetorical, 173, 181, 182, 184, 186, 187, 201
methodologies, xvi, 14, 27, 31, 192; compositional, 44; digital, 28–32, 44; interview, 30; rhetorical, 44; transfer, 81
Miller, Carolyn, 110, 112
Mina, Lilian W., 126, 128, 133
mindful abstraction, 128, 129, 135, 212
modalities, 63*n1*, 79, 80, 98, 150, 165, 166*n1*, 184; agency of, 78; communication and, 10; composing, 179; digital, 73; language and, 68; leveraging, 66; media and, 147, 148; multiple, 147, 148; semiotic, 149; technology and, 184; transfer across, 12–14, 67, 69
model programs, 174–79, 182, 183, 185, 186
modeling, xiii, 111, 114, 147, 158, 223
modes, 4, 48, 50, 63, 92, 171, 172, 173, 184, 186; individual, 230; knowledge across, 116; linguistic, 230; multiple, 55, 95, 120; semiotic, 7, 16, 51, 149, 151, 166*n1*, 181; writing across, 139
MoE. *See* medium of education
Moeller, Ryan (Rylish) M., 211
Montgomery, D. Philip, 68
Monty, Randall, 68, 73
Moore, Jessie L., 11, 48, 49, 51, 63
multilingualism, 67, 71, 80
multiliteracy, 5, 70, 100, 170; pedagogy of, 12, 13, 172, 173

multiliteracy autobiography, 70, 71, 72; translation from, 73–74
multiliteracy centers, 8, 211, 217, 218
multimodal, 38, 197; term, 166*n1*
multimodal advocacy campaigns, 52, 58; collaborative design of, 49
multimodal composition, 52; critical vocabulary for, 100–101; disposition toward, 213; enacting, 175, 178, 209; knowledge transfer and, 213; rhetorical aspects of, 94; value of, 97, 209
multimodal projects, 27, 34, 49, 51, 52, 53, 63, 209, 211
multimodal transfer, 5, 14, 27, 52, 183, 192, 198, 199, 200, 201, 221, 231; approaches to, 148; curriculum and, 172–74; demonstrating, 184, 187; fostering, 16–17, 18, 171, 172, 174, 175–76, 178, 181, 182, 185, 187, 191; future of, 204; potential for, 28; remediation and, 180–81; requirements for, 173; research on, 28–32, 163, 164, 165
multimodal writing, 43, 53, 54, 86–87, 137, 186, 201, 204, 230; approach to, 94; assessment practices and, 97; developing writing practices from, 133; excluding, 131; exploring, 138; map of, 232; prior, 96; social media and, 134, 136; transfer of, 97, 99–101; understanding, 128
multimodality: dimensions of, xv*f*; examples of, 230; experiencing, 37; focus on, 68; goals/values around, 13; incorporating, 171; lens of, xiv–xv; research on, 3, 5, 13, 16, 19*n2*, 67, 220; rhetoric and, 180; state of, 18; term, 6–9; theory of, 117; transfer and, 4–5, 12, 14, 62, 67, 147–48, 172
musical compositions, reworking, 50

Naftzinger, Jeff, 18, 229
Naming What We Know: Threshold Concepts of Writing Studies (Taczak and Yancey), 194
narratives, 33, 37, 114; cultural, 115; literacy, 30; spoken, 34, 35, 39, 42
nature, nurture and, 229, 231
networks, 209; historical, 149–50; spatiotemporal, 150
New Literacy Studies (NLS), xii, xiv
New London Group (NLG), 4, 6, 12, 170, 172, 185, 230; technical communication and, 19*n2*; transfer/multimodal composition and, 13
NLG. *See* New London Group
NLS. *See* New Literacy Studies

Nora, 107, 108; on shareability, 109
Nowacek, Rebecca S., 95, 105, 117
nurture, nature and, 229, 231

"Old Ways" (Lovato), 40, 42
outcomes, 11, 170, 174, 175, 215; foundational, 188; learning, 118; multimodal, 179*t*, 183, 211; programmatic, 187, 194; rhetorical, 177, 177*t*; vertical, 181–88

Palmeri, Jason, 28
Papper, Carole C., 32
pathos, ix, 7, 34, 37, 52, 54, 55
pedagogy, x–xi, 3, 9, 14, 48, 69, 101, 118, 127, 171, 172, 173, 174, 192, 209; alternate, 138; conceptualization of, 6; development of, 190; digital, 210, 215, 222, 223, 224; evidence-based, 12; FYC, 215, 219; multimodal, 7, 13, 63, 105, 218; problems with, 222; research and, 79–81; writing, 10, 12, 49, 63, 119, 130
"Pedagogy of Multiliteracies: Designing Social Futures" (NLG), 6
Perelman, Les, 121*n4*
performance, xii, 92, 112, 174, 176; layered, 78; rhetorical, 173, 179, 187; semiotic, 149, 151
Perkins, David N., 128
Perryman-Clark, Staci, 228
photography, 111, 114, 115, 116, 228
Pinterest, 148
platforms: animation, 55, 57, 59; brochure, 55, 57, 62; cloud-based, 56, 63; challenges with, 60*f*; comparisons across, 54–57, 57–59; design, 54, 55, 56, 59, 60; digital, 48–49, 52, 53, 54, 61, 62, 63; micro-blogging, 113; online, 100; social media, 108, 148; technological, 51, 212; visual, 108
podcasts, 87, 89, 97
politics, 44, 111; language, 71
Portz, Josie Rose, 16, 44, 63, 230
posters, 8, 87, 88, 97, 102*n1*, 185
PowerPoint, 8, 53, 75, 89, 90, 91, 94
Powtoon, 53, 59
presentations: face-to-face, 57, 61; multimodal, 42, 75–79; Pecha Kucha, 87; peer-reviewed, 31; Prezi, 27, 34, 35, 38, 39*f*
prior knowledge, xi, xv, xvi, 4, 90–96, 104–6, 120, 193, 195; applying, 10; transforming, 10, 49
Prior, Paul, 147, 151, 158, 162, 166*n2*, 166*n3*; on becoming, 165; on historical networks, 149–50; literate action and, 150; semiotic histories and, 148

Professional Writing and Rhetoric (PWR), 88, 94, 97
proficiency: gaining, 177; multimodal, 186, 187; rhetorical, 177–78
public spheres, 51–52
PWR. *See* Professional Writing and Rhetoric

Qualtrics surveys, 52, 191

race, 49, 52, 224*n*3; teacher/student identity and, 44
reading, 90, 106, 125; writing and, 166*n*3
Reddit, 136
reflection, 4, 50, 135, 170; encouraging, 198
Reflection in the Writing Classroom (Yancey), 194
Reiff, Mary Jo, 170
remediation, 28–29, 98, 100, 176; adaptive, 105, 110, 111–117, 171; multimodal transfer and, 180–81; semiotic, 149
Remediation Project, 180
remixing, 29, 44, 50, 100, 180
representation, 228; ethics of, 29; language, 74, 75, 77, 78, 80, 81; modes of, 172
repurposing, 10, 231; semiotic, 147–48, 164
research, 11, 14, 61, 69, 86, 96, 146, 162, 163, 180; agendas, 212; conceptualizing, 32; data-informed, 15; design, 49; ecological, 33; empirical, 190; future, 18, 70, 81; methods, 3, 175; pedagogy and, 79–81; qualitative, 70, 73, 75–79; social justice–informed, 105; theory and, 118; video, 34
resources, 104; communicative, 173, 179, 181; linguistic, 80; marketing, 9; semiotic, 51, 54, 56, 57, 58, 61, 62, 114, 147, 148, 149, 150, 151, 162, 163, 164, 165, 181; technological, 14, 59
Reynolds, Thomas, 29
rhetoric, 11, 13, 30, 47, 54, 58, 61, 62, 66–67, 73, 86, 97, 99, 100, 109, 119, 171, 173, 174, 184, 187; composition programs and, 181–82; enacting, 177, 178, 179; metacognitive, 202–4; multimodal, 105, 180; public, 49, 52; studying processes of, 29; transfer and, 28; transforming, 3; understandings of, 194
rhetorical knowledge, 4, 10, 14, 48, 49, 53, 172, 175–76, 182, 183, 186, 191, 201; transfer of, 51, 52
rhetorical situations, 51, 91, 92, 95, 185, 231; addressing, 178; public, 56
Rhodes, Jacqueline, 7
Rickly, Rebecca J., 32

Ringer, Jeffrey M., 9, 10, 13, 110, 113, 147, 171; inventorying and, 114; remediation and, 28–29
Robertson, Liane, 10, 18*n*1, 28, 135, 908
Roozen, Kevin, 17, 105, 195, 228
Rosinski, Paula, 13, 29, 51, 63
Rounsaville, Angela, 105, 110, 113–14, 117
RSL. *See* Russian Sign Language
rubrics, 118, 119
Russian Sign Language (RSL), 66, 69, 71, 72, 75, 76, 77, 78, 79, 80
Rylish, Ryan, 211

Salomon, Gavriel, 128
scaffolding, 13, 99, 229
Script, 35
Selber, Stuart, 209
self-efficacy, xv, 212, 213, 217, 218, 220, 222
Selfe, Cynthia L., 6
Selfe, Richard J., 213
semiotics, 148, 149, 150, 151, 162–66, 171, 173
shareability, 108, 109
Shepherd, Ryan P., 13, 17, 29, 63, 110, 198, 204, 229; blogging and, 112; multimodal transfer and, 148
Shilling, Laura, 17, 228; art/medicine and, 159–62; artwork of, 58, 145, 146, 151–53, 156, 158, 160, 163; engagement by, 148, 151, 163, 164; focus for, 154–58; literate activity and, 163; Medical Terminology and, 155; sketches by, 145, 146*f*, 153–54, 153*f*, 155*f*, 156*f*, 157*f*, 159, 160*f*, 161–62, 161*f*, 164
Shipka, Jody, 147, 148, 150
Shivers-McNair, Ann, 30
Shor, Ira, 127
skills, xi, 4, 39, 108; composing, 7; computer, 53; digital, 7; linguistic, 7; metacognitive, xii; multimodal transfer, 185; rhetorical, 7; set of, 129; technological, 7; thinking, 127. *See also* writing skills
Smagulova, Juldyz, 74, 79, 80
Smith, David W., 147, 151
Snapchat, 136, 148
social issues, 49, 111, 180
social media, 14, 17, 63, 70, 95, 106, 119, 139, 145, 164, 196, 197; academic writing and, 132–33, 136; English classes and, 107–11; marketing, 73–74; multimodal, 133, 134, 136, 137; perceptions of, 126; posting on, 136; practices on, 128; writing lessons and, 135; writing on, 112, 126–27, 128, 129, 130–34, 136
social worlds, 151, 166
socialization, 67; language, 68, 74, 80, 81

software, 9, 217; Adobe Creative Suite, 199; Adobe Illustrator, 53; Adobe Photoshop, 53, 199; animation, 57, 58; brochure, 57, 58; composing, 217; image editing, 53; InDesign, 199; iMovie, 53, 216; sound editing, 53; statistical, 89; video editing, 40; Windows Movie Maker, 53
Sommers, Jeff, 228
sound bites, 29, 43
sounds, 40; analyzing, 43; peer-reviewed presentations of, 31; triangulating evidence with, 34–35, 37
Spinuzzi, Clay, 32
strategies, 51; pedagogical, 101; translation, 76; tutoring, 94; writing, 31
Street, Brian V., xii
Sweetland Digital Rhetoric Collaborative book series, 31

Taczak, Kara, 10, 18*n1*, 28, 98, 135, 194
Takayoshi, Pamela, 6
Tatar language, 66, 71, 75, 76, 77, 78, 79
TC. *See* threshold concepts
teaching, 4, 106, 118; artifacts, 119; improving, 3; language and, 5
Teaching Literature as Reflective Practice (Yancey), 194
Teaching for Transfer (TFT), xii, 11, 98, 185, 187
techne theory, 81*n*2
technical issues, 59, 61, 62
technology, xiv, 7, 8, 29, 32, 33, 44, 59, 60, 62, 81, 106, 148, 172, 186, 214, 217, 230; cloud-based, 63; composing, 182, 198, 204; digital, xv, xvi, 209, 215, 216, 219, 220, 221, 224*n*3; limits of, 212; modalities, and, 184; multimodal, 179, 184, 212; text, 13, 194; understanding of, 213
text length, 109; genres and, 117–19; requirements for, 118; rhetorical weight of, 119
texts, 184, 186; academic, 51; alphabetic, 91, 93, 94, 97, 99, 100, 110; analysis of, 88, 92–93; breaking up, 109; digital, 8, 16; multimedia, 14; multimodal, 8, 13, 48, 86–89, 90–91, 92–101, 171; new-media, 6; persuasive, 182; visual, 8, 92–93
textuality, 108, 146, 148, 166, 174; dialogic histories of, 149; semiotic, 163; sociohistoric landscapes, 165
TFT. *See* Teaching for Transfer
theory, 3, 116, 117; framing, 11; multimodal, 8, 172; research and, 118; transfer, 48; visual, 8; writing, 14, 228, 232

Thorne, Steve, 149, 158
threshold concepts (TC), xi, 12, 229–30
time management, 54, 60, 61, 62
tools, xv, xvi, 101, 171, 230; compositional, 10, 186; digital, 44; semiotic, 146, 149, 150, 163, 164, 165; technological, xiv
training, 9, 99, 193; multimodal, 98; rhetorical, 200
transfer, 3, 4, 13, 44, 48, 49, 57, 67, 80, 81, 100, 101, 105, 138, 173; adaptive, 147, 163, 231; alumni, 194, 206; awareness in, 38; challenges of, 106; concept of, ix, 9, 14; concurrent/subsequent, 198–201; cross-media, 228; defining, ix, 10, 231; digital, 28, 29; dimensions of, x*f,* xiv*f;* dynamics, 10, 11, 193, 231; effectiveness of, xii–xiii, xiii–xiv; encouraging, 198, 204; facilitating, 12, 49, 50, 62, 191; high-road, 128, 129–30; implications for, 104; just-in-time, 198; learning, ix, 9–12, 128; low-road, 128; map of, 232; media and, 14, 104; multimodality and, 4–5, 14, 62, 67, 147–48, 172; nature of, xvi, 9, 15–16; other curriculum and, 126–30; pedagogical goal of, 10; potentials for, 55*f;* research on, 3, 4, 5, 10, 11, 13, 15, 28, 31, 34, 67, 162, 190; rhetoric and, 28; understanding, xi–xii, xiii, xiv, 16, 67; uptake in, 110, 111–17. *See also* multimodal transfer
Transfer of Learning in the Writing Center (Devet and Driscoll), 95
transfer mind-set, 11, 170, 182
transfer research, 67, 206; alumni studies and, 192–94
transformation, 10, 68, 80, 147; curricular, 175, 180, 187; knowledge, 50, 77; multimodal, 183
translanguaging, 72
translation, 77, 80, 93; digital, 70; labor of, 78; literacy and, 69, 70–73, 76; multimodality and, 70; resistance in, 81; rhetoric of, 66–67; transfer and, 69
translingualism, 68, 74, 81
tutoring, 86, 92, 93, 95, 96, 98, 210; misconceptions about, 99; multimodal, 87, 94, 99–100; opportunities for, 101
Twitter, 108, 113, 136

University Writing Center (UWC) (Baylor), 86, 87, 97, 98
usability, 54, 56, 57, 58, 59
UWC. *See* University Writing Center

values: reinforcing dispositions around, 221–22; writing/learning, 13

VanKooten, Crystal, 50, 63, 176, 178, 228; data collection and, 16
vernacular, 66, 76, 101
video, 8, 27, 31–32, 52, 59, 94, 133, 136, 185, 202; academic, 29; analysis process for, 35, 37, 40; animated, 58; Animoto, 34; digital, 30, 42; video, 28, 29, 30, 53; peer-reviewed presentations of, 31; products, 32, 34, 35, 37–38, 49; research, 33, 35
visual, 31–32, 40, 88, 108, 230; analyzing, 43; aural and, 33; triangulating evidence with, 34–35, 37
vocabulary, 93, 95, 170, 186, 230, 231; building, 5; common, 231; critical, 99, 100–101; rhetorical, 176, 177, 181; technical, 93

WAC course, 68, 70, 71, 72, 73, 75
Wardle, Elizabeth, 10, 11, 80, 190
WCs. *See* writing centers
website design, 197; processes for, 55–56
websites, 52, 54, 56, 57, 59, 60, 62, 94, 97; potentials for, 55*f*
Weebly, 53
Weisser, Christian, 192
Wells, Jennifer, 21, 210
Westby, Carol, 172
Williams, Robin, 88
Wilson, Joseph Anthony, 16, 44, 63, 230
Wix, 49, 52, 53, 56, 61, 216
WordPress, 216
words: analyzing, 43; triangulating evidence with, 34–35, 37
WPA Outcomes Statement for First-Year Composition (3.0), 185
Wright, Frank Lloyd, ix
writing: academic, 48, 51, 106, 109, 111–17, 120, 131, 132–33, 136, 137, 139, 193; alphabetic, 14, 96, 97, 98, 171, 187; alumni, 192, 193, 194, 196, 197, 201, 204, 205, 206; argument-driven, 113; co-curricular, 193; conception of, 91, 97, 232; defining, 130, 131–32, 133, 137;

digital, 47, 51, 105, 106; dimensions of, x*f*; extracurricular, 126; learning about, 126, 129; non-academic, 193; online, 108, 112, 115, 202; practices, 15, 31, 134, 137, 195; processes, 14, 51, 52, 205; professional, 4, 15, 137, 186, 192, 193, 194, 198, 201, 202, 203–4, 205, 231; real, 97, 127; recomposing/repurposing, 182; social media, 126–27, 128, 129, 130–34; studying, 3, 4, 29; teaching, 4, 138–39; technical, 15; understanding of, 8, 16, 231, 232
Writing across Contexts (Yancey, Robertson, and Taczak), 10
writing centers (WCs), 9, 12, 85, 86, 87, 96, 97, 99; consultants and, 100; as generative sites, 95; literacy linking and, 100; structures/dispositions/practices of, 95; training, 92; tutors for, 193; work of, 101
writing courses, 12, 127, 128, 130, 135, 137, 138, 194; digital, 8; foundational, xi; new-media, 8; reshaping, 3
Writing for Digital Media course, 39
writing knowledge, 10, 34, 86, 95, 101, 104, 110, 120, 148, 190, 192, 210; alphabetic, 198; alumni, 199; leveraging, 100; prior, 87; transfer, 106, 170, 191, 193, 205
writing skills, 128, 129, 194; alphabetic, 183; multimodal, 40; student, 127
writing studies, 14, 67, 95, 106, 117, 147, 171, 190, 206, 231; curriculum development in, 8; funding for, 120*nI*; multimodality in, 18*nI*, 49; professional development in, 120*nI*

Yancey, Kathleen Blake, 6, 18, 28, 98, 135, 147, 148, 165, 191, 194, 198; curricular framework of, 195*f*; meta-awareness and, 50; writing studies and, 190; on writing transfer, 10
Yelland, Nicola, 173
Yosso, Tara J., 105

ABOUT THE AUTHORS

Kara Poe Alexander is professor of English in professional writing and rhetoric and director of the University Writing Center at Baylor University. She is also co-editor of *Literacy in Composition Studies*. Her research centers on literacy, identity, and the teaching of writing. Her work has appeared in *College Composition and Communication, College English, Composition Forum, Composition Studies, Computers and Composition, Journal of Business and Technical Writing, Literacy in Composition Studies, Rhetoric Review, Technical Communication Quarterly*, and several other scholarly journals and edited collections. Preferred email address: kara_alexander@baylor.edu.

Chris M. Anson is distinguished university professor and Alumni Association distinguished graduate professor at North Carolina State University, where he is executive director of the Campus Writing and Speaking Program. He has published 19 books and over 140 articles and book chapters relating to writing research and instruction and has spoken widely across the US and in thirty-four other countries. He is past chair of the Conference on College Composition and Communication and past president of the Council of Writing Program Administrators and is currently chair of the International Society for the Advancement of Writing Research. His full CV is at www.ansonica.net. Preferred email address: canson@ncsu.edu.

Logan Bearden is associate professor in the Department of Communication, Media, and the Arts at Nova Southeastern University, where he teaches courses in composition, rhetoric, and digital media. He studies writing program administration, programmatic documents, and curricular reform. His research can be found in the *Journal of College Literacy and Learning, WPA: Writing Program Administration*, and various edited collections. His book, *Making Progress: Programmatic and Administrative Strategies for Multimodal Curricular Transformation*, is available from Utah State University Press. Preferred email address: lbearden@nova.edu.

Becca Cassady is director of the Graduate Writing Center at Baylor University, where she leads and trains a team of writing consultants from across disciplines as they work with graduate students on projects and publications. She also oversees Baylor's Dissertation and Thesis Office and is closely involved with graduate student professional development. Before joining Baylor's Graduate School staff in 2022, Becca earned her PhD in English from Baylor with a focus in rhetoric and composition. Her research interests include learning transfer, writing center theory, and literacy. She has taught various composition, rhetoric, and literature courses in Baylor's English Department and Honors College, and she enjoys mentoring undergraduate students. Preferred email address: becca_cassady@baylor.edu.

Matthew Davis is associate professor of English and director of the Center on Media and Society at the University of Massachusetts Boston. He is the current co-editor of *Composition Studies* and incoming co-editor of *College Composition and Communication*. He has has published in *College Composition and Communication, Computers and Composition, enculturation, Kairos, WAC Journal*, and several edited collections. Preferred email address: Matthew.Davis@umb.edu.

ABOUT THE AUTHORS

Michael-John DePalma is professor and director of professional writing and rhetoric at Baylor University. He is the author of *Sacred Rhetorical Education in Nineteenth-Century America: Austin Phelps at Andover Theological Seminary*. With Jeff Ringer, he edited *Mapping Christian Rhetorics: Connecting Conversations, Charting New Territories*, which was awarded the 2015 Book of the Year by the Religious Communication Association. His work has appeared in journals such as *College Composition and Communication*, *College English*, *Computers and Composition*, *Rhetoric Review*, *Rhetoric Society Quarterly*, and several edited collections. His most recent book, co-edited with Paul Lynch and Jeff Ringer, is *Rhetoric and Religion in the Twenty-First Century: Pluralism in a Postsecular Age*. Preferred email address: Michael-John_DePalma@baylor.edu.

Jialei Jiang is a teaching assistant professor of composition at the University of Pittsburgh. Her research interests include digital composition, feminist posthumanism, and multimodal pedagogy. Trained in qualitative research, she examines the use of emerging technologies and multimodal projects in college composition courses. Her works have appeared in *College Composition and Communication* (forthcoming), *Composition Forum*, *Computers and Composition*, *Journal of Technical Writing and Communication*, *Kairos*, and edited collections. Preferred email address: j.jiang@pitt.edu.

Anna V. Knutson holds a PhD in English and education from the University of Michigan. For three years, she served as a tenure-track writing program administrator before leaving academia during the pandemic to live near family in Seattle, Washington; she now works in tech as a qualitative researcher. Her writing studies research explores learning transfer across academic and non-academic contexts, as well as students and faculty in transition. Her academic work can be found in *Across the Disciplines*, *College English*, *Composition Forum*, *Computers and Composition*, *Kairos*, *WPA: Writing Program Administration*, and *Writing across the Curriculum Journal*, as well as the collections *Developing Writers in Higher Education: A Longitudinal Study* and *Class in the Composition Classroom: Pedagogy and the Working Class*. When she's not conducting research, Anna is enjoying living near her family, participating in the Seattle music scene, or spending time with her dogs, Biscuit and Bernadette. Preferred email address: avknutson@gmail.com.

Travis Maynard is assistant professor of English at Elon University, where he teaches in the Professional Writing and Rhetoric and First-Year Writing Programs. Beyond alumni study in undergraduate major programs in writing and rhetoric, his research interests include digital multimodal composition and assemblage pedagogy in the composition classroom. His prior work has appeared in the edited collections *Assembling Composition* and *Teaching through the Archives: Text, Collaboration, and Activism*. Preferred email address: tmaynard3@elon.edu.

Lilian W. Mina is associate professor of English and director of freshman English at the University of Alabama at Birmingham. She is president of the Council of Writing Program Administrators (CWPA). Her research is situated in three major areas: digital writing, writing program administration, and multilingual composition. Her research in digital writing focuses on multimodal composing, teachers' use of digital technologies, and using social media in teaching writing. Research in writing program administration is focused on professional development of writing instructors, programmatic assessment, and reflective practices in teacher training programs. Finally, her research in multilingual composition is centered around multilingual writers' experiences with and response to (digital) pedagogies in the writing classroom. Her work has appeared in prestigious journals and edited collections from university presses. Preferred email address: lilian.mina@gmail.com.

About the Authors

Jeff Naftzinger is assistant professor of rhetoric, composition, and writing at Sacred Heart University, where he teaches undergraduate courses on everyday writing, academic writing, and digital rhetoric. His research focuses on understanding how and why people write in both academic and non-academic contexts. His recent publications have appeared in the edited collection *Approaches to Lifespan Writing Research* and the journal *South Atlantic Review*. Preferred email address: naftzingerj@sacredheart.edu.

Josie Rose Portz is a doctoral student in English at the University of Arizona. She is a former Fulbright grantee to Sri Lanka. Her research explores classical rhetorical conceptions of religious identity, material religious practice, and their implications for contemporary rhetorical scholarship and transnational research methodologies. Preferred email address: portz.josie@gmail.com.

Kevin Roozen is professor of writing and rhetoric at the University of Central Florida. His research argues for richer, fuller, and more dialogic perspectives on how people and their textual practices come to be across moments and lives. In addition to *Expanding Literate Landscapes* (2017), his book with Joe Erickson, Kevin's scholarship has appeared in journals including *College Composition and Communication*, *Research in the Teaching of English*, and *Written Communication* and in a number of edited collections. Kevin's current research focuses on a series of longitudinal studies examining the role that acting with inscriptions plays in shaping the emergent, ongoing development of people, their literate practices, and the social worlds they are making. Preferred email address: Kevin.Roozen@ucf.edu.

Ryan P. Shepherd is associate professor of English and director of first-year composition at Northern Illinois University, where he teaches graduate courses in composition pedagogy, multimodality, and learning transfer. In particular, he is interested in helping new teachers and scholars create pedagogical approaches that are steeped in composition research and build toward practical and achievable goals in the classroom. Ryan's scholarship focuses primarily on connections between the writing students do for school and writing they do outside of it, particularly multimodal writing and writing for social media. He is also interested in illuminating pedagogical approaches to graduate education in rhetoric and composition. His work has appeared in *Composition Studies*, *Computers and Composition*, *Kairos*, and elsewhere. Preferred email address: rshepherd@niu.edu.

Crystal VanKooten is an associate professor at Michigan State University, where she teaches courses in Writing, Rhetoric, and Cultures and first-year writing and serves as co-managing editor of *The Journal for Undergraduate Multimedia Projects* (*JUMP+*). Her work focuses on digital media composition through an engagement with how technologies shape composition practices, pedagogy, and research. Her publications appear in journals that include *College English*, *Computers and Composition*, *Enculturation*, and *Kairos*. VanKooten's digital book, *Transfer across Media: Using Digital Video in the Teaching of Writing*, was funded by a Conference on College Composition and Communication Emergent Research/er Award and is available online from Computers and Composition Digital Press. The book is a qualitative research project that provides an in-depth look at the experiences of eighteen first-year students as they completed different kinds of video composition assignments in their writing courses. Preferred email address: vankooten@oakland.edu.

Joseph Anthony Wilson is assistant professor of Composition and Literacy at Syracuse University, where his research interests include translingual and transnational orientations to writing studies, queer methodologies, and critical applied linguistics/TESOL. His work has appeared in *English for Academic Purposes* and *Technical Communication and Social Justice*, as well as multiple edited collections. Preferred email address: jwilso56@syr.edu.

ABOUT THE AUTHORS

Kathleen Blake Yancey, Kellogg W. Hunt Professor of English and distinguished research professor emerita at Florida State University, has served as president of the National Council of Teachers of English (NCTE), chair of the Conference on College Composition and Communication (CCCC), and president of the Council of Writing Program Administrators (CWPA). A co-founder and co-editor of the journal *Assessing Writing* (1994–2001), she also served as editor of *College Composition and Communication* (2010–2014). Author, editor, or co-editor of seventeen scholarly books—among them *Reflection in the Writing Classroom*; *Writing across Contexts: Transfer, Composition, and Sites of Writing*; *Assembling Composition*; *and ePortfolio-as-Curriculum*—she has authored more than 100 articles and book chapters, often with colleagues. She is the recipient of several awards, among them the CCCC Research Impact Award, the CWPA Best Book Award (twice), the FSU Graduate Teaching Award (twice), the Purdue Distinguished Woman Scholar Award, and the CCCC Exemplar Award. Preferred email address: kyancey@fsu.edu.

www.ingramcontent.com/pod-product-compliance
Lightning Source LLC
Chambersburg PA
CBHW060555080526
44585CB00013B/572